GOURMET COOKING ON A BUDGET

KNACK

GOURMET COOKING ON A BUDGET

Essential Recipes & Techniques from Professional Kitchens

Michalene Busico and Jennifer Clair

Photography by Viktor Budnik

KNACK
MAKE IT EASY

Guilford, Connecticut
An imprint of Globe Pequot Press

To buy books in quantity for corporate use
or incentives, call **(800) 962-0973**
or e-mail **premiums@GlobePequot.com**.

Editorial Director: Cynthia Hughes
Editor: Katie Benoit
Project Editor: Tracee Williams
Cover Design: Paul Beatrice, Bret Kerr
Interior Design: Paul Beatrice
Layout: Melissa Evarts
Cover Photos by: Viktor Budnik
Interior Photos by: Viktor Budnik

Library of Congress Cataloging-in-Publication Data

Busico, Michalene.
    Knack gourmet cooking on a budget : top chefs recipes for great taste at low cost / Michalene Busico and Jennifer Clair ; photographs by Viktor Budnik.
       p. cm.
    ISBN 978-1-59921-913-4
  1. Low budget cookery. I. Clair, Jennifer. II. Title.
    TX652.B882 2010
641.5'52—dc22
                                            2010001558

The following manufacturers/names appearing in *Knack Gourmet Cooking on a Budget* are trademarks:
All-Clad®
Le Creuset®
STYROFOAM™
TABASCO®
Wondra®

Printed in China

10 9 8 7 6 5 4 3 2 1

For my mother, Rose
~Michalene Busico

To my father, Ivan G. Herman, who would have been so proud
~Jennifer Clair

Acknowledgments

My deepest thanks to the chefs, food journalists and home cooks whose work inspired this book. To Leslie Brenner, Regina Schrambling, Amy Albert, and Jenni Barnett, friends and food lovers who generously shared some of their best recipes and offered so much encouragement along the way. And to Maureen Graney, Katie Benoit, and the team at Knack, who made it all happen.
~Michalene Busico

Much gratitude is due to my students who have helped me learn something new from every class I teach. It is because of them that I wanted to write this book, so I could finally have a place to jot down all the lessons and secrets I have learned from over a decade on the cooking soapbox.
~Jennifer Clair

Photographer's acknowledgements

I would like to thank all those at Knack. Thanks to my crew of gifted and talented people: Claire Stancer, a wonderful and talented food stylist who created beautiful food to photograph; Celeste, for her perfect shopping and props for all the recipes and setups; and Sespe Creek Organics, for the wonderful oranges and other items that were prepared for the shoot. Thank you to the organic farmers' markets in Thousand Oaks: Trader Joe's (Westlake Village, CA), Whole Foods (Thousand Oaks, CA), Jimenez Family Organic Farms (Santa Ynez, CA), and Sespe Creek Organics (Fillmore, CA). Cheers!
~Viktor Budnik

CONTENTS

INTRODUCTION

No one wants to make sacrifices at the table—certainly not two people who love good food and good cooking as much as we do. So this book isn't about that.

In fact, it is really about the luxury of cooking and eating well without spending a lot of money on ingredients or a lot of time fussing over complicated recipes. It ranges through some of the best kitchens in America, and serves up a wide-ranging selection of appetizers, entrees, side dishes, and desserts—casual but sophisticated dishes (and a few show-stoppers for entertaining, too). It explains which tools you need to own, and which you can skip. It tells you how to get the most for your money at the farmers' market and the supermarket, how to throw a rollicking party without breaking the bank, and much more.

We've come to share a philosophy about cooking—it's about taste, not money; intelligence, not deprivation—after two very different careers in the culinary world.

After cooking school in New York City, Jennifer spent her formative culinary years working at *Martha Stewart Living*, developing recipes in the test kitchen and writing cookbooks. Drawing from her experiences, she went on to open her own mobile cooking school, Home Cooking New York, eight years ago, where she teaches students how to prepare the foods they love to eat in their own kitchens. This has allowed her to see first-hand how people really cook for themselves, and it has helped shape the recipes that were chosen for this book: accessible recipes that are full of flavor and easy to accomplish in any kitchen space.

Michalene, a journalist for more than 20 years, has been the editor of the nation's top food newspaper sections at *The New York Times* and *Los Angeles Times*. She has spent most of her career discovering and distilling the best of the food scenes on both coasts for readers who have grown more interested and knowledgeable about food than they have ever been. She has learned that even the most elite chefs go into their kitchens night after night with an eye on the bottom line. And if we follow their lead, we too can revel in deeply satisfying flavors and inventive preparations, and be the richer for it.

A Look at What's Inside

Cooking on a budget starts with shopping, and the first three chapters of this book are a helpful guide for stocking your kitchen, pantry, and refrigerator with the essentials. Having the right equipment on hand, like a large Dutch oven, will allow you to cook tough (read: inexpensive) cuts of meat down into meltingly tender meals. It will also give you the room you need to make large batches of soups and

stews for guests or the freezer. Cooking in volume is one of the greatest cost-cutting measures around.

Filling your larder with the right staples will keep you from having to run to the supermarket quite so often. (This alone will save you, since every trip leads to the purchase of a few items that weren't actually on your list.) Having canned beans, canned tomatoes, a selection of spices and seasonings, and a variety of dried grains and pasta means a good meal is always at your fingertips. A freezer full of soups and other pre-made meals means you won't have to order takeout after a long day at work.

Just as essential as the pantry, we have included a chapter on how to shop for fresh produce and meats. Luckily, many of the most inexpensive foods are also the freshest and healthiest. Buy "whole foods"—our shopping motto—as much as you can. The more food is packaged and tampered with, the more manufacturers have to charge and

the less nutritional value it has. Fresh vegetables, fresh fruit, fresh meat, and whole grains will give you the most flavor for your money—and the dishes you'll create will be infinitely more nutritious than any precooked items you could buy.

And there are plenty of ways to keep your costs down. First, buy in bulk when you can. Nuts, beans, grains, and rice can all be purchased at significant savings from the bins at health food stores. Buy seasonally—produce will be at its peak of flavor, and at its cheapest. Choose cuts of meat that will give you the most for your money: pork shoulder, brisket, and turkey breasts are great bargains. And keep an open mind: If you find an item on sale, buy it and rework your recipe.

Learn from the Experts

Since all chefs spend a good deal of time devising cost-cutting measures to trim their restaurant budgets, they are natural models for how to trim the fat in your own kitchen. Nothing is left to waste: At most restaurants, all vegetable and meat trimmings are made into stock. You can employ this same idea by devoting a gallon-size zip bag in your freezer for storing these odds and ends to turn into a stock when the bag is full. Chefs transform ingredients that have slipped past their prime into all sorts of dishes: bread puddings, or crostini for quick hors d'oeuvres or salads, just to name two. And chefs definitely know how to turn last night's unsold entree into a new dish for the next day's menu. A seared salmon with green herb sauce on the dinner special menu is a grilled salmon sandwich with a green herb mayonnaise for lunch the next day.

That sandwich, of course, might be better known to the home cook as "leftovers." But look at it this way: Cook once (doubling the recipe) and eat two or three times without any extra work. In the restaurant kitchen and at home, the economics of time count as much as the bottom line, so use it wisely. When you cook up a soup, stew, braised meat dish, or a batch of sauce—anything blanketed with sauce freezes beautifully—think about cooking ahead and at least doubling the recipe for future meals.

A visit to the farmers' market always yields an excellent selection of seasonal produce—some of it quite pricey. But many farmers will also have a bin of ugly—but marked down, and still delicious—tomatoes or fruit, perfect for canning, pies, and sauces. And, beyond the savings, shopping directly from the farmers in your area not only feeds your family but also feeds your local economy. Good eating starts with these local farmers—a fact that often escapes us in the day-to-day rush, especially if we live in a city.

In the end, we think you'll find that cooking on a budget is immensely satisfying. To create a classic dish with roots in any number of cuisines, or to reproduce the creativity of a top chef, is something to be proud of. These pages are filled with the recipes we use in our own kitchens every day, and the essential techniques that will take you far beyond these pages. Cook at home for yourself and your family, and reap the rewards in every way.

Jennifer & Michalene

POTS & PANS

The right cooking equipment ensures you can easily cook for one person or a crowd

Good cooking starts with the right pots and pans. That said, those pots and pans need not be the priciest, top-of-the-line skillets and saucepans. The food you cook does not notice how much you paid for your sauté pan, but it does notice poor quality and crowded conditions. So it is important to make sure you have a few key items to choose from so you can make the best-tasting food possible.

First, size matters. Cooking a dish for two people does not require the same size pot or pan than that for eight guests.

Second, you need to consider the desired outcome when choosing your cooking vessel. If you want browned food,

Cast-Iron Grill Pan

- Heat the pan over medium-high heat for 3 minutes before using to achieve a true grill-like heat.

- Brush your pan with a little oil after you heat the pan and before you add the food to prevent sticking.

- Perfect for cooking steaks, chops, chicken breasts, sliced vegetables, shrimp, and scallops.

- To protect the pan's non-stick coating, don't scrub it with anything more abrasive than nylon bristles when cleaning it.

Nonstick Cookware

- Always use wooden or silicone utensils to cook food in a nonstick pan; metal will scratch off the nonstick coating.

- Like cast-iron cookware, nonstick cookware should not be cleaned with anything stronger than a soft nylon brush or sponge.

- Nonstick pans are perfect for cooking foods that are notorious for sticking: fish, eggs, potatoes, and pancakes.

- Choose a heavy nonstick pan to avoid scorching your food; avoid light and flimsy cookware across the board.

you must choose something with low sides, so the natural moisture that is released from the food doesn't get trapped by the pan's tall sides, which inhibits browning. On the other hand, braised foods or long-simmering soups need high sides to contain the moisture so it doesn't evaporate before the food is fully cooked.

And third, you need to choose a pot or pan made from the best material for your cooking needs. Cast iron is terrific for searing meats and lousy for acidic foods like tomatoes and wine, which react with the iron and draw some of its metallic flavor into food. Nonstick pans are great for sticky ingredients, like fish, potatoes, and eggs, and a poor choice if you want to make a pan sauce, since nothing will have stuck to the bottom of the pan to start your sauce with. And the heavier the pan, the better it will treat you and your food. Thin metal pans, with no heat-diffusing base, will scorch your food directly where the gas or electric burner touches it.

Stainless Steel Sauté Pan

- This is the best, all-purpose cooking pan. A 12-inch sauté pan is the standard size and can cook enough food for four to six people.

- Buy a sauté pan with an all-metal handle so it can easily be transferred from stove top to oven.

- Sauté pans and frying pans (the same thing) have sloped sides, whereas skillets have straight sides.

- Your sauté pan should have a heavy bottom to ensure that heat is evenly dispersed along the cooking surface.

Large Dutch Oven

- The heavy metal material and tall shape helps food retain its heat during cooking, making the Dutch oven a very efficient cooking vessel.

- They are perfect for long-simmering dishes like braised meats and hearty soups and stews.

- Enamel-coated cast-iron Dutch ovens allow you to cook acidic foods that would normally react with the uncoated iron.

- Use this when cooking for a crowd, especially when you need to double or triple a recipe.

KITCHEN TOOLS
The simplest utensils can help you be more efficient in the kitchen

The right kitchen tools can make cooking so much easier, and luckily the best ones are also the least expensive. Natural wooden spoons make the best stirrers and offer a soft welcoming sound when scraping up the browned bits on the bottom of your pans (try to avoid metal utensils in pans; they scratch the surface and make an unpleasant sound).

An instant-read thermometer, which is priced under $10,

will take all the guess work out of "Is it done yet?" You will never need to cut into your steak or chicken again to see how it's cooked. The temperature is the most accurate judge. Metal cooking tongs (not salad servers) help you turn food in a controlled way, while avoiding the splattering of oil that often accompanies turning hot food with a spatula.

It is also a good idea to rescue your most-used utensils from

Wooden Spoons

- Wooden spoons are very economical, so invest in a few different lengths to accommodate both deep pots and shallow pans.

- Wooden spoons stain easily, so be aware when stirring pots of food seasoned with turmeric, curry, or beets.

- Make sure a few of your wooden spoons have a squared-off, spatula tip for getting into the corners of pots.

- Use them when cooking anything in a nonstick pan; wood is naturally soft and won't scratch your pans.

Tongs

- Tongs allow you to gently grip and turn foods in a hot pan, avoiding the splatter of flipping them with a spatula.

- Use tongs to avoid touching raw meat: Transfer seasoned meat to a hot pan using the tongs and not your fingers.

- Buy tongs with a locking mechanism to keep them closed in storage so they don't get tangled in your utensil drawer.

- Silicone-tipped cooking tongs are a good choice when cooking in a cast-iron or nonstick pan.

the depth of the kitchen drawer and place them right next to the stove in a tall utensil holder so they are right at your fingertips when you need them. As important, your knives should also be stored on the countertop (sharp knives in a drawer are always a bad idea), either in a countertop knife holder or on a wall-mounted magnetic holder.

MAKE IT EASY

Holding Your Knife Correctly: Grip both sides of the blade with your thumb and forefinger, right at the very top of the knife blade, just forward of the handle (this gives you the most control over the blade). Curl the rest of your fingertips underneath the handle. Angle the tip down while cutting down to the cutting board with the back of the blade (don't use it like a cleaver!).

Knives

- An 8-inch chef's knife is the most useful knife you can own. It is deep enough to cut up large vegetables and big cuts of meat, but can also dice smaller herbs, garlic, and ginger.

- Buy a sharpening stone from the hardware store (they are more expensive at a housewares store) and ask how to use it. A sharp knife is the safest knife.

- Use a serrated knife when cutting bread, bagels, and tomatoes, which need the teeth of the knife to cut through their tough exteriors.

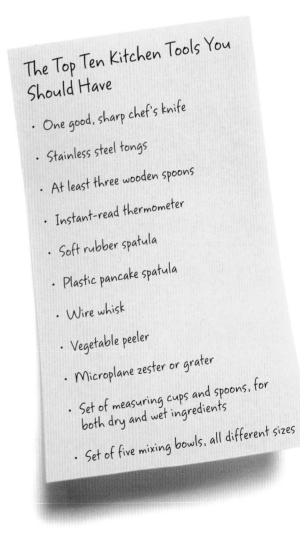

The Top Ten Kitchen Tools You Should Have

- One good, sharp chef's knife
- Stainless steel tongs
- At least three wooden spoons
- Instant-read thermometer
- Soft rubber spatula
- Plastic pancake spatula
- Wire whisk
- Vegetable peeler
- Microplane zester or grater
- Set of measuring cups and spoons, for both dry and wet ingredients
- Set of five mixing bowls, all different sizes

USING YOUR FREEZER
That small door next to your refrigerator is filled with endless options for saving you money

For the longest shelf life and to be sure you always have the ingredients you need on hand, there are many foods that belong in your freezer at all times. The list includes extra sticks of unsalted butter (for last-minute baking projects), nuts that won't be eaten for a few weeks, fresh ginger (makes grating a snap and there is never a need to peel it first), leftover

wine frozen in ½ cup portions, the raw trimming of chicken and vegetables (for making broth and soups), and, of course, leftover dinners. It is always good practice when making any amount of sauce or stew, which all freeze beautifully because of their high liquid content, to double or triple the recipe and freeze the remainder in small portions for future use. Imagine

Making Bread Crumbs

- Fill the bowl of a food processor with fresh or stale bread pieces and process until very fine.

- For seasoned crumbs, add 2 cloves fresh garlic, fresh or dried parsley, thyme, or oregano, 1 teaspoon lemon zest, ½ teaspoon salt, and black pepper.

- Walnuts, almonds, or pecans also make an excellent addition to bread crumbs for coating lamb, chicken, or fish. Store in the freezer until ready to use.

- Mark on the bag what seasonings, if any, you added to the crumbs.

Freezer Meals

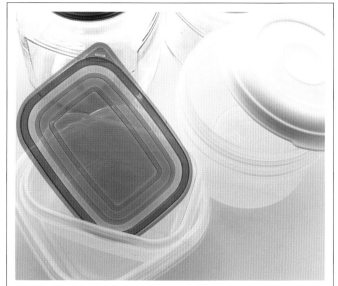

- Foods that have a good deal of liquid (sauces, stews, soups, thickly sauced meats) make the best freezer meals. The liquid protects the food from getting dry freezer burn.

- Use the right size container when storing food.

- The food should fit snugly with minimum air, where ice crystals can form. And since food expands when it freezes, don't fill right to the top.

- Make sure the food is completely cooled before freezing.

coming home from work or vacation late in the day and not having to worry about a good, hot meal. One will always be waiting for you in the freezer if you just plan ahead.

Also, good-quality frozen vegetables (peas, corn, lima beans, mustard greens) make surprising additions to soups in winter, and frozen berries (raspberries, strawberries, and blueberries) and frozen peaches make excellent breakfast smoothies and do wonders for breakfast pancakes.

MAKE IT EASY

Frozen Baby Food: For new parents, the best way to save money is to make your own baby food, and the freezer is practically the only tool you need. Roast several butternut squashes at a time (see page 6) and freeze the soft flesh in ice-cube trays, then store in freezer bags for when you need it. The same can be done with steamed spinach and zucchini (puree before freezing) and sweet potato.

Inexpensive Homemade Chicken Broth

- In a tall pot, cover 8 chicken legs and 8 wings, 2 halved onions, 3 celery stalks, and 3 carrots with 3 inches cold water. Bring to a boil, reduce heat, and simmer for 1 hour.

- Remove any "scum" that floats to the top for a clear broth.

- Strain the broth; cool. The vegetables will be too cooked to use again, but the cooked chicken can be shredded and used in soups, quesadillas, or chicken salad.

- Store in 1-cup portions in the freezer.

Ingredients to Have in Your Freezer

- Stale bread, for bread crumbs

- Chicken and vegetable trimmings, for broth

- Shrimp

- Ground meat, easily thawed for quick dinners

- Leftover wine in 1/2-cup portions

- Rinds of Parmesan cheese, for seasoning bean soups

- Leftovers, for quick microwave dinners

- Fresh ginger, for grating

- Nuts, to keep them from going rancid

- Peas, because they go with everything

COOKING AHEAD
Cook once and keep enjoying fresh food meal after meal

The best way to save money is to have a surplus of ingredients on hand at all times. So, in addition to dipping into the pantry for dried and canned staples, it is also a good idea to stock the fridge and freezer with a few cooked fresh foods for when you need dinner in a pinch. Roast a few chickens, grill some extra steaks, or slow roast another pork shoulder; the leftovers will last for up to 3 days in your refrigerator for the foundation of countless other lunches and dinners.

Since you always want to have a fresh vegetable at every meal (and may not always have fresh produce on hand), frozen cooked vegetables are both practical and healthy. The obvious frozen peas and corn are good to have in stock, but so are portions of fresh-cooked tomato sauce and steamed bell peppers. A package of cooked greens—like spinach, mustard greens, kale, or Swiss chard—or roasted squash can be defrosted easily and served as a side dish when heated

Roast Chicken

- Use leftover chicken or a supermarket rotisserie chicken. Shred meat before storing.

- Cashew Chicken: Stir-fry ginger, garlic, snow peas, sliced peppers, and cashews until brown. Add soy sauce, a bit of dark sesame oil, and shredded chicken. Serve with rice.

- Chicken Puttanesca: Simmer tomato sauce with capers, olives, anchovies, and hot pepper flakes. Add chicken and serve over pasta.

Roasted Butternut Squash

- Cut the squash in half lengthwise, scrape out seeds, and place facedown on a foil-lined baking sheet. Roast at 375°F until soft, 45 minutes. Scrape out soft flesh. Freeze in 1-cup portions.

- Use to make squash soup, seasoned with fresh ginger and apples.

- Serve as a side dish for ham or turkey, seasoned with orange zest, butter, and honey.

- Add it to macaroni and cheese to enrich it and add nutritional value.

in a pan with a little butter and salt (or plenty of other variations).

To stock your frozen pantry most efficiently, make large quantities of sauces and cooked vegetables when the time allows and then cool and portion into containers the right size to feed your family.

Cooked Leafy Greens

- Steam, squeeze dry, and chop several pounds of greens and freeze in 1-cup portions for future use.

- Use to make quick side dishes: heat with heavy cream and lemon zest; sauté in butter with fresh ginger and sesame seeds; or sauté in olive oil with sliced garlic and red pepper flakes.

- Add to main dishes for tremendous nutritional value: layer into lasagna; fold into baked ziti; pair with cheese in an omelet; sauté with canned beans and crumbled sausage.

Tomato Sauce

- Homemade tomato sauce is best, but there are plenty of good-quality jarred sauces on the market. Just check the ingredients: no sugar and only ingredients you would use to make your own sauce.

- Poached Eggs in Tomato Sauce: In a nonstick pan, simmer 1½ cups tomato sauce. Make four small wells, crack in eggs, cover, and poach until gently set, 4 minutes. Serve with crusty bread or over pasta.

- Add browned meat and/ or sautéed eggplant and zucchini to enrich premade sauce.

CHEF SECRETS
Learn a few time-saving and flavor-boosting tricks from the professionals

Chefs certainly know a thing or two when it comes to making the most of their ingredients. Their tight food budgets require them to come up with tricks for making the most delicious food with a minimum of waste and expense. Lemons and limes are always zested before they are squeezed for juice, so all parts are used (you can store the zest indefinitely in a bag in your freezer for future pound cakes or puddings).

Vegetable and meat trimmings are saved for broth; pasta cooking water is used to thin sauces to the perfect consistency; day-old bread is made into bread crumbs or croutons. And they know how to coax the most flavor out of a dish. To season your food, think beyond the traditional salt and

Mise en Place

- This is a French culinary term that means "everything in its place."

- It is a cooking concept that allows cooks to keep organized in the kitchen by preparing each ingredient before they start cooking: chopping the onion, mincing garlic, peeling and cubing potatoes, cutting chicken breasts into strips.

- Lay out the prepared ingredients in piles on your cutting board (or in small bowls) and bring the piles over to the stove when you begin cooking. That way everything will be at your fingertips when you need it.

Pan Sauces

- Use the drippings left behind after browning a steak or piece of chicken to make a rich sauce.

- Remove the cooked meat and keep the pan over medium-high heat. Add 1 cup broth, ⅓ cup wine, and a sprig or pinch of dried thyme and cook, scraping the bottom of the pan to remove bits.

- Simmer liquid for 5 minutes to concentrate flavors. Remove from heat and swirl in 2 tablespoons butter until melted and season with salt and a dash of vinegar to brighten it.

pepper and try perking it up with a squeeze of citrus juice, a dash of vinegar, a few capers or chopped garlic, a handful of chopped fresh herbs, a pinch of cayenne or other hot pepper product, a pat of unsalted butter, or a splash of cream. Having a few tricks up your sleeve will guarantee that you'll be eating restaurant-quality food without the expense of leaving the house.

Caramelized Onions

- In a large skillet over medium heat, melt 2 tablespoons butter. Add 3 large onions, sliced; cover and steam for 5 minutes. Remove cover and cook onions, stirring occasionally, until they are golden brown, 20 minutes.

- Use onions to top pizzas or as an omelet filling when paired with Swiss or Brie cheese.

- Toss onions with a little vinegar and serve as a condiment for grilled sausages and meats.

Crostini

- Arrange ½-inch thick slices of bread (baguettes are good) on a baking sheet, brush both sides with olive oil, and toast in a 350°F oven until crisp, 8 minutes.

- Use as salad croutons: Rub crostini with a raw garlic clove and cut into small cubes.

- Serve with soups: Spread with soft cheese or melt grated cheese on top and float on top of soup or serve alongside.

- Make appetizers: Top with fresh mozzarella cheese, basil leaves, and roasted red peppers.

9

ENTERTAINING ON A BUDGET
Learn how to cook for a crowd without breaking the bank

The key to cooking for a large group of people is to choose a main course or a cut of meat that is both inexpensive and large enough to feed a crowd. Check out Chapter 18: Showstoppers, for the best of the best.

Since the most inexpensive cuts of meat are also the toughest, they all work beautifully as braised or slow-roasted dishes, which frees up your time to work on the rest of the party.

Cheaper yet, choose a vegetarian showstopper to take center stage, like a roasted vegetable lasagna, homemade pizza, or rich bean soup.

Choose side dishes that can also be made ahead of time; you don't want to be preparing dishes while you should be enjoying your guests. Salads are ideal, dressed up with some colorful vegetables and fruits, and most vegetables (string

Quick Appetizers

- Crostini (see page 9) topped with soft goat cheese, sliced roasted mushrooms, and balsamic syrup (cook ½ cup balsamic vinegar with ½ teaspoon sugar until syrupy, 7 minutes).

- Platter with red grapes, walnuts, blue cheese, and crackers.

- Fresh Guacamole: Mash 4 ripe avocadoes until smooth. Add 2 diced and seeded plum tomatoes; ½ small red onion, diced; ¼ cup chopped cilantro; juice of 2 limes; ¼ teaspoon cumin; and ½ teaspoon salt. Serve with blue and yellow corn tortilla chips.

Easy Side Dishes

- Romaine salad with sliced oranges, black olives, and pickled red onions (toss 1 sliced red onion with 2 tablespoons red wine vinegar and marinate for 30 minutes).

- Orange Sweet Potatoes: Thinly slice 4 peeled sweet potatoes and layer in large

heavy pot. Pour over 1 cup heavy cream or broth, cover, and steam until tender. Mash with 1 teaspoon grated orange zest, 2 tablespoons honey or maple syrup, and salt to taste.

beans, broccoli rabe, asparagus) can be steamed ahead of time and then rinsed under cold water to cool them. They'll be fine at room temperature for hours until you serve them, tossed with some vinaigrette during the summer months or warmed in a pan with melted butter and sesame seeds and seasoned with fresh lemon juice and salt.

Think about color when you cook for a party; imagine what the plate will look like as you plan the menu. Think sweet potatoes, butternut squash, fuschia beets, slender green vegetables, orange and yellow bell peppers, cherry tomatoes, yellow squash, orange carrots; these vibrant-colors can be snuck into most dishes to add a visual appeal that will set your party apart.

Desserts on a Dime

- Fresh peaches, plums, or nectarines (halved and pitted) taste great topped with fresh ricotta cheese, toasted sliced almonds, and a generous drizzle of honey.

- Chocolate Fondue: Put 12 ounces chocolate chips in bowl. Pour over 1½ cups hot heavy cream; let stand 5 minutes and stir until smooth. Serve with fruit (bananas, strawberries, orange sections).

- Lime Syrup: Combine ½ cup water, ½ cup sugar, grated zest of 2 limes in saucepan; heat until sugar dissolves; cool. Serve over any sliced tropical fruit.

The Tough Cuts

Consider these meats for your next party; they are both inexpensive and cook slowly in an unattended oven.

- Brisket
- Oxtail
- Short ribs
- Chicken thighs and legs
- Lamb shanks
- Lamb ribs
- Pork shoulder butt (or Boston butt)
- Fresh ham (uncured fresh pork)
- Pork ribs (country style or St. Louis style)

BEANS & LENTILS
With a pantry filled with colorful legumes, dinner is just around the corner

When it comes to inexpensive and convenient, canned beans can't be beat. They are also quite low in fat and high in protein and fiber, and last practically forever on pantry shelves. And, with so many varieties to choose from, you can eat them frequently without getting tired of the same old, same old. Black, kidney, and pinto beans are the mainstay

of a good chili, while creamy cannellini and roman beans (another name for borlotti or cranberry beans) are terrific tossed with braised bitter greens, like broccoli rabe, escarole, or mustard greens.

For even greater savings, buy dried beans when you can, which are available in 1-pound bags in the supermarket or in

KNACK GOURMET COOKING ON A BUDGET

Dried Beans, Dos and Don'ts

- When cooking dried beans, don't add any salt or acidic ingredients (tomatoes, vinegar, wine) to the liquid they are cooking in. Acid toughens the skins.

- To check when the beans are done (short of popping a hot bean in your mouth), pick one up on a spoon and

- blow lightly on it. If its skin ripples and pulls away from the bean, the bean is done.

- A pinch of baking soda added to the cooking water will make a soft, tender bean.

Lentils

- Lentils are most commonly available in brown, French green, and red.

- They are the quickest cooking of the legume family and don't need to be soaked.

- Split lentils cook up soft and creamy, while whole lentils keep their shape.

- Their flavor is earthy and mild and pairs well with spices.

- Indian *Dal*: Combine 4 cups water, 1 cup red split lentils, 1 teaspoon turmeric, ¾ teaspoon salt. Boil, cover, simmer until creamy, 25 minutes. Serve with rice and plain yogurt.

bulk at health food stores, which offer an even better savings. Some varieties of beans are less than $1 a pound, which can make enough food to feed six people. Especially when buying in bulk, be extra careful about checking for small stones. Just rinse the beans in a colander and toss through them with your hands. The small stones will be more visible that way.

Dried lentils cook much faster than dried beans, so they are a good option when you want a hearty dinner on the table in under 30 minutes.

MAKE IT EASY

Soaking Beans: Since dried beans need to be soaked for at least 6 hours before cooking, it is handy to have a quick-soaking method to fall back on when you are short on time. Put the beans in a large pot and cover with 2 inches cold water. Bring to a boil, immediately cover the pot, and remove it from the burner. Allow to stand for 1 hour. Drain the beans, and they are ready to use.

Chickpeas

- Chickpeas, also called garbanzo beans, are a sturdy legume and take the longest to cook.

- Because of their meaty texture, they are a good vegetarian substitute for meat in dishes like curries, stews, and soups. Add to salads for extra protein.

- Fresh Three-Bean Salad: Combine 1 cup cooked chickpeas, 1 cup cooked kidney beans, and ⅓ pound cooked string beans cut into 1-inch lengths. Toss with ¼ cup olive oil, 2 tablespoons wine vinegar, salt, and pepper.

Dried Beans in a Pressure Cooker

- A pressure cooker shaves hours off bean cooking time. Keep your eyes open at tag sales or discount stores; new ones are around $50.

- Pressure cookers work by trapping hot steam inside the pot, which builds up extreme pressure. This causes the temperature inside to rise dramatically, which cooks the beans faster.

- You need to presoak beans before pressure cooking, but not more than 4 hours.

- Most beans will be tender after only 15 minutes.

OILS & VINEGARS

Flavorful food starts with a diversity of oils and vinegars to choose from

While you'll find olive oil and balsamic vinegar in most cupboards, it is a good idea to broaden your selection. Since olive oil is the healthiest all-purpose cooking and seasoning oil, you want a big bottle of extra-virgin to use for all your cooking. For occasions when olive oil is not the right choice, like when baking or making Asian food, make sure to stock a neutral oil like light olive oil (this only refers to the color and flavor, not calories). Toasted dark sesame oil, which is available in the Asian aisle of most supermarkets, adds a fragrant nutty note to all Asian dishes and stir-fries. Store all toasted nut oils in the fridge to keep them from going rancid prematurely.

On the vinegar front, while balsamic is a fine choice for salad

Extra-Virgin Olive Oil

- This is the finest quality olive oil on the market.

- Extra-virgin oil is what is released the first time the olives are pressed. This dark green oil is rich in aroma, color, and flavor.

- "Light" olive oils are simply lighter in color and flavor (from second pressings); they are not lower in fat.

- Store it out of the way of light and heat, both of which hasten the rancidity of olive oil. Extra-virgin olive oil has a shelf life of one year.

Seasoning with Vinegar

- Vinegar is not just for salad dressings; its acidic bite helps sharpen the flavors of many foods.

- Cooked greens are light on flavor and benefit tremendously from a splash of vinegar (red wine and apple cider are best).

- When making a pan sauce for steak or chicken, add a teaspoon of balsamic or wine vinegar to the finished sauce for the best flavor.

- Vinegar not only adds flavor to marinating meats, its acid also tenderizes it by breaking down connective tissue.

dressing, its strong, sweet flavor often overpowers more delicate lettuces and milder dishes. In addition, consider white balsamic vinegar (for the same sweet taste but less intense in both flavor and color), red and white wine vinegars, sherry wine vinegar, and rice vinegar. All have their own wonderful qualities, and variety will help you expand your seasoning abilities, whether it is a splash of red wine vinegar on your sautéed Swiss chard or a tablespoon of sherry vinegar to perk up your black bean soup.

ZOOM

Here is how to read the labels on extra-virgin olive oil to choose the best bottle: Look for "grown, pressed, and bottled" in a single country ("Product of Italy" only means the oil was bottled there). "Cold-pressed" means the oil was never subjected to heat, a good thing for its flavor. Look for a "pressing" date, avoiding oil that is more than two years old.

Homemade Vinaigrette

- Start with one part vinegar to two parts oil. Use extra-virgin olive oil as your base, adding small amounts of nut oils (walnut, hazelnut, toasted sesame) for occasional flavoring.

- For acid, choose citrus juices (lemon, lime, grapefruit, or orange) or vinegars (red wine, balsamic, white balsamic, rice, sherry wine, or champagne).

- Enhance your vinaigrette with Dijon mustard, chopped shallots, minced garlic, fresh or dried herbs (tarragon, basil, mint, parsley, or oregano), or spices (cumin or coriander).

Upgrading Your Pantry

It is helpful to have a variety of ingredients to choose from when seasoning your food. Consider stocking your pantry with a few new oils or vinegars.

- Oils: pistachio, walnut, toasted pumpkin seed, toasted dark sesame, Asian hot chile.

- Vinegars: rice (white and black Chinese), unfiltered apple cider, sherry, and white balsamic.

GRAINS & PASTA

Healthy cooking starts with a pantry filled with whole grains

Variety is the spice of life, and that adage should be applied to your grain and pasta pantry. While nearly everyone has a package of spaghetti and a bag of white rice on hand, there are many more staples that can bring color and flavor to your dinner plate.

Consider pasta in all shapes and sizes. Italians pair their pasta to the sauce they are using, and that is a very good practice to get used to. Twisted or cupped pastas are best to catch the sauce of chunky ragùs, thin sauces like white clam cling to the long strands of linguine and spaghetti, and penne and pesto sauce are a classic pairing.

On the rice front, add a wild rice blend (plain wild rice is too strong to eat on its own), a sticky short-grain brown rice (great for Asian food), or a fragrant brown basmati rice to your

Polenta

- Polenta is a thick, cornmeal porridge.

- It is traditionally used as a side dish with hearty meat and vegetable stews.

- Polenta can be served creamy or left to firm up in a greased baking dish and cut into in thick slices.

- Polenta, or cornmeal, is available in regular medium-grain or instant (precooked cornmeal). Choose the variety based on the time you have.

- The longer you cook cornmeal, the richer the flavor will be. Stir frequently to prevent it from scorching.

Risotto

- Risotto is a creamy rice dish made from a starchy, short-grain rice like arborio.

- Hot broth is added gradually to the cooking rice to maximize the starchy liquid released from the rice.

- Risotto is finished with some cold butter and grated Parmesan cheese to enrich it.

- Add different ingredients at the end of cooking to vary its flavor: sautéed mushrooms, steamed asparagus and lemon zest, cooked spinach and fresh basil, roasted butternut squash, or fresh peas and diced ham.

shelves. Short, white arborio rice is a must for creamy risotto, fish and rice dishes like paella, and unbeatable rice puddings. Other grains, like cornmeal (for making polenta), pearl barley, couscous, and quinoa, also make hearty and healthy starch alternatives to the standard rice and pasta choices.

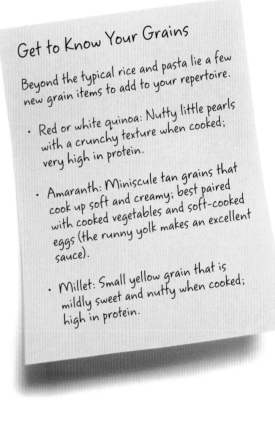
YELLOW ● LIGHT

Storing Your Grains: To avoid the occasional pantry or grain moth outbreak, which can infiltrate your pantry from a poorly packaged bag of flour or the bulk grain bin at the health food store, store all your grains in glass containers. The least expensive way to do this is to slowly accumulate glass jars from spent condiments, honey, and juices. Clean and dry them and then fill with colorful grains (and beans). They make for a more artful display and easier access.

Fresh and Dried Pasta

- Choose fresh pasta when you are pairing it with a chunky meat sauce, like Bolognese. Its toothsome bite can hold its own with the hearty sauce.

- Choose a shaped pasta (like penne or fusilli) when tossing it with vegetables or cubes of meat or cheese, so the ingredients can get trapped in the pasta's twists and turns.

- Consider whole wheat pasta, not only for its added nutritional value, but also for its nutty flavor, which pairs well with pesto and creamy Alfredo sauce.

Get to Know Your Grains

Beyond the typical rice and pasta lie a few new grain items to add to your repertoire.

- Red or white quinoa: Nutty little pearls with a crunchy texture when cooked; very high in protein.

- Amaranth: Miniscule tan grains that cook up soft and creamy; best paired with cooked vegetables and soft-cooked eggs (the runny yolk makes an excellent sauce).

- Millet: Small yellow grain that is mildly sweet and nutty when cooked; high in protein.

17

FRESH HERBS & SPICES

Having a selection of seasonings on hand helps make food taste vibrant and flavorful

To maximize the flavor of food, it is important to have a variety of seasonings readily available. First and foremost is salt, which can be simple table salt or, even better, flaky kosher salt (for texture) or briny sea salt (for flavor), both preferred by most chefs.

Sea salt comes in both a fine and coarse grain. Fine is good for cooking and seasoning, while coarse grain is used in a salt grinder, which produces a ground salt with a beautiful, crystalline texture. After salt, a good peppermill with a supply of black peppercorns (which you can buy inexpensively in bulk) is a close second; powdery preground pepper is a poor substitute.

A Basic Spice Rack

- Bay leaves
- Black peppercorns
- Cayenne pepper and pepper flakes
- Cinnamon, sticks and ground
- Cloves, whole and ground
- Coriander, ground and seeds
- Cumin, ground and seeds
- Curry powder
- Dried oregano and or/basil
- Dry mustard
- Fennel seeds
- Ground ginger
- Nutmeg (whole provides the best flavor)
- Paprika (regular and smoked)

Using Salt

- Salt can be harvested from a mine or from the sea.

- A dash of salt will draw the moisture out of food, helping it evaporate quickly so food can brown.

- Salt brings out the flavors of food; just enough will intensify the flavors already in a dish, too much will make it just taste salty.

- Sprinkle a bit of salt over your salad just before serving to bring out the flavor of the lettuce and dressing and to give it a pleasing crunch.

Supermarkets also sell plastic peppermills with whole peppercorns inside. They are much better than ground, but be aware that you can't alter the texture of the pepper (it generally comes out very coarse) and you can't reuse the container.

The shelf life of well-kept dried spices and herbs—kept away from light and heat—is at least one year, but fresh herbs need to be replaced a bit more often. Woody herbs like rosemary keep longer than leafy herbs like basil, so keep that in mind when you buy your next bunch.

ZOOM

For woody herbs (thyme, rosemary, and sage), the bane of their existence is moisture. When possible, buy them in small plastic boxes, which protect them from the moisture of the refrigerator. Otherwise, wrap them loosely in paper towels and seal in a plastic bag. Treat leafy herbs (cilantro, basil, parsley) like flowers and set the stems in a jar of water. Loosely cover leaves with a plastic bag.

Drying Herbs

- When you find yourself with too many fresh herbs to use before they wilt, dry them.

- Tie the stems loosely together and hang upside down.

- Store in a well-ventilated area until the leaves are brittle.

- Once they are dried, crumble the leaves off the stems and store in a glass jar, away from light and heat.

- Dried herb bouquets look nice, but the longer they hang, the less flavorful they become.

Fresh Herb Sauces

- Extend the life of fresh herbs by making an herb sauce.

- In the jar of a blender, combine the fresh herb leaves and enough olive oil to make a puree.

- You can add any of the following to increase the flavor: nuts (no skin), salty hard cheeses like Parmesan or pecorino, lemon zest, or fresh garlic.

- Store in the freezer (or in the 2 tablespoon wells of an ice-cube tray) until you cook something that needs that fresh herbal boost.

TOMATOES, TOMATOES, TOMATOES

From fresh to paste, the tomato has a way of perking up the flavor of food

Is it a fruit or a vegetable? No matter which camp you are in, everyone agrees with the power of a good tomato. Raw and fresh from the garden is the ultimate, but luckily there are plenty of other ways to enjoy tomato's unique sweet and acidic punch: in cans (whole peeled or crushed), in a tube of paste, sauced in a jar, and dried into tomato leather. In all its nonfresh forms, tomatoes are perfect pantry items, laying in wait for your next bean soup, chili, or meat sauce, where they would be sorely missed.

Tomatoes also contain lycopene, which is a known antioxidant and cancer fighter. The more concentrated the tomato (think tomato paste and ketchup), the more lycopene it has.

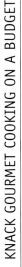

Canned Tomatoes

- When fresh seasonal tomatoes aren't at your disposal (or in your budget), opt for canned tomatoes to make soups, sauces, and braised dishes.

- The tomatoes are picked ripe then peeled and canned in tomato juice or a thick tomato puree. Opt for ones packed in juice for a lighter flavor. The puree often tastes heartily of cooked tomato paste.

- Diced tomatoes are often harder than whole peeled; better to buy whole peeled and shred them with your hands for the best texture.

Roasted Tomatoes

- This is the number one way to extend the shelf life and usefulness of any fresh tomato.

- It turns bland, watery tomatoes into sweet tomato bliss.

- Cherry tomatoes and plum tomatoes are the best all-purpose roasting tomatoes, due to their small size and sturdy skin.

- Cut tomatoes in half (for plum) or leave whole (for cherry) and toss gently with a bit of olive oil. Roast in a 350°F oven until soft and collapsed; 1 hour at least.

Tomato Paste

- Look for tomato paste sold in long tubes instead of small cans. Most recipes don't call for a whole can and then you are forced to repackage the leftovers. With the tubes you squeeze out just what you need. Store in the refrigerator.

- If you can't find tubes, store extra tomato paste in the 2-tablespoon wells of an ice-cube tray, then transfer frozen paste to a freezer bag to store for future use.

Peeling Fresh Tomatoes

- Sometimes you don't want tomato's tough skin in your food.

- Make a small X in the bottom of each tomato using a sharp knife.

- Fill a pot with 6 inches of water and bring to a boil. Use a slotted spoon to lower the tomatoes into the pot; leave in until the X starts to pull away from the tomato, about 1 minute.

- Remove the tomatoes and transfer to a colander in the sink; run cold water over them until cool. Slip off skins.

FLAVORFUL INGREDIENTS
Discover the world of seasonings beyond salt and spices

After the ubiquitous salt and pepper, there is still a whole host of pantry and refrigerated condiments items that can help boost foods' flavor: Kalamata olives, capers, anchovies, roasted red peppers, roasted garlic, sun-dried tomatoes, dried mushrooms, dried chiles (like ancho or guajillo), canned chipotle peppers in adobo sauce, hot sauce (anything from Tabasco to Asian sambal), Dijon mustard,

chicken or vegetable broth, canned tomatoes, individual-serving wine bottles (both red and white) for cooking, coconut milk, and soy sauce.

By having a collection of add-ins in your pantry, you will never tire of the food you make, which often happens when you reach for the same seasoning dish after dish.

Capers belong in almost any fish dish; their salty flavor

Roasted Red Peppers

- On the grill or gas burner: Blacken skin of whole peppers all over on a very hot grill or gas stove burner set on high.

- Under the broiler: Cut peppers in half and lay, skin side up, on a baking sheet. Flatten halves with your hand for even charring.

- Place under broiler until skin is blackened.

- Transfer peppers to a bowl and cover for 10 minutes to loosen skin. Use fingers or paper towel to remove the skin (don't run under sink!).

Olives and Capers

- Add chopped capers and olives to tomato sauce and chicken dishes and sprinkle over fish and salads as a salt or vinegar substitute.

- Quick marinated olives for parties: Combine 2 cups unpitted olives marinated in 1 teaspoon dried herbs (oregano, thyme, rosemary),

2 smashed garlic cloves, pinch of pepper flakes, 1 strip orange zest, ¼ cup olive oil, 1 tablespoon balsamic vinegar, salt, and pepper.

complements the briny flavor and perks up milder tasting fish like cod and sole. Dried mushrooms and sun-dried tomatoes can be soaked in hot water until soft, then chopped and added to soups, stews, and sauces. Smoky chipotle peppers are wonderful with black beans, pinto beans, sweet potatoes, and butternut squash. Coconut milk makes terrific curries and soups and sweetens cooked rice. Use it for desserts, too, as in coconut rice pudding or coconut tapioca pudding flavored with a little ground cardamom or chopped pistachios.

MAKE IT EASY

Roasted Garlic: Preheat oven to 400°F. Cut ¼-inch off the top of the garlic head to expose the tips of all the cloves (this will make it easier to remove). Place the bulb on a piece of foil and drizzle with a little olive oil, rubbing it into the cut tips so they don't dry out. Wrap the foil around the garlic and roast until it is soft and golden brown, 45 minutes. Cool before squeezing out.

Citrus

- Remember that citrus juices (and vinegar) are flavor boosters, too. Don't let salt have all the fun. Reach for a lemon wedge before you add more salt.

- Cooked vegetables, vegetable soups, and beans take especially well to a squeeze of fresh lemon or lime juice. The juice perks up their flavor more than salt can.

- Citrus juices don't like heat, which breaks down its delicate zesty taste. If you reheat a dish with fresh lemon or lime juice, you need to add more before serving again.

Asian Condiments

- Add coconut milk in place of half the water when cooking white or brown rice for delicious coconut rice.

- Use rice vinegar to season your sautéed vegetables. Use a dash of sesame oil and soy sauce to a pan of sautéed chicken or beef.

- Whisk a bit of soy sauce into your scrambled eggs in lieu of salt.

- Hot chile sauces, like Sriracha or sambal, wake up the flavor of stir-fried greens, quesadillas, and even fried eggs.

DAIRY & EGGS
All hail cows, sheep, goats, and chickens

Ah, dairy. It is the stuff of life. Milk, cream, yogurt, cheese, sour cream, cream cheese—where would we be without these foods? We have our cows to thank for this abundance of dairy, and it is important to remember that these products all come from a living animal. The food that cows eat is directly related to the quality of the milk we drink. These days there are so many choices to be made in the dairy aisle,

and you should take time to understand what they all mean. Organic milk is a good place to start. This milk is free of any bovine growth hormone (which makes cows produce more milk) and antibiotics (which are given to commercially raised cattle to ward off potential diseases from living in such tight quarters). Organic dairy is slightly more expensive than commercial dairy, but the health benefits outweigh the minimal

Butter

- If a recipe calls for "butter," it is safe to use either salted or unsalted. However, in case unsalted butter was used to test the recipe, taste the dish before adding the prescribed amount of salt.

- Unsalted butter is in fact a fresher product than salted; the salt used acts as a pre-

servative and increases the shelf life.

- European-style butter (now available in many supermarkets) has a higher fat content and a more luxurious texture. It makes unbeatably tender baked goods.

Yogurt

- Yogurt is filled with friendly bacteria for good digestive health.

- Greek yogurt is strained of most of its whey, creating a thick and creamy yogurt. It is a great way to enjoy low-fat yogurt.

- Stir Greek yogurt into sautéed spinach for healthy creamed spinach or serve for dessert topped with honey and walnuts.

- Yogurt is also made from goat, sheep, and buffalo milk (the richest of the milks). Try them all.

cost. Look for store-brand organic milk for the best savings.

Eggs, too, come from a living source, so the chickens' care is an important component of their quality. Farmers' markets provide the best and most direct source of eggs, usually from real free-range, farm-raised birds. But if that is not feasible, look for cartons marked "cage free" and certainly "no antibiotics," all clearly displayed to set them apart from the conventional Styrofoam-packed variety.

Soft Fresh Cheeses

- Fresh cheeses are not aged and hardened before being consumed.

- Fresh ricotta, cottage cheese, farmers' cheese, pot cheese, *queso fresco*, and goat cheese are among the most popular.

- The shelf life is shorter than aged and salted cheese, and these cheeses are beloved for their creamy sweetness.

- Add fresh goat cheese to salads and fold into scrambled eggs.

- Crumble salty *queso fresco* on top of tacos and beans.

Eggs

- Buy the freshest eggs you can; look to farmers' markets or friends with chickens. Pastured chickens make healthier eggs, higher in omega-3s.

- Fresher eggs at room temperature make the fluffiest beaten egg whites.

- When making hard-boiled eggs, don't overcook them (no more than 10 minutes), or they will develop gray green rings around the yolks.

- Tap and crack the boiled egg all over for the easiest peeling.

FRESH INGREDIENTS

FRESH VEGETABLES

The key to enjoying the freshest produce is to buy local and in season whenever possible

When it comes to shopping for fresh produce, it is said that local is the new organic, but let us explain. When choosing the healthiest possible fruits and vegetables, buying organic produce (and countless other products) is a good place to start. It simply means that the food is grown without the use of chemicals or pesticides, all of which are good things

to avoid. The resulting cost is a bit higher, because organic farming methods are more costly. Of course, choosing to spend extra money on an organic head of lettuce versus a conventionally grown one is a matter of personal choice (and finances).

It should be noted that getting the "organic" seal of approval

Leafy Greens

- Make greens a part of your everyday diet.

- The darker the green, the richer it is in vitamins and minerals (like iron and calcium). Choose dark collards, kale, and Swiss chard for optimal nutrition.

- Wash salad greens and lay in an even layer on a dish towel or paper towels. Roll up and store in a plastic bag for maximum shelf life. This keeps the leaves moist but not too wet.

- Discard the woody ribs from kale and collards before cooking.

Summer Squash

- Tender yellow squash and zucchini are the "summer squashes," while the hard, orange-fleshed varieties are the "winter squashes."

- Wrap summer squashes in paper towels to prevent them from rotting in the refrigerator.

- Grilled and roasted are excellent ways to enjoy these vegetables. Just toss cubes or strips with olive oil and salt and cook until golden and tender.

- Zucchini will "melt" when it's cooked for a long time, making it a terrific vegetable to add to cooked pasta.

from the FDA is a costly procedure, and many small farms (who sell directly from their own farms or at farmers' markets) opt not to get it, even though their farming practices are organic to the letter.

The recent national push to buy local (sometimes choosing it above buying "organic") focuses on supporting local businesses and cutting out the extreme distances most food has to travel to get to consumers, thus saving energy. Most people can't get local bananas and lemons, so your choices are dependent on where in the country you live

Broccoli and Cauliflower

- For quick steamed broccoli: Heat 1 inch water with ½ teaspoon salt. Bring to a boil, add bite-size florets, cover, and cook for 4 minutes.

- Drain and toss with melted butter (the water will already have salted the broccoli) or enjoy plain.

- Roast cauliflower to bring out its sweetness: Toss bite-size florets with olive oil and lay in an even layer on a baking sheet. Sprinkle with salt; roast at 375°F until soft and golden, 25 minutes.

Blanching Green Vegetables

- Blanching refers to cooking something in boiling water until it is less than perfectly cooked. This ensures that foods that are reheated (to season or serve them) will not be overcooked.

- Bitter vegetables like brussels sprouts and broccoli rabe are often blanched to rid them of some of their sharp taste.

- Blanching and "shocking" (cooling in cold water) helps green vegetables retain their bright green color.

- Blanch string beans, broccoli, snow peas, and asparagus.

ROOT VEGGIES & WINTER SQUASH
Thanks to cold storage, we can enjoy these vegetables all year long

We differentiate between fresh vegetables and root vegetables/winter squash because while they are technically fresh, their shelf life far exceeds more tender, watery vegetables that belong in the refrigerator. Luckily you can keep these hard beauties on hand for a long while, ensuring that you always have a choice when making dinner, even if the produce drawer of the refrigerator is empty.

Since so many root vegetables and most squashes tend toward the sweet side (sweet potatoes, parsnips, carrots, rutabagas, butternut squash, beets), they pair well with many foods: pork, chicken, beans, turkey, duck. Their rich, deeply hued colors are also a culinary inspiration, making any dish that includes them that much more impressive (and nutritious; think tons of vitamin A and C).

How to Cut an Onion

- Cut the onion in half lengthwise (through the root, which holds all the layers together). Place cut-side down on a board. Remove papery skin.

- With the root end away from you, make lengthwise cuts across the onion, leaving ¼ inch of the onion still attached at the root end; this will hold the onion together while you cut.

- Rotate the onion 90 degrees and cut across the slices you just made, cutting toward the root for uniform cubes.

Winter Squash

- Roasting squash intensifies its sweetness: Cut squash in half, scrape out seeds. Place cut side down in a foil-lined roasting pan. Roast at 375°F until very tender, 45 minutes.

- Spaghetti squash: Once it is roasted and cooled slightly, use a fork to scrape out the strands of squash from the tough, leathery shell. Toss with butter and Parmesan cheese or top with tomato sauce. It has a wonderful crunchy texture and mildly sweet flavor.

Store winter squashes on the countertop or in the refrigerator if there is room (although they don't require the cold unless their skin is cut). Squashes will only start to rot if there is a small blemish or nick on the skin. If they do, just cut out the "bad" part and use the rest, which will be unaffected.

Carrots and parsnips do best in the refrigerator and will last for at least a month. Keep them wrapped in a plastic bag to avoid bendable carrots. If they do lose moisture and become soft, just use them for a batch of carrot soup, where they will be perfect.

A word about pumpkins: For a cooking pumpkin, you will need to buy a "sugar pumpkin" or "pie pumpkin," which are small and heavy and have a sweet pumpkin taste. Also, if you can find it, a "cheese pumpkin" has the richest flavor, with the deep orange nuttiness that is most often associated with canned pumpkin. It has a thickly ribbed tan skin, much the color of a butternut squash.

Potatoes

- Keep potatoes away from light, as they will develop a bitter green flesh just beneath the skin.

- Store in a cool, dry place, preferably in a paper bag. This allows the potatoes to breathe, preventing rotting or sprouting. Don't store in the refrigerator.

- Don't store with onions, or they will produce gases that rot both.

- Buy purple Peruvian potatoes when you can find them. They make gorgeous mashed or roasted potatoes.

Roasted Beets

- Don't boil your beets! They leech out too much of their sweet flavor and bright color into the water.

- Instead, roast them: Scrub and cut in half or quarters, if large. Tightly wrap in aluminum foil, keeping them in a single layer (important for quick, even roasting). Roast at 375°F until very tender, 1 hour. Cool and rub off skins while still warm.

- Roasted beets pair well with oranges, arugula, goat cheese, walnuts, red onions, and balsamic vinegar.

CHICKEN & TURKEY

Poultry is a wise choice for economical eating

Chicken and turkey provide a great way to get the most out of your money at the supermarket. Chickens can be roasted whole (for the greatest savings), carved, and served as is, or shredded for countless other dishes. Roasted chicken wings or dishes made from braised drumsticks and thighs utilize inexpensive cuts to create delicious meals. The dark meat is richer in flavor and moisture and is the best bet for both

your palate and your wallet. Roasting a whole turkey, or even just a large turkey breast, creates enough food for a crowd or enough to take you through a week's worth of meals (which can be stored in the freezer so you don't tire of turkey all at once!).

As a word of caution when cooking poultry: Most cases of salmonella come from cross-contamination, when people

Dark Meat

- Most chefs agree: Dark meat is more succulent than white.

- Dark meat does not dry out as fast during cooking.

- Dark meat does have slightly more fat and calories than white, but the difference is small enough

not to choose one over the other.

- Dark meat depends on muscle use. Flightless chicken and turkeys have white breasts because they don't fly, and dark legs and thighs because they walk. Ducks have dark breasts and legs.

Pan-Roasted Chicken

- Crisping chicken skin in a hot skillet before transferring it (skillet and all) to the oven creates perfectly browned skin coupled with tender roasted meat.

- The direct heat of the skillet is required to make the skin as crispy as it can be.

- The indirect heat of the oven is required to cook chicken all the way through when it is on the bone. The cold bone makes it difficult to cook evenly in a pan.

- Pan roasting chicken provides plenty of drippings for a quick pan gravy.

eat foods tainted with raw chicken, not from eating improperly cooked chicken. So when you are cutting raw chicken or handling it in any way, make sure you do it on a surface (like a thin plastic cutting board) that can easily be whisked to the sink and washed with hot soap and water. Clean each utensil used (and the sink!) before moving on to the next ingredient or preparing another dish.

Braised Chicken

- *Braising* refers to foods that are cooked, covered, in a flavorful liquid or sauce.

- Braising allows the juices from the cooking chicken to fall back into the sauce it is cooking in, so no flavor is lost.

- There are two types of braising: Brown braising is when the chicken is lightly covered in oil or butter before being braised in a flavorful liquid. White braising is when raw chicken is added directly to the cooking liquid.

Roasted Turkey

- Throw out the pop-up timers that come with turkeys; they only lead to overcooked meat. Use an instant-read thermometer and take the turkey out when it registers 165°F in the thickest part of the thigh.

- Allow the bird to rest for at least 15 minutes before carving so you don't lose precious juices.

- For the easiest carving, cut the wings off first, then the breast meat, then the legs and thighs.

FRESH INGREDIENTS

BEEF, PORK & LAMB
Choosing the right cut and cooking technique are the keys to delicious meat dishes

There is a lot of information out there about the different cuts of meat, how to shop for them, and how best to prepare them. We have narrowed down the most popular cuts of meat to help clarify the process.

In the most general terms, tough, inexpensive cuts (like pork ribs, beef stew meat, brisket, lamb shoulder) require the longest cooking times to soften their tough connective tissue to render them tender and moist. Steaks, chops, and tenderloins, whether bone in or boneless, are meant to be cooked until just done, since they cook up tender much more quickly and dry out with extended cooking.

When possible, opt for grass-fed beef, which is free of

Bone-In Cuts

- Bones add a tremendous amount of flavor to food while it is cooking, so opt for the bone-in cut when possible.

- If a recipe calls for boneless, you can substitute bone in, but you will need to increase the cooking time to accommodate the bone.

- When the bone is removed from a leg of lamb, it is called "butterflied."

- Save leftover bones (cooked or uncooked) for making flavorful broth or seasoning tomato sauce.

Boneless Roasts

- Cooking a large roast affords you the most leftovers with the least amount of fuss.

- A boneless roast will not take as long to cook as a bone-in roast, so adjust your cooking times accordingly.

- Pork and beef roasts should be cooked until just done, as these lean cuts tend to dry out with overcooking. Pork should be 150°F and beef 135°F (both for medium). The internal temperature will rise slightly as it rests.

antibiotics and growth hormones and comes from cows that are raised in a pasture (hence, they eat grass). The meat is a bit leaner (and a bit more expensive, so you will have to budget yourself), so it cooks faster than conventional beef. It is also higher in omega-3 fatty acids, which gives it the added benefit of being a healthier choice.

 If you know what kind of meat to buy and how to cook it properly, that is most of the battle of getting a delicious meal on the table.

Ground Meat

- Use a variety of ground meats when making a meatloaf. The standard mix is equal parts beef, pork, and veal. This mixture has a more complex flavor than 100 percent ground beef.

- For a quick meat sauce: Brown 1 pound ground beef, turkey, or pork (or a combination), then add a 28-ounce can crushed tomatoes, 2 crushed garlic cloves, a pinch of oregano, and salt. Simmer uncovered until thick, 20 minutes.

- Choose a good-looking roast or shoulder cut and ask the butcher to grind it fresh.

Sausages

- Sausages are extremely versatile. They can be grilled, roasted, panfried, or removed from their casings and sautéed.

- Best sausage recipe we know: In 2 tablespoons olive oil, brown any kind of uncooked sausage; remove from pan. Add 1 onion, sliced, and cook 4 minutes. Add 1 bunch chopped greens (kale, collards, chard, mustard); wilt 1 minute. Add sausages, 1 tablespoon cider or wine vinegar, and ¼ cup chicken broth, cover and cook until greens are wilted and sausage cooked. Serve over rice or polenta.

FRESH INGREDIENTS

33

FISH & SHELLFISH
Learn how to choose among all the fishes in the sea

Fish is an exceptionally healthy food. It is high in protein, low in saturated fat, and the oily varieties (such as wild salmon, sardines, Arctic char, herring, and trout) are excellent sources of essential omega-3 fatty acids, one of the "good fats" that help your heart, joints, brain, and body function at their best.

As a main course ingredient, fish is relatively inexpensive, if you know which kind to look for. Tilapia, catfish, and trout are all farm-raised fish that are affordable and raised in a way that is healthy for you and the environment. Whole fish is the least expensive and takes very little effort to cook to perfection (recipe to follow). In general, fish cooks up much more quickly than meat does, so it makes a quick after-work meal.

In a fish store or large supermarket, fish is available both whole and filleted. Judging the freshness of a whole fish is

KNACK GOURMET COOKING ON A BUDGET

Roasting Whole Fish

- Count on buying 1½ pounds whole fish (before it's cleaned) per person.

- Have the fishmonger gut and scale the fish for you, as you don't want to do this at home!

- Despite its look, keep the head intact during roasting.

- There are delicious nuggets of fish in the head and collar region.

- Stuff the cavity with fresh herbs and citrus to perfume the fish.

- Roast at 400°F for 10 minutes per inch of fish; measure at the thickest part.

Fish Fillets and Steaks

- Count on buying ⅓ to ½ pound fish fillet per person.

- Choose center-cut portions whenever possible; they cook more evenly than the skinnier tail pieces.

- Fish steaks (which are a cross-section of the fish) are often less expensive than

- fillets, but also have bones and skin still attached.

- Steaks are sturdy enough for the grill, but tender fillets are best browned in a nonstick skillet.

- Clean you fish skillet well; stubborn fish oils cling to the pan.

easier than it is for fillets, since the markers of freshness are still intact. If you have the choice, choose a whole fish and ask the fishmonger to fillet it for you, ensuring the freshest product.

When considering what to serve with fish, remember that fish pairs well with citrus (orange, lemon, and lime), salty items like capers and olives, fresh tomatoes, and fresh herbs (parsley, dill, chives).

Whole fish provide more clues to freshness than fillets. Whole fish should have bright red gills under the collar, clear bulging eyes (no signs of milky whiteness), tight scales, and taught skin. It should smell briny and fresh like the ocean, and not at all "fishy." Fish fillets should have pearly opalescent flesh and no brown spots. Try to buy fillets directly from a fishmonger or fish counter.

Mussels and Clams

Frozen Shrimp

- For wild mussels, make sure to remove the furry "beards" that peak out of the shells. Use your thumb pressed against the flat of a small knife to yank them out.

- Scrub all shellfish before use to remove any grit. Soak fresh clams in a bowl of salted water for 30 minutes before using.

- Cultivated clams and mussels, which make up most of what is available in supermarkets, don't have the grit of wild seafood.

- Discard any shellfish that doesn't open after steaming.

- Frozen uncooked shrimp is an excellent ingredient to always have in your freezer. Buy the kind that still has the shell on (for making broths and to prevent freezer burn).

- When you want to cook it, just defrost as much as you need in a bowl of cold (not warm) salted water. It will usually take about 30 minutes to thaw them. Peel and use.

- Fresh shrimp in the store has been previously frozen and thawed, so don't freeze it again.

WHITE BEAN CROSTINI

Crispy toast rounds set the stage for a lemony white bean puree infused with sage and garlic

Crostini, the thin crispy toasts that support countless appetizer toppings, are the answer to leftover bread. Crostini can be made out of almost any kind of loaf, stale or fresh. Once they are toasted, either plain or brushed with oil, they can be used to dress up salads (slathered with some goat cheese) or to provide a canvas for so many ingredient combinations:

roasted bell peppers and fresh mozzarella, fresh ricotta cheese and sliced fruit, or a garlicky bean puree, like the tangy white bean and sage mash here. Since there is always a can of beans somewhere in your pantry, these crostini are a snap to make and don't require a trip to the market. *Yield: 12 crostini*

Ingredients

1 tablespoon chopped sage

2 cloves garlic, divided

1/2 cup olive oil

1 15-ounce can cannellini beans, rinsed and drained well

3/4 teaspoon salt

Zest of 1 lemon

1 baguette, fresh or day old

White Bean Crostini

- In a small saucepan over low heat, steep sage and 1 clove garlic, minced, in olive oil for 15 minutes.

- Put beans in a small bowl with salt and lemon zest. Reserve 2 tablespoons oil, and add remaining oil with herbs.

- Mash together with a potato masher or the back of a fork until creamy, but still rough textured.

- Serve on garlic crostini topped with a drop or two of sage oil.

Fresh Ricotta–Black Pepper Crostini: Mix 2 cups fresh ricotta cheese with 2 cloves garlic, finely minced; 3 tablespoons any chopped fresh herb; salt; and plenty of fresh cracked pepper. Spread a few tablespoons on each crostini, then place under the broiler until the cheese is very warm to the touch. Finish with a drizzle of extra-virgin olive oil and a few more crystals of salt.

Bitter Greens–Prosciutto Crostini: Sauté a bunch of bitter greens (mustard, turnip, or broccoli rabe) in olive oil with 3 cloves garlic, thinly sliced, and a pinch of crushed red pepper flakes. Cook until the greens are wilted and very tender, then season with salt. Place a mound of greens on top of each toasted crostini and finish with a ribbon of thinly sliced prosciutto.

Making Garlic Crostini

- Heat oven to 350°F. Cut baguette on a slight diagonal into 12 ½-inch-thick slices.

- Brush with reserved sage oil, to the edges. You will have leftover oil for drizzling on finished crostini.

- Set bread, oil side up, on a baking sheet in a single layer. Toast in oven until golden.

- Cut a garlic clove in half and rub the oiled side of each crostini with garlic.

Making Herb-Infused Oils

- You can buy herb-infused oils, but they are expensive and often have a slightly off, commercial flavor.

- It's better and cheaper to make them yourself, using the basic procedure here for any sturdy herb, including rosemary, thyme, oregano, and sage.

- For every ½ cup of oil, use 1 tablespoon chopped herbs. Bring the heat to a bare simmer and let the mixture steep 15 minutes or longer.

- Store covered in the refrigerator.

APPETIZERS

TURKISH RED PEPPER DIP

A chile-spiked pepper dip enriched with toasted nuts and crème fraiche

This luxurious dip was created by Leslie Brenner, food critic for the *Dallas Morning News* after a trip to Turkey.

You can use fresh red peppers and roast them yourself when they go on sale at the supermarket (which they so often do). Otherwise, use less expensive jars of roasted peppers to make this dip. Nuts are a traditional thickener, adding a richness of texture and flavor to dips, sauces, and soups. Add the basil just before serving, as it darkens in color soon after it is cut. You can substitute fresh cilantro or flat-leaf parsley, too, which don't lose their vibrant green color after being chopped. The dip is also a delicious condiment for sandwiches. *Yield: 6 servings*

Ingredients

¼ cup walnuts

3–4 roasted red peppers

1 teaspoon harissa (or ¼ can chipotle chile)

2 tablespoons chopped basil (optional)

1 tablespoon crème fraiche

Salt to taste

Cauliflower

Carrots

String beans

Radishes

Fennel

Celery

Turkish Red Pepper Dip

- Preheat oven to 350°F and toast walnuts until lightly brown and fragrant.

- Put slightly cooled walnuts into a food processor or blender with the red peppers and harissa (or chipotle). Process until smooth but slightly gritty.

- Add basil if you're using it, and process till smooth again.

- Put mixture in a small bowl and stir in crème fraiche and some salt, if needed. Cover and refrigerate at least 2 hours and up to 24, to let flavors meld. Serve with crudité basket.

Preparing the Vegetables

- Choose a variety of vegetables, thinking flavor, color and what's in season. Then prepare them so they look as natural as possible.

- Wash and trim cauliflower, radishes, fennel, and celery. Peel carrots, and quickly blanch string beans in salted boiling water.

- Cut everything into attractive bite-size pieces.

- If you have small carrots and radishes, leave some green sprigs on the tops. Leave tails on string beans, too.

A Crème Fraiche Substitution

- Crème fraiche, the silkier and more buttery cousin of sour cream, is delicious stirred into soups or sauces or served over vegetables or with fresh fruit.

- You can make a version by combining 2 tablespoons cultured buttermilk with 2 cups heavy cream and heating until tepid (no more than 85°F).

- Pour into a clean jar, cover partially, and let stand at room temperature 8 to 24 hours, until thickened.

- Stir and refrigerate at least 24 hours before using. It keeps for 2 weeks.

APPETIZERS

39

HUMMUS WITH CRISPY LAVASH

A good splash of lemon returns this hummus to its authentic Mediterranean roots

If you've never made hummus, prepare for a surprise: it's as simple as it gets and has more bright flavor than the expensive prepared versions from the market. The secret is the balance of garlic and lemon juice. Most commercial hummus makers scale back on both—especially the lemon—and a great version of this spread needs that citrus zing.

The first time you make it, you'll need to invest in a jar of tahini, the sesame seed paste that gives hummus its rich, earthy flavor. But just a little flavors a whole batch, and once you know how good fresh hummus can be, you'll always want a jar on hand. *Yield: 4 servings*

Ingredients

1 15-ounce can chickpeas

3 tablespoons tahini

2 garlic cloves, chopped

3-4 tablespoons lemon juice

2 tablespoons olive oil

Pinch of cayenne pepper

Salt to taste

Additional olive oil, as needed

2 sheets lavash

Hummus with Crispy Lavash

- Rinse and drain chickpeas.

- Put the chickpeas, tahini, garlic, lemon juice, 2 tablespoons olive oil, cayenne pepper, and some salt in a food processor or blender; pulse until the mixture is smooth.

- Add a little water or olive oil to get the right consistency; it should have a slightly fluffy, whipped quality (but not be "wet" or runny).

- Transfer hummus to a bowl, drizzle a swirl of olive oil as a garnish, and serve with crispy lavash.

Seasoned Lavash: With just a little effort, you can make gorgeous seasoned lavash. Brush the triangles with olive oil and top with a seasoning you like, such as sesame seeds, fennel seeds, paprika, a favorite spice blend, or even nori (seaweed) powder. Then bake until crispy in a 350°F oven.

Marinated Olives: For a small splurge, serve marinated olives alongside. Toss a cup of good olives with 1 teaspoon crushed fennel seed, the grated zest of 1 orange, 3 smashed garlic cloves, 1 bay leaf, 1 teaspoon red wine vinegar, and 3 tablespoons olive oil. The longer they marinate, the deeper the flavor, but even an hour will do.

Preparing the Lavash

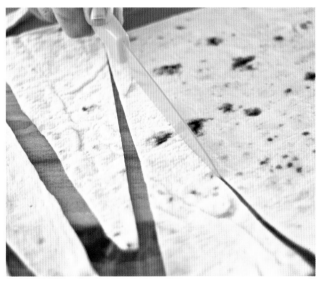

- Preheat the oven to 350°F.

- Using kitchen scissors, cut the lavash into irregular triangles, about 6 to 8 inches long, and set in a single layer on a baking sheet.

- Bake 20 minutes, or until crisp and lightly browned. This can be done several hours ahead.

- Hummus can also be served with warm pita or raw vegetables, but these big, dramatic shards make an impressive scoop.

Adjusting the Flavors

- As you adjust the hummus's consistency, be sure to taste.

- Depending on how tart your lemon is, you may want a little more juice (which will mean a little less water or oil).

- The cayenne should add a subtle note of pepper, not a blast of heat.

- If you like, hummus can also be garnished with a very fine mince of parsley or a light sprinkling of paprika or cumin. You can also reserve 6 or 8 whole chickpeas.

APPETIZERS

ROASTED RED PEPPER SALAD

This brilliant Mediterranean appetizer is a delicious partner to hummus or a stand-alone side dish

This is a dish to make in the late summer, when bright red and yellow bell peppers are at their sweetest—and cheapest. Buy them by the bagful to roast and store for the months ahead, when you'll be craving this luxurious dish but wouldn't dream of paying $6 a pound for the peppers.

The Kalamata olives and feta cheese are flavorful ingredients used in small quantities, so keep that in mind at the supermarket: You're shopping for a few olives, not a whole tubful! And you're bound to have some feta left over. Try it tossed with chunks of fresh watermelon and a grinding of black pepper for an equally delicious, but very different, salad. *Yield: 6 servings*

Ingredients

Zest of 1 lemon

$1/2$ cup olive oil

3 red bell peppers

2 yellow bell peppers

12 cherry tomatoes

12 Kalamata olives, pitted

Additional olive oil, for roasting

2 ounces feta cheese, cut into small cubes

Chives, for garnish (optional)

Roasted Red Pepper Salad

- Grate lemon zest into olive oil; let stand.

- Roast and peel peppers, slice into ¼-inch strips, and toss with lemon oil to coat. Cut cherry tomatoes and olives in half; add to peppers and gently toss to distribute (adding lemon oil as needed).

- Cut feta into ¼-inch cubes and gently mix through salad (without breaking up cubes). Transfer to a serving bowl and, if you have chives on hand, top with a few long snips as a garnish.

Red Pepper Relish: Use a little less lemon oil, and the salad becomes a terrific relish served alongside grilled fish or chicken. You can also use it as a sandwich filling with prosciutto or cold roasted meats piled on top of a soft roll. Or, put little mounds on top of slices of baguette that you've brushed with olive oil and toasted or grilled.

Roasted Pepper Antipasto: Roast extra peppers, toss them with olive oil, and store them in the refrigerator or freezer; you'll always have an easy antipasto on hand. Just top them with some salt, pepper, garlic, and a splash of olive oil and let them marinate for a few hours or a few days in the refrigerator. Serve with crusty bread and, if you like, some thinly sliced salami or prosciutto.

Roasting the Peppers

- Preheat oven to 400°F.

- Cut peppers in half, removing seeds and stems. Lightly brush both sides with olive oil, place cut side down on a baking sheet lined with foil. Roast about 45 minutes, until skins are blistered and burnt. Transfer peppers to a bowl and cover with a plate for 10 minutes to help loosen the skins. When cool enough to handle, remove skins over a bowl to catch juices. Place roasted peppers (don't rinse!) in the bowl after you remove skins.

Lemon Olive Oil

- Lemon olive oil adds delicate, sunny flavor without the acidity of lemon juice.

- Make it quickly by grating zest into olive oil and letting it infuse while the peppers roast.

- Or you can make it ahead: For each cup of oil, add the zest of 2 lemons (grated into big strips), warm over very low heat for about 10 minutes, remove zest, and cool.

- You can also buy pressings of lemons and olive oil—but they are expensive.

APPETIZERS

43

JERK-STYLE CHICKEN WINGS

Move over Buffalo! These sweetly spiced wings pack a world of flavor in every bite

No matter how you plan to prepare them, there is nothing more economical than a package of chicken wings. It is worth the extra few minutes to make a homemade jerk spice rub to season your next batch of wings or "drumettes" (wingless wings).

Jerk chicken is a staple of Jamaican cooking and has an addictive spice-and-herb coating. Wings, which should be cooked for a long time to achieve maximum tenderness, benefit even more from the jerk rub's warm spices, which bath the wings for hours in a low oven. Since the list of spices for making the jerk seasonings runs long, consider tripling the dry spice mix for future batches. *Yield: 10 servings*

Ingredients

- ¹/₄ cup soy sauce
- ³/₄ cup white wine
- ¹/₄ cup brown sugar
- ¹/₂ medium onion, chopped
- 1 clove garlic, quartered
- ¹/₂ teaspoon allspice
- ¹/₂ teaspoon thyme
- ¹/₄ teaspoon cayenne pepper
- ¹/₂ teaspoon black pepper
- ¹/₄ teaspoon nutmeg
- ¹/₂ teaspoon cinnamon
- ¹/₂ teaspoon ground cloves
- 1 teaspoon ground ginger
- 1 4-pound bag frozen chicken wing drumettes

Jerk-Style Chicken Wings

- Preheat oven to 300°F. Mix soy sauce, wine, and brown sugar together until sugar is dissolved. Finely chop onion, garlic, and spices in a food processor and slowly add liquid until textured sauce.

- Place frozen wings into a large roasting pan. Do not defrost. Pour sauce over wings and toss to coat.

- Bake uncovered for 2½ hours, turning every 30 minutes. Raise heat to 400°F and cook 30 minutes more. Serve warm or at room temperature, with pan sauce poured over the top or served alongside for dipping.

44

Jerk Chicken on the Grill: For your next barbecue, marinate an entire chicken, cut into 8 pieces, in the same marinade the wings are baked in. Marinate for up to 2 days. Grill skin side down with the lid down (watch for flare-ups), until the skin is crisp and the chicken is cooked through, turning occasionally.

Asian-Spiced Wings: Combine ⅓ cup soy sauce; ¼ cup rice vinegar; ¼ cup brown sugar; 3 garlic cloves, crushed; 3 scallions (white and green parts), finely minced; 1 tablespoon finely chopped fresh ginger; 2 tablespoons toasted sesame oil; 2 tablespoon sesame seeds; and 1 teaspoon hot chile sauce or hot sauce. Pour over the wings and proceed with the recipe.

Turning the Chicken

- There are a lot of ways to add flavor to meat—marinades, rubs, stuffing, grilling. This is one of the easiest.

- The chicken is cooked at a low temperature, literally bathing in jerk-style season-ings. And because it cooks slowly, the meat will be flavored to the bone and meltingly tender.

- Turn the wings every 30 minutes to keep them evenly moist and evenly exposed to the sauce.

Getting the Most from Spices

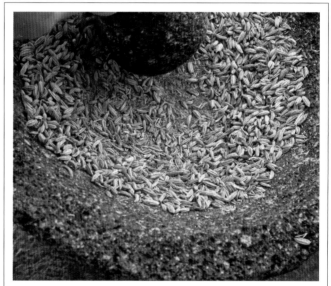

- Whole spices generally have more flavor than spices you buy already ground in a jar.

- For this recipe you can easily crush allspice berries, black peppercorns, and whole cloves in a mortar and pestle. Or you can place them between two sheets of wax paper and crush them with a rolling pin or heavy pan.

- Just break a cinnamon stick in half.

- The nutmeg can be grated with any fine grating tool.

SCALLION PANCAKES

Crispy tortillas with scallions and sesame create a unique twist on a favorite Chinese appetizer

Flour tortillas are a staple in most kitchens and provide an easy and budget-friendly template for so many dishes. Chef Tom Douglas from Seattle uses tortillas to build his version of scallion pancakes. They provide a good shortcut from the traditional recipe, which uses the same ingredients a tortilla already has in it (flour and water).

Use dark sesame oil for this dish. The seeds are toasted before being pressed into oil, providing it with a rich fragrance and flavor. If you cannot find hot sesame oil at your supermarket, just use plain dark sesame oil and add some cayenne pepper. Don't skimp on the filling ingredients for these pancakes; the more the better! *Yield: 8–10 servings*

Ingredients

1 large egg

2 teaspoons hot sesame oil

¼ teaspoon salt

8 8-inch flour tortillas

2 tablespoons toasted sesame seeds

1⅓ cups finely chopped scallions, green and white parts

Peanut oil or vegetable oil for frying

Scallion Pancakes

- Beat the egg with the sesame oil and salt.

- Assemble four pancakes by making a "sandwich" with 2 tortillas and the egg mixture, sesame seeds, and scallions.

- Heat 2 teaspoons oil in a large skillet over medium heat. Cook pancakes one at a time, until lightly browned.

- Remove to a platter lined with paper towels; keep warm. Continue with remaining pancakes, adding oil to the skillet as needed. Serve cut into wedges.

Dinner Scallion Pancakes: Add one of the following ingredients along with the scallions: 6 cooked shrimp, cut in half lengthwise; ¼ cup finely shredded cooked chicken breast or pork; ¼ cup black beans; or 2 scrambled eggs. Brush tortillas with extra egg to hold the bulky ingredients inside.

Dipping Sauce: In a medium bowl, combine ¼ cup soy sauce; ¼ cup rice vinegar; 2 scallions, finely minced; 1 teaspoon sugar; 1 teaspoon ginger, finely minced; 1 tablespoon toasted sesame seeds; and dash of hot sesame oil or pinch of cayenne pepper. Let sit for 10 minutes before serving.

Assembling the Pancakes

- To assemble the scallion pancakes, brush one side of 4 tortillas with the egg mixture.

- Sprinkle the sesame seeds and green onions evenly on top—don't worry about overfilling. You want plenty of scallion and sesame.

- Brush the remaining 4 tortillas with remaining egg mixture and lay each tortilla, egg side down, on top of the scallion-sesame tortillas. Press to seal edges.

Brown Evenly

- To get a good, evenly browned surface, give the skillet and the oil a couple of minutes to get evenly heated over a medium flame.

- Be sure you have a nice, even film of oil covering the surface—use a paper towel to distribute it, if necessary. Test the temperature by touching the edge of the pancake to the pan; if it doesn't sizzle on contact, the pan is not hot enough yet.

APPETIZERS

SOFT-SCRAMBLED EGGS

Take the extra time to scramble the eggs slowly for an unbeatably custardy treat

Eggs are one of the most inexpensive and versatile of the protein sources. You may wonder why scrambled eggs would warrant their own cookbook recipe, but the secret here is in the low heat and gentle stirring that creates a scrambled egg well beyond the diner variety. When eggs are traditionally scrambled fast in a hot pan, the proteins bind quickly and

tightly, leaving you with something the texture of a chopped omelet. But when you lower the heat and take the time to gently stir them, the eggs maintain their innately creamy texture, leading to a much more delicious and custardy result. Adding a little extra fat to the whisked eggs before cooking them also helps maintain their soft texture. *Yield: 4 servings*

Ingredients

4 slices crusty bread

1 tablespoon olive oil

1 clove garlic, cut in half

6 large eggs

2 tablespoons butter, divided

Salt to taste

Pinch of white pepper

4 thin slices prosciutto

Soft-Scrambled Eggs

- Brush the bread with olive oil. Heat a skillet to medium high and toast until browned on both sides. Rub slices with the garlic.

- Lightly whisk together the eggs, 1 tablespoon butter cut into small pieces, salt, and white pepper. Melt 1 tablespoon butter in a

nonstick skillet over low heat. Add eggs and cook, stirring constantly, until they thicken and become custard-like, about 15 minutes.

- Spread eggs onto the toasted bread and top each with a slice of prosciutto.

No Rushing

- Soft-scrambled eggs take some time and patience. You can speed things up a little by starting with room-temperature eggs, but don't be tempted to raise the heat, or you'll lose that luscious texture.

- As soon as the butter has melted, pour in the eggs. You can be a little remiss about stirring at the beginning. But once the eggs begin to set at the bottom, you'll need to stir them constantly until they are ready.

Gently from the Start

- Whisking the eggs gently with a bit of butter makes them even richer and more decadent. You can also add a little bit of oil or some crème fraiche in place of the butter.

- Or, you can skip the extra bit of fat entirely. If you simply whisk the eggs with some salt and pepper and give them a long, slow scramble, you'll be amazed at the results.

EGGS

SPINACH & RICE TORTA

A savory baked rice tart studded with fresh spinach and Parmesan cheese

Rice, whether you cook a fresh batch or use that leftover Chinese take-out rice (no shame in that), is an economical ingredient. In this torta recipe from Regina Schrambling (a gifted food writer who also blogs about frugal cooking at Epicurious.com), sweet spinach and salty Parmesan cheese combine with cooked rice and eggs to make a richly flavored dish that is ideal for lunch, a light dinner, or even breakfast. It's even good cold.

Rice tortas are an excellent insurance that no leftover rice will ever languish too long in your refrigerator. *Yield: 4–6 servings*

Ingredients

1 cup rice

5 tablespoons butter, divided

1 pound spinach leaves, steamed and chopped

2 tablespoons olive oil

1/2 onion, chopped

3 eggs, beaten

1/4 cup grated Parmesan cheese

Salt and black pepper

Spinach and Rice Torta

- Preheat the oven to 400°F.

- Cook the rice until al dente and toss with 1 tablespoon butter. Steam spinach; drain and chop.

- Heat olive oil and 4 tablespoons butter in a large skillet. Sauté the onion, rice, and spinach for a few minutes. Remove from heat and stir in the eggs and cheese.

- Season well with salt and pepper, spread into a 9-inch baking dish, and bake until golden brown, about 20 minutes.

・・・・ RECIPE VARIATIONS ・・・・

Play with Your Rice: Since a rice torta is the lighter cousin of baked risotto, try using a creamy risotto rice like arborio instead of a standard long-grain white rice. The starchy lusciousness of arborio rice mixed with the eggs and cheese will further enrich this dish. Or choose a brown rice (it will take about 15 minutes longer to cook to al dente) for a whole-grain boost.

Spinach-Basil and Butternut Squash Tortas: To brighten the flavors of this dish, add 10 basil leaves, thinly sliced, or ½ teaspoon grated lemon zest when you fold in the eggs and cheese. Or in place of the cooked spinach, substitute small cubes of butternut squash and sauté with the onions until cooked through, about 10 minutes.

Make the Rice

- This is an unusual way to cook rice—actually, it's exactly the way you normally cook pasta. Bring a large pot of salted water to a boil, add the rice, and cook until al dente. Drain and toss with 1 tablespoon butter.

- You can also use leftover cooked rice. Just drop it into boiling water for a minute to moisten and separate the grains, then toss it with the butter.

Steam the Spinach

- Fill a pot with 1 to 2 inches of water, depending on how high your steamer basket sits (you want to keep it above the water level). Cover and bring to a boil.

- Add spinach leaves and steam until tender, about 3 minutes.

- Remove to a colander or strainer and press out excess water. Chop.

BISTRO SALAD

A classic French salad combines creamy poached eggs, bitter greens, and smoky bacon

The dinner salad is the best way to eat healthy on a budget. By combining plenty of flavorful ingredients, you will feel satisfied with very little effort. In this classic bistro salad, found in every cafe in France, bitter curly endive creates a bed for soft-poached eggs and crisp smoky bacon pieces. When the egg yolk is broken (which should be your first order of business), it mixes with the vinaigrette to create a rich sauce for the salad.

Pair this salad with a slice of crusty baguette or country bread and you have a full meal. If you can't find curly endive or prefer a sweeter lettuce, substitute fresh baby spinach leaves. *Yield: 4 servings*

Ingredients

1 tablespoon Dijon mustard

3 tablespoons red wine vinegar

¹/₂ cup olive oil

Salt and pepper to taste

4 thick slices crisp bacon

6 cups curly endive

4 eggs

Bistro Salad

- Make the vinaigrette by combining the mustard, vinegar, oil, and salt and pepper. Cut bacon into ½-inch pieces and fry until brown but soft. Wash, trim, and tear the endive into bite-size pieces. Poach the eggs.

- When ready to serve, place the greens into a large bowl and toss with the vinaigrette, coating the leaves thoroughly and evenly. Add bacon and toss to distribute.

- Divide salad among four plates. Place a warm poached egg at the center of each and serve.

• • • • RECIPE VARIATIONS • • • •

Poached Eggs over Asparagus with Creamy Pesto: Mix ¼ cup prepared pesto sauce with 2 tablespoons cream; set aside. Steam 1 bunch trimmed asparagus and poach the eggs. To serve, place the poached eggs over the asparagus and top each portion with the pesto sauce.

Lardons: Thick-cut pieces of bacon called lardons add a sweet bite of smoky meatiness to many salads, especially ones made from bitter lettuces (like endive) and spinach. To make, buy an uncut 1-inch slab of bacon (ask your butcher). Cut the bacon into ½-inch cubes and cook in a pan over medium heat until they are crisp and brown, about 8 minutes. Use instead of bacon in the recipe.

Poaching the Eggs

- Fill a pot with 3 inches of water and bring to a simmer. Add a few drops of vinegar.

- One at a time, crack eggs into a small bowl and gently slip into the simmering water.

- Poach 3 to 4 minutes, until loosely set. Remove with a slotted spoon and blot gently on a towel. Trim edges.

- If not serving immediately, refrigerate and reheat with a quick dip in simmering water.

Making the Vinaigrette

- This is a classic vinaigrette, based on the 3-to-1 ratio: 3 parts oil to 1 part acid.

- You can make numerous vinaigrettes based on this ratio—try using different oils and vinegars, or even lemon juice. Or substitute minced shallot in place of the Dijon mustard.

- Whisk together vinegar and salt and pepper in small bowl, until salt is dissolved.

- Add Dijon mustard; whisk until smooth. Slowly add oil, whisking continually, until emulsified.

EGGS

53

ZUCCHINI FRITTATA

A baked vegetable omelet seasoned with rosemary and Parmesan cheese

Frittatas provide an excellent way to create a full meal out of just a few eggs. Essentially a baked omelet, frittatas are an Italian dish most often seasoned with Parmesan cheese and seasonal vegetables. The filling ingredients are fully cooked before being mixed with beaten eggs. The mixture is then partially cooked on the stove top (don't brown the bottom!)

before being transferred to the oven to finish cooking, which gives the finished frittata a puffy, soufflé-like texture and appearance. This frittata is further lightened with a bit of fresh ricotta cheese, which is mixed with the eggs before cooking. The finished frittata is sliced into wedges and can be served warm or at room temperature. *Yield: 4 servings*

Ingredients

3 tablespoons butter, plus more if needed

2-3 medium zucchini, cut into matchsticks

1 large shallot, minced

¹/₂ teaspoon rosemary

5-6 large eggs

¹/₂ cup ricotta cheese

2 tablespoons Parmesan cheese

Salt and pepper to taste

Chopped parsley, for garnish (optional)

Zucchini Frittata

- Preheat oven to 350°F. Melt butter in a large nonstick skillet over medium heat and cook zucchini, shallot, and rosemary until zucchini is tender, but crisp.

- Meanwhile, beat together eggs, ricotta, Parmesan, and salt and pepper. Turn skillet heat to low, pour in egg mixture, and gently stir for a minute.

- Cook, without stirring, until egg begins to set. Put skillet into the oven and cook until egg is set and slightly puffed, 5 minutes. Remove and let rest for a minute, cut into wedges, top with parsley, and serve.

Mushroom and Goat Cheese Frittata: Heat 3 tablespoons butter in a nonstick skillet over medium heat and cook 4 ounces sliced mushrooms with ½ teaspoon thyme leaves until the mushrooms are golden, about 7 minutes. Whisk together 6 large eggs, 2 ounces fresh goat cheese, 2 tablespoons grated Parmesan cheese, and salt and pepper. Add the egg mixture to the skillet with mushrooms and cook frittata as directed.

Rustic Frittata Sandwiches: Use leftover frittata to make sandwiches. The crustier the bread, the better, but even well-toasted sandwich bread will do. Enjoy the sandwich plain or embellished with a juicy tomato slice, roasted peppers, or smear of pesto or mayonnaise.

Cutting the Zucchini Matchsticks

Finishing the Frittata

- You'll make a more elegant frittata if you cut the zucchini into matchsticks instead of the usual rounds.

- The shape—technically called a julienne—is easy to make with zucchini, carrots, or any cylindrical vegetable.

- Trim the ends from the zucchini and cut them into 2-inch chunks.

- Stand them on end and cut into ¼-inch slices. Lay the slices in a stack (make two stacks per chunk, with a flat side on the cutting board), and cut the slices into matchsticks.

- Many frittatas are cooked at high heat, which gives them a dark brown layer of egg that distracts from all the wonderful flavors within.

- This frittata is cooked gently and finished in an oven instead of under a broiler.

- It's ready when the eggs are set and a little puffy—don't look for any browning.

- If you'd prefer a little crust, just increase the skillet heat to medium or medium high and finish the cooking under a broiler instead.

EGGS

DEVILED EGGS
The most ubiquitous hors d'oeuvre is also one of the most delicious

Everyone loves hard-boiled eggs. And while the most nostalgic version is made with just mayonnaise and maybe a little mustard, it never hurts to update a classic, here embellished with sweet curry powder, spicy cayenne, fresh herbs, or salty olives and bacon.

Most important: Don't overcook your hard-boiled eggs! If you do, the whites will be rubbery and there will be an unpleasant greenish gray ring around the yolks. And if you have a tough-to-peel egg, your egg may be too fresh (lucky you!); older eggs are much easier to peel. So to hedge your bets, gently crack the egg all over when attempting to peel it—that breaks any tight seal that might make it difficult to peel. *Yield: 6 servings*

Ingredients

12 large hard-boiled eggs

6 tablespoons mayonnaise

2 tablespoons Dijon mustard

Salt to taste

$1/2$ teaspoon curry powder or cayenne pepper, or either to taste

Garnishes such as chopped fresh tarragon, dill, chives, or parsley; paprika or smoked paprika; ground black pepper; finely minced olives, capers or cornichons; bits of bacon

Deviled Eggs

- Peel the eggs, cut them in half lengthwise, and carefully remove the yolks to a medium bowl. Arrange the halved whites on a large serving platter and refrigerate until ready to fill.

- Add the mayonnaise, mustard, salt and curry powder or cayenne to the yolks and mash together until the mixture is smooth.

- Fill each egg half with a little mound of yolk mixture and top with a combination of any of the garnishes.

Curried Egg Salad Sandwiches: Leftover deviled eggs can be made into a curried egg salad. Roughly chop 4 hard-boiled eggs. Add 3 tablespoons mayonnaise, 1 teaspoon mustard, 1 teaspoon curry powder, 1 tablespoon finely chopped celery, and 1 tablespoon currants (or finely chopped raisins). Serve on slices of whole grain bread with sliced cucumbers and/or tomatoes.

Deconstructed Deviled Eggs: A favorite restaurant used to have this version of deviled eggs on its menu. Cut 2 hard-boiled eggs in half and spread each half with a generous tablespoon of mayonnaise. Top each half with a few thin slices of cornichon or regular pickle. Finish with a dusting of smoked or regular paprika.

Perfect Hard-Boiled Eggs

- Bring a large pot of water to a boil.

- Gently place the eggs in the water with a slotted spoon. Continue to boil, but lower heat slightly so the boil isn't strong enough to crack the eggs against each other or the side of the pot.

- After 12 minutes, remove the eggs with the slotted spoon and plunge into a bowl of ice water. After 2 minutes, remove from the ice water and peel.

Garnishing the Eggs

- Deviled eggs can be garnished with just about anything you can think of.

- You can make a great-looking party platter by choosing a few complementary garnishes—think in terms of flavor and color—and then "painting" the platter of eggs with the toppings.

- Don't hesitate to combine garnishes. Try bacon and chives, for example, or parsley and dill or capers and tarragon—you get the idea.

EGGS

GRUYÈRE CHEESE SOUFFLÉ
The success of this nutty cheese soufflé is in the egg whites

The common egg takes on an uncommon appeal when whisked into a frothy soufflé. For this cheese soufflé, nutty Gruyère is laced with a bit of warm nutmeg to create a light lunch or brunch treat.

Be mindful not to overbeat the egg whites. They should hold their shape in small, soft peaks when the beaters are gently pulled out. This happens just after you start to see the beaters leave a trail behind in the fluffy egg whites. Overbeaten whites (when they start to break apart in clumps due to lack of moisture) make a dry soufflé and are difficult to incorporate into the base. Let the egg whites sit out for an hour or so before beating for maximum volume. *Yield: 6 servings*

Ingredients

5 tablespoons butter, plus more for the baking dish

¹/₄ cup flour

1¹/₂ cups milk

6 large eggs, separated

¹/₄ teaspoon nutmeg

Salt and pepper to taste

1 cup grated Gruyère cheese, divided

¹/₈ teaspoon cream of tartar or salt

Gruyère Cheese Soufflé

- Preheat oven to 400°F. Generously butter a 2-quart soufflé dish or deep 2-quart baking dish.

- Make a base with butter, flour, milk, egg yolks, nutmeg, salt, pepper, and Gruyère, reserving 1 tablespoon cheese. Beat egg whites with cream of tartar or salt, to soft peaks.

- Fold whites into the base, scrape into buttered dish, and run your finger around the rim to ensure an even rise. Sprinkle with reserved Gruyère and bake until high and lightly brown, about 30 minutes. Serve immediately.

Making the Base

- Melt the butter over medium heat, whisk in the flour, and cook until it foams and darkens a little.

- Whisk in the milk slowly, bringing to a boil and whisking until thickened. Remove from heat and whisk in the Gruyère (reserving 1 tablespoon for topping),

salt, pepper, and nutmeg. Whisking constantly, beat in the egg yolks.

- You can make the base up to 5 hours ahead. Cover with plastic wrap pressed to the surface and hold at room temperature; when ready, reheat mixture but do not boil.

Folding in the Egg Whites

- You want to incorporate the beaten egg whites gently to retain as much air as possible and get the highest rise.

- Using a rubber spatula, fold about a fourth of the beaten egg whites into the base mixture to lighten and loosen it. To fold, the edge

of the spatula should cut through the mixture, be drawn upward and toward you, then turned to softly deposit the mixture on top.

- Using the same motion, carefully fold in the rest of the whites.

EGGS

HERBED ROAST CHICKEN
The ultimate comfort food perked up with fennel and thyme

Roasting a whole chicken is a lesson in economy. Not only are you buying the least expensive kind of chicken (parts are always pricier), but there are almost always some leftovers for another meal. At the very least there is a carcass to start a batch of chicken broth en route to your freezer or a pot of chicken noodle soup.

Roast chicken meat is always the juiciest it can be, as the skin and bones baste and season the meat as it cooks, while also protecting it from drying out in the hot oven.

Add a few small whole potatoes and thickly sliced carrots to the bottom of the pan at the start of cooking; you'll be rewarded with the perfect side dish.

This particular roast chicken recipe is from Paul Bertolli, formerly the chef at Chez Panisse in Berkeley. *Yield: 4 servings*

Ingredients

1 4-pound roasting chicken

1 teaspoon fennel seeds

1/4 teaspoon cayenne pepper flakes

1 1/2 teaspoons kosher salt, plus more to season chicken

1/2 teaspoon ground black pepper

1 small bunch fresh thyme or 1 teaspoon dried thyme

Herbed Roast Chicken

- Preheat oven to 400°F. Clean and prepare chicken.

- Crack the fennel seeds in a mortar and pestle (or between sheets of wax paper, under a rolling pin). Mix with cayenne, salt, and pepper.

- Salt the prepared cavity and put the thyme inside. Season the bird all over with the fennel mixture.

- Set in a roasting pan without a rack and cook for 1 hour. Remove from oven; let rest 5 minutes and carve.

• • • • RECIPE VARIATION • • • •

Onion Pan Gravy: Set the whole chicken on a bed of thickly sliced onions in a large, deep skillet (so it can transfer easily to the stove top). Roast the chicken as instructed. Remove chicken, leaving behind the browned onions, and transfer skillet to the stove top. Turn heat to medium high and bring the pan juices to a simmer. Add 2 tablespoons flour and cook, stirring constantly, until the flour has dissolved and the mixture is smooth, 1 minute. Add 1 cup chicken broth, ⅓ cup white wine or sherry, and ½ teaspoon thyme; stir until smooth, scraping up the browned bits on the bottom of the pan. Simmer until thickened into a rich gravy, 3 minutes. Season with salt and pepper and serve alongside the roast chicken.

Preparing the Chicken

- Cut away any visible fat from the cavity of the chicken. Rinse inside and out and pat dry inside and out. Let it come to room temperature.

- Salt the cavity and tuck the thyme inside. Tie legs together loosely with kitchen twine—be sure all leg surfaces are exposed to the heat, especially the inner thigh, so the chicken cooks evenly.

- Tuck wing tips behind the neck so the bird looks like it is basking.

Carving the Bird

- Using a sharp knife, cut directly down from the top of the breast, using a fork to help separate the meat away from the ribs. Cut breasts in half, if you like.

- Use the tip of the knife to feel for the joint where the wing joins the body. Cut through the center.

- Slice along the body to release the leg and thigh. Then, using the tip of the knife to feel for the joint at the body, cut through the center.

CHICKEN CACCIATORE

Tender chicken thighs are braised in a savory tomato sauce with peppers and mushrooms

Chicken thighs are less expensive than chicken breasts, which is lucky for those who appreciate its richer flavor and juicier meat. Buying the whole thigh is best, but even the boneless, skinless variety holds up to long slow braise in a flavorful sauce, like this rich tomato sauce seasoned with sweet bell peppers and earthy mushrooms. Thighs are even great on the grill, and resist drying out as quickly as boneless skinless chicken breasts so often do.

Cacciatore just refers to food prepared in the "hunter-style," a popular way to cook up game birds. Chicken thighs (and chicken legs which are also dark meat) are a logical substitution for the rich taste of game meat. *Yield: 4 servings*

Ingredients

8 bone-in chicken thighs, with or without skin

Salt and pepper

4 tablespoons olive oil

3 cloves of garlic, sliced thin

3 bell peppers, sliced into wide strips

12 whole button mushrooms

1 15-ounce can tomato sauce or crushed tomatoes

$1/2$ cup red or white wine or water

Cooked white rice, for serving

Chicken Cacciatore

- Rinse chicken and pat dry. Salt and pepper both sides. Heat olive oil in a large skillet over medium-high heat; brown well. When you turn chicken, scatter garlic slices over the top as the bottom browns.

- Crowd peppers and mushrooms into pan. Pour tomato sauce over the top. Rinse can with wine or water and pour into pan.

- Reduce heat, cover, and simmer, turning occasionally, until tender and almost falling off the bone, 45 minutes to 1 hour. Serve with sauce over white rice.

• • • • RECIPE VARIATIONS • • • •

Lemon-Rosemary Chicken: Brown the chicken thighs in ovenproof pan and top with slivered garlic, as below. Pour over a sauce made from ⅓ cup lemon juice, 3 tablespoons olive oil, 1 tablespoon red wine vinegar, 2 teaspoons chopped fresh rosemary, ¼ teaspoon salt, and black pepper. Bake in 375°F oven until chicken is cooked through, about 20 minutes.

Chicken Provençal: Brown chicken thighs and top with slivered garlic, as below. Crowd pan with 2 zucchini or squash, cut ½-inch thick, ½ cup chopped Kalamata olives, 1 teaspoon thyme, and pour over a 15-ounce can crushed tomatoes and ½ cup red wine. Cover and simmer until chicken is tender and vegetables are soft, about 45 minutes.

Browning the Chicken

- Browning the chicken develops and melds the flavors in this recipe. The trick is to brown the chicken well, but not the garlic—which gets bitter.

- If you leave the skins on, brown the thighs skin side first to get the most attractive surface. When the surface is a deep golden brown, turn the chicken and place the garlic on top of the browned skin.

- Don't worry if a piece or two slips into the oil, as long as most stays out.

Cutting the Bell Pepper

- You can use any color bell pepper in this recipe, although green peppers tend to be the least expensive. Avoid any that feel heavy; you'll just be paying for additional seeds.

- To core, cut a circle around the stem with a paring knife and pull out the stem and most of the seeds. Cut in half and rinse out the remaining seeds.

- Slice halves into 2-inch strips.

CHICKEN IN GINGER BROTH

Asian herbs spice up this simple poached chicken dinner

Poaching is a simple and flavorful method that yields a double result: moist, cooked food plus a savory sauce to serve it with. You can season your poaching liquid with any aromatic vegetable and herbs you have on hand: scallions, leeks, shallots, fresh ginger, fresh herbs (thyme, dill, and parsley), lemon or lime slices, whole peppercorns, or fennel or cumin seeds.

You can serve your poached food with the broth it was cooked in, or you can reduce the poaching liquid to a sauce-like consistency by bringing the poaching liquid to a boil and reducing it until it is rich and flavorful. Remove from heat and swirl in a tablespoon of cold butter until melted.

This version of poached chicken is based on a recipe from Donna Hay. *Yield: 4 servings*

Ingredients

6 cups chicken broth

3 tablespoons fresh ginger, cut into matchsticks

2 coriander roots (or substitute a handful of fresh cilantro stems)

2 small or 1 large sweet potato, peeled and sliced into rounds

4 boneless, skinless chicken breasts

Salt to taste

4 scallions, cut into 3-inch matchsticks, green included

Chicken in Ginger Broth

- Put the chicken broth, ginger, and coriander roots (or cilantro stems) in a deep skillet over medium-high heat and let simmer 2 minutes. Add the sweet potatoes and simmer about 4 minutes.

- Cut each chicken breast into 2 long halves. Add to the pan and simmer about 5 minutes, until tender and cooked through.

- Check for seasoning and add salt if needed.

- Serve chicken and sweet potato in shallow bowls with plenty of broth and sprinkled with scallions.

Ginger-Poached Salmon and Asparagus: In a deep skillet combine 4 cups vegetable broth; ½ cup white wine; 2 slices fresh ginger, crushed; and 15 cilantro stems. Simmer for 20 minutes. Add 4 6-ounce skinless salmon fillets and 16 spears asparagus. Bring to the barest simmer. Remove asparagus after 4 minutes and salmon after it flakes, about 4 minutes.

Broth for Every Occasion: Since many recipes call for only 1 cup chicken broth, and sometimes even less, it is a good idea to keep a frozen stash on hand. When you find yourself with leftover broth from a large can or box or in the form of poaching liquid, freeze some of it in 1-cup portions in small freezer bags, and store the remainder in clean ice-cube trays for 2-tablespoon portions.

Coriander Root

Poaching the Chicken

- Coriander root is simply the root of the cilantro (coriander) plant.

- If you grow your own, you have a ready supply. If you buy cilantro with the root still attached, there it is.

- The roots themselves can be found in Asian and farmers' markets and in some well-stocked grocery stores.

- You can also flavor the broth with a handful of cilantro stems—just tie them together in a bundle or two so you can remove it before serving.

- Poaching simply means cooking in a light-simmering broth or water.

- You can flavor the liquid in endless ways, and in the end, serve the broth as a light sauce with the finished dish.

- It's important not to let the liquid boil, which results in tough chicken breasts.

- If you have leftover broth, strain it and save it for making soups or sauces.

DEVILED CHICKEN

Roast chicken spiced up with mustard and extra-crispy bread crumbs

Don't let the name scare you . . . the devil in this recipe is just the mustard, which adds a spicy kick to the chicken. Make sure to use a whole chicken that is cut into pieces (with a pair of poultry shears either by the butcher or you); it provides a great savings over buying single cuts like whole chicken breasts. The chicken pieces are slathered with two kinds of

mustard—both dry and prepared—for an extra depth of flavor. A drizzle of melted butter adds richness, and a layer of super-crunchy bread crumbs, called panko, creates a crackly crust that enhances the chicken's crispy skin. Make sure to press the bread crumbs firmly onto the mustard mixture so it stays put. *Yield: 4 servings*

Ingredients

1 teaspoon dry mustard

¹/₂ teaspoon water

6 tablespoons Dijon mustard

4 tablespoons olive oil, divided

1 chicken, cut up

¹/₂ cup panko bread crumbs

2 tablespoons unsalted butter, melted

³/₄ pound green beans

1–2 cloves garlic, sliced thin

Deviled Chicken

- Preheat oven to 400°F. Dissolve dry mustard in water and mix into 6 tablespoons Dijon.

- Warm 2 tablespoons oil in a large skillet over medium heat. Brown chicken, remove from pan, and brush skin sides with mustard mixture and top with panko, patting it in.

- Set chicken in a roasting pan and drizzle with melted butter. Roast 25 to 30 minutes, until juices run clear.

- Turn on broiler. Run chicken under broiler until crumbs are brown and crisp. Serve with braised green beans.

• • • • RECIPE VARIATION • • • •

Deviled Pork Chops: Season 4 1-inch-thick pork chops with salt and pepper. In a hot skillet with 2 tablespoons oil, brown 3 minutes per side; transfer to roasting pan. Combine ¼ cup mustard with 1 teaspoon fresh thyme. Spread evenly over pork chops. Press 2 tablespoons panko on top of each chop; drizzle with melted butter. Roast at 375°F until meat is 150°F, 15 minutes.

Coating the Chicken

- In addition to the piquant taste of mustard and spices, this chicken gets its kick from the contrast of very crispy skin and tender meat.

- To maximize the crispness, the chicken is seared on the stove top before it's coated with mustard.

- And then it's coated with panko, the flakier Japanese bread crumbs that have become a mainstream grocery item.

- Give the panko a gentle press into the mustard to be sure it stays in place. You wouldn't want to miss a crunchy bite.

Braise the Green Beans

- Wash and trim green beans, but leave whole with tails attached.

- Cook garlic a couple of minutes in 2 tablespoons olive oil in a skillet over medium-low heat. Stir in green beans and add enough water to come about a quarter of the way up the greens.

- Cover and cook at a low simmer, stirring occasionally, about 30 minutes.

- Add water if needed to keep beans moist as they cook—but water should be evaporated when the beans are done.

SLOW-COOKED DUCK LEGS
Finally a luxurious duck confit that everyone can make at home

Duck confit—that is, duck legs braised in duck fat—is a succulent bistro classic. But believe it or not, duck legs are an inexpensive treat.

This particular method for making a quick confit—although you will need to set aside a full day to let the legs marinate with the spices before you plan to serve them—was discovered by Regina Schrambling, popular food writer and blogger on Epicurious.com. She uses the same spices as traditional duck confit, but she cooks the duck legs slowly over low heat instead of simmering them in vats of duck fat. The result is shockingly good, very versatile (in terms of leftovers), and virtually foolproof. *Yield: 4 servings*

Ingredients

1 teaspoon allspice

1 teaspoon thyme

1 teaspoon cumin

$\frac{1}{4}$ teaspoon ginger

$\frac{1}{4}$ teaspoon cloves

$\frac{1}{4}$ teaspoon nutmeg

8 duck legs

4 tablespoons kosher salt

8 cloves garlic

1 bay leaf

Slow-Cooked Duck Legs

- Combine the spices in a small bowl and rub into duck legs. Sprinkle evenly with kosher salt. Marinate 24 hours in the refrigerator.

- Preheat oven to 300°F. Wipe off salt and crowd legs skin side up (in a single layer) into one or two 3-inch-deep roasting pans. Toss in garlic and bay leaf, cover tightly with foil, and cook 2½ to 3 hours, until meat is extremely tender.

- Crisp skin and serve.

• • • • RECIPE VARIATION • • • •

Leftover Duck Confit: This is a rich dish, so only a little duck goes a long way. If you find yourself with leftovers (double this recipe!), rejoice! You can shred the meat and toss with bitter baby arugula leaves and sections of grapefruit for an outstanding lunch salad. Or enjoy the crisped whole legs with cranberry sauce or applesauce; duck pairs very well with fruit.

Rubbing in the Spices

- Make a confit-style seasoning mixture by combining allspice, thyme, cumin, ginger, cloves, and nutmeg.

- Pat the duck legs dry with a paper towel and rub seasonings into flesh. Sprinkle evenly with kosher salt.

- Put legs in a single layer into a glass dish, cover with plastic wrap, and marinate 24 hours in the refrigerator.

- When ready to cook, carefully wipe off all salt with a paper towel.

Crisping the Skin

- The legs can be slow roasted up to 2 days ahead and refrigerated.

- Just before serving, crisp the legs. Heat a nonstick skillet over medium-high heat (if you want to do all the legs at once, heat two skillets). Or preheat the broiler.

- Sear the duck legs in the skillet, skin side down, just until crisp. Or crisp under the broiler, skin side up, 2 to 3 minutes.

- Serve with mashed potatoes, grits, braised greens, or a lightly dressed mesclun salad.

ROAST TURKEY BREAST

The star of Thanksgiving dinner can be enjoyed year-round

Like all holiday birds, a roast turkey breast is the meal that keeps on giving, night after night. Unless you are feeding an army, you will have leftovers for a few more lunches or dinners.

This recipe is based on one from Chef Emeril Lagasse, who adds crumbled bacon to the traditional herbed butter mixture that is tucked under the skin, which bastes the meat

with a sweet smokiness. To ensure a moist and juicy bird, throw away the little pop-up timer that comes with most turkey breasts. Instead, invest in an inexpensive instant-read thermometer to tell you when the bird is done (165°F, then let rest 15 minutes). The plastic timers tend not to pop until well after the meat is cooked, leaving you with dry meat. *Yield: 8 servings*

Ingredients

3 strips thick-cut bacon

1¹/₂ tablespoons minced garlic

1 tablespoon chopped fresh sage

1 tablespoon chopped fresh parsley

1 teaspoon chopped fresh thyme (optional)

3 tablespoons butter

2 teaspoons salt, divided

1 teaspoon pepper, divided

1 5¹/₂–6-pound whole turkey breast

Roast Turkey Breast

- Preheat oven to 375°F. Line a roasting pan with foil. Cook bacon until crisp; reserve 1 tablespoon fat. Chop bacon fine.

- Mix together bacon, garlic, herbs, butter, salt and pepper. Spread under the skin of the turkey, then season

the outside with 1 teaspoon salt and ½ teaspoon pepper. Brush with bacon fat.

- Roast uncovered about 1 hour, until breast is 165°F at center. Let rest 20 minutes, carve, and serve with pan drippings.

• • • • RECIPE VARIATIONS • • • •

Jamaican Curried Turkey Stew: Heat 2 tablespoons olive oil in a large skillet. Add 1 chopped onion and cook until golden. Add 1 tablespoon flour and 2 tablespoons curry powder and cook, stirring, 1 minute. Add 2 cups chicken broth and bring to a boil. Add 1 cup diced potato and 2 carrots, diced, and cook until tender, 10 minutes. Add 1 cup shredded leftover turkey and ½ cup frozen peas; cook 4 minutes. Serve over hot rice.

Thanksgiving Turkey Salad: Combine 2 cups diced leftover turkey, ¼ cup mayonnaise, 1 tablespoon Dijon mustard, ¼ teaspoon fresh thyme or minced fresh sage leaves, 3 tablespoons dried cranberries, ½ chopped apple (unpeeled), and ¼ cup toasted and crumbled pecans.

Seasoning the Breast

- The mild breast meat gets a double dose of seasoning, both under and over the skin.

- First the bacon-sage paste is gently spread under the skin. Loosen the skin with your fingertips, being careful not to tear it, then distribute half of the paste over each side of the breast.

- Next salt and pepper the outside and—in a very nice bit of economy—add even more flavor with a brushing of the bacon drippings.

Carving the Breast

- The breast is a simple cut to carve well.

- First cut the breast meat off the ribs. With the knife parallel to the table, slice along the rib bones until you hit the breastbone.

- Then slice straight down along the breastbone to free the meat. Remove the breast meat to a cutting board and slice along the length of the breast, front to back. Repeat for the other side.

- Slice thicker for a main course, thinner for sandwiches.

71

SLOW-COOKED BRISKET

Tender slices of brisket are served with turnips and an apple cider gravy

Brisket is a very affordable and versatile cut of beef, able to feed large groups of people with a minimum of hands-on work. It is also a tough cut of meat, which requires a slow-cooking technique like braising, smoking, or low-temperature roasting to create tender slices of meat.

This flavorful recipe is from Chef Daniel Boulud, who uses inexpensive apple cider instead of pricier wine to build his sauce.

Brisket needs to be cut "across the grain" in order for the meat to shred properly, otherwise it will be stringy and tough. *Yield: 6 servings*

Ingredients

For the marinade:

¼ cup packed light-brown sugar

1 cup dry white wine

5 cloves garlic, peeled and crushed

1 teaspoon thyme

2 bay leaves, broken in half

For the brisket:

1 2-pound beef brisket

Salt and pepper to taste

2 tablespoons olive oil

5 cups unsalted beef broth

3 turnips, peeled, trimmed, and quartered

3 onions, trimmed and quartered

½ cup apple cider

¼ cup cider vinegar

Slow-Cooked Brisket

- Marinate brisket 24 hours, refrigerated.

- Preheat oven to 325°F. Remove meat, reserving marinade. Pat dry; season with salt and pepper. In a Dutch oven, brown in olive oil over medium-high heat. Add marinade and bring to boil; add beef broth, return to boil. Cover and braise in the oven for 2 hours.

- Add turnips and onions and braise, uncovered, 2 hours more, basting regularly.

- Slice brisket across the grain. Make sauce, pour over meat and vegetables, and serve.

•••• RECIPE VARIATION ••••

Brisket with Horseradish Cream: Horseradish cream's sharp lusciousness makes it the perfect condiment for the sweet lean meat. To make cream, combine ½ cup sour cream, ½ cup mayonnaise, 1 teaspoon Dijon mustard, and 2 tablespoons prepared horseradish. Serve with warm brisket slices or as a slather for cold brisket sandwiches, piled on toasted rye or eggy challah bread.

•••••• GREEN ● LIGHT ••••••

Marinating plays two roles: flavor enhancer and tenderizer. The acid in a marinade (whether it is citrus juice, vinegar, yogurt, or wine) adds flavor while also helping to tenderize the meat by breaking down tough connective tissue. You can marinate meat for up to a day, but any more may break the meat down too much, causing it to lose valuable juices.

The Marinade

- Make the marinade by mixing together the brown sugar, wine, garlic, thyme, and bay leaves.

- To get the most from the marinade, put the brisket in a snug shallow pan and turn it at least once during its 24-hour soak in the refrigerator.

- The marinade becomes the braising liquid when the brisket goes into the oven.

- Scrape off all the herbs and garlic when you remove the meat from the marinade and reserve them with the liquid.

Making the Sauce

- When the brisket and vegetables are finished cooking, remove them to a covered platter and make a quick reduction sauce.

- Skim the fat off the braising liquid and put the roasting pan or Dutch oven on a burner over medium heat.

- Add the cider and cider vinegar, bring to a boil, and cook until sauce is reduced enough to coat the back of a spoon.

- Taste and add salt and pepper, if needed. Strain over sliced meat and vegetables, and serve.

CARNE ASADA TACOS

Soft beef tacos are accented with cilantro and grilled scallions

Authentic carne asada tacos, made with seasoned and sliced skirt steak, are a far cry from the tacos that most Americans are used to—crisp taco shells filled with ground beef and shredded cheddar. Here, soft corn tortillas enclose grilled steak slices and whole grilled scallions, which are then brightened with fresh cilantro, tomatoes, and tomatillo salsa, made from small green tomatoes in a papery husk. Serve the tacos with the lime wedges on the side so everyone can squeeze over the juice just before eating for the maximum citrus effect (lime juice loses its zing the longer it is exposed to heat). Soft corn tortillas can be made from yellow, white, or blue corn; store them in your refrigerator for maximum shelf life. *Yield: 4 servings*

Ingredients

1 bunch scallions, trimmed and dark green tops removed

1 pound skirt steak, trimmed of fat, cut lengthwise in half

Salt and pepper to taste

$1/2$ teaspoon garlic powder, divided

12 5-inch corn tortillas, warmed

1 avocado, thinly sliced

$1/2$ bunch cilantro, stemmed, leaves chopped

2 tomatoes, diced

2 limes, cut into wedges

Tomatillo Salsa (optional)

Carne Asada Tacos

- Heat an outdoor grill or indoor grill pan until very hot. Grill scallions until they are charred on all sides.

- Put steak halves on the grill, fat side down. Season with salt, pepper, and half the garlic powder. After about 7 minutes, when browned and slightly crusty, turn and season the other side. Cook another 7 minutes.

- Let rest, slice and serve on warm tortillas topped with grilled scallions, avocado, cilantro, and tomato.

- Serve with lime wedges and, if you like, Tomatillo Salsa.

Tomatillo Salsa: In a large bowl combine 1 pound chopped tomatillos (papery husks removed); 1 jalapeño pepper, seeded and chopped; 2 garlic cloves, minced; ½ small white or red onion, chopped; ½ teaspoon salt; 2 tablespoons fresh lime juice; and ¼ cup chopped fresh cilantro. Allow to sit at room temperature for 1 hour to allow flavors to meld. Blend for a smoother salsa.

Grilled Shrimp Tacos: Marinate 1 pound large shrimp in 3 tablespoons olive oil, 1 tablespoon fresh lime juice, ½ teaspoon garlic powder, and ½ teaspoon salt for 30 minutes. Grill shrimp until cooked through and pink, 2 minutes per side. Use in place of steak.

Using an Indoor Grill Pan

- You can buy a cast-iron grill pan for less than $20, and it will last just about forever.

- The pan, or rectangular griddle, has ridges that mimic the grids of an outdoor grill and impart a surprisingly smoky, "outdoors" flavor.

- The grill pan needs to be as hot as possible. Preheat it for 4 to 5 minutes over the highest heat on your stove.

- Sear the meat, then turn down the heat a little, if needed, to let meat cook through.

Cutting the Steak

- The steak's cooking time will vary a bit with the heat of the grill and the thickness of the steak.

- You want the meat juicy and just cooked through, an internal temperature of about 140°F.

- When they're done, remove steak halves to a cutting board and let rest 5 minutes.

- Cut each into thin slices across the grain. If you don't go across the grain, you'll have tough, chewy tacos.

STEAK WITH ONION MARMALADE

Asian-spiced steaks are served with a tangle of sweet-and-sour onions

This recipe hails from Jenni Barnett, an incredible home cook with a unique talent for pairing uncommon ingredients. While any cut of steak will work for this marinade and preparation, rump steak offers a meaty flavor at an affordable price. After the meat is soaked in a sweet Asian-spiced marinade, it is seared, then sliced and served over white rice to catch the quickly prepared pan sauce.

A sweet-and-sour onion marmalade is made while the steaks are marinating. Balsamic vinegar is added to the browned onions just before serving, providing a nice condiment for the sliced steak. This dish is finished with a handful of cilantro and thinly sliced scallions. *Yield: 6 servings*

Ingredients

¼ cup soy sauce

¼ cup Marsala or any sweet wine, plus a splash for the sauce

2 cloves garlic, crushed

Juice of 1 lime

1½ pounds rump steak, 1–1½ inches thick

Freshly ground black pepper to taste

1 teaspoon ground ginger (optional)

2 tablespoons vegetable oil

4 cups cooked long-grain rice, preferably basmati or jasmine

½ cup scallions, chopped, including green

½ cup cilantro, chopped

1 tablespoon butter

2 red onions, sliced

Salt to taste

1 teaspoon balsamic vinegar

Steak with Onion Marmalade

- Mix soy sauce, wine, garlic and lime juice. Rub pepper and ginger into steak; cover with the soy marinade for 1 hour or overnight.

- Put oil in a large skillet over very high heat. Sear steak, 4 to 8 minutes per side. Remove to a shallow bowl to catch juices; cover.

- Put rice on a platter. Slice steak thin, lay on rice, grind pepper over meat. Make a sauce with juices; pour on.

- Sprinkle with scallions and cilantro and serve with caramelized onions.

Steak with Red Wine Pan Sauce: Heat 2 tablespoons oil in skillet over medium-high heat. Sear any 1-inch steak (we prefer hanger, sirloin, and rib-eye) to desired doneness, 4 to 8 minutes per side. Remove steak and add 5 sliced shallots to hot pan and cook until browned. Add 1 tablespoon flour; cook 1 minute. Add 1 cup red wine, 1 teaspoon balsamic vinegar, ¼ cup chicken or beef broth, and pinch of dried thyme. Simmer until thickened, about 5 minutes. Remove from heat and add 1 tablespoon butter; swirl until melted. Season with salt and serve over sliced steak.

Make the Caramelized Onions

- Start the onions as you begin preparing the meal. They get sweeter and more delicious the longer they cook.

- In a medium skillet over medium heat, melt the butter and gently fry red onion slices, seasoned with a little salt.

- When onions have just begun to soften, turn heat to low and cover the pan.

- Continue cooking, stirring occasionally, until onions are translucent and soft. Drizzle on balsamic vinegar and serve.

Make the Sauce

- Take all the juices from the meat—the juices in the shallow bowl and whatever juices you can collect after the steak has been sliced—and return them to the pan that you seared the meat in.

- Turn heat to medium high and splash in a little sweet wine and a dash of salt.

- Let bubble and reduce a little, scraping the pan for browned bits, then pour over sliced steak, top with scallions and cilantro, and serve.

KOREAN GRILLED SHORT RIBS

Sticky sweet short ribs are paired with a pickled cabbage for an authentic Korean meal

These short ribs (a richly flavored and inexpensive cut) are a mainstay on the popular Korean barbecue menu. In a Korean barbecue restaurant, you will be given marinated short ribs (called *kalbi*) to cook yourself on the grill set into the middle of your table. The ribs are often sliced across the bone into thin pieces, making them quicker to grill and easier to eat with chopsticks. An assortment of condiments will be provided for you to enjoy with the sweet and meaty short ribs, most importantly steamed white rice and *kim chee*, the ubiquitous Korean side dish of spicy pickled cabbage. At home, the meal is just as easy to prepare and a perfect party idea for a warm summer night. *Yield: 6 servings*

Ingredients

2 tablespoons brown sugar

¹/₄ cup toasted sesame oil

¹/₄ cup tamari soy sauce

1 1-inch piece fresh ginger, grated

¹/₄ cup apple juice

2 tablespoons dry white wine

4–5 cloves garlic, pressed

Black pepper to taste

3¹/₂ pounds beef short ribs, preferably cut across the bone for kalbi (from an Asian grocer)

2 scallions, thinly sliced, including green part

1 tablespoon toasted sesame seeds

White rice for serving

Kim chee for serving

Korean Grilled Short Ribs

- Mix together brown sugar, sesame oil, soy sauce, ginger, apple juice, wine, garlic, and black pepper to taste.

- Put the short ribs in a shallow glass dish, pour on marinade, and toss well, making sure all surfaces are coated. Sprinkle sliced scallions and sesame seeds on top, cover, and refrigerate at least 2 hours and up to 24, turning occasionally.

- Grill over a hot fire, on a stove top grill pan, or in a skillet until browned. Serve with rice and kim chee.

- Boil marinade to use as a dipping sauce.

• • • • RECIPE VARIATION • • • •

Kim Chee Rice: Kim chee is made from sliced Chinese cabbage or other vegetables that is pickled with salt, chile powder, and sometimes shrimp. Heat 2 table-spoons toasted sesame oil in a nonstick pan. Scramble 1 beaten egg mixed with 1 tablespoon soy sauce. Add 2 cups cooked white rice, ¼ cup sliced scallions, and ¼ cup chopped kim chee. Stir until rice is hot.

MAKE IT EASY

Toasting Nuts and Seeds: Toasting dramatically enhances flavor and aroma and it is a good idea to toast some extra for future recipes. Store toasted nuts and seeds in reseal-able bags in the freezer until ready to use (toasted nuts and seeds go rancid quickly). Place an even layer in a dry skillet over medium heat. Toast, shaking, until lightly golden and fragrant, 6 minutes.

Choosing the Short Ribs

- You can find short ribs cut for kalbi in Asian markets and in most other meat markets, too. Or you can request it.

- The cut, which is sometimes called flanken, is simply a thin strip of rib meat cut across the bone. It should be about ¼-inch thick.

- Kalbi are deeply flavored, and marbled with a good amount of fat.

- Look for the leanest ribs—all that visible fat will melt away when you cook it.

Making the Marinade

- This marinade imparts a lot of flavor.

- Make sure you use toasted sesame oil and not plain sesame oil, which is pallid in comparison. Tamari soy sauce, as opposed to standard soy sauce, also has more dimension.

- When you cut the onion, do it on a diagonal so you get long, oval shape slices instead of little circles.

- Cutting the onions this way gives the dish an authentic look—and they cling to the meat better as it cooks, too.

LAMB SHANKS WITH POLENTA

Lamb shanks are braised in an herb and tomato sauce for a rich Mediterranean flavor

Lamb shanks provide a great way to enjoy lamb's unique flavor without breaking the bank. The tough shank cut requires a slow-cooking technique to tenderize the meat, unlike the quick-cooking method of the more expensive rib or loin chops. Lucky for the shanks, the longer they are braised in their tomato and herb sauce, the better they are seasoned and the more tender the meat becomes. The phrase "falling off the bone" is a perfect description for these shanks, whose meat will shred easily from the bone when they are finished cooking. It is an impressive entertaining dish as well, especially when paired with the creamy polenta. *Yield: 6 servings*

Ingredients

6 lamb shanks, patted dry

Salt and pepper to taste

2 tablespoons olive oil, plus more if needed

2 onions, chopped

6 cloves garlic, minced

1 28-ounce can tomatoes, including juices

1¹/₂ cups red wine

2 cups chicken broth

1 heaping tablespoon rosemary (minced fresh, or dried)

1 teaspoon thyme

1 bay leaf

1 cup coarsely ground polenta (cornmeal)

Butter to taste (optional)

1 tablespoon minced fresh parsley (optional)

Lamb Shanks with Polenta

- Salt and pepper lamb shanks. Heat 2 tablespoons olive oil in a flameproof casserole over medium heat. Brown shanks in batches.

- Pour out all but 2 tablespoons oil; add onions and garlic. Cover and cook until tender. Add tomatoes, wine, chicken broth, rosemary, thyme, bay leaf, pepper, and salt. Break up tomatoes and scrape pan to loosen browned bits.

- Add shanks; bring to a simmer, cover, and braise in a 350°F oven for 90 minutes. Finish sauce and serve over polenta, sprinkled with parsley.

• • • • RECIPE VARIATION • • • •

Lamb Shanks for Company: The sauce served with these shanks is a "rustic" sauce with whole pieces of vegetables still visible. For a more "elegant" presentation, transfer the sauce to a blender to puree the tomatoes, onions, and garlic. Wipe out the pan, pour in the sauce, and bring to a boil. Reduce heat, skimming as needed, until reduced by a third. Continue with recipe.

MAKE IT EASY

True polenta is made from simmering coarse cornmeal until it is soft and creamy. The coarser the cornmeal the better the flavor the polenta will have (the long cooking time develops the corn's flavor). When you don't have 30 minutes to spend making polenta, you can use a finer grain of cornmeal, which cooks up faster; just reduce the water to 4 cups for 1 cup dry polenta.

Finishing the Sauce

- When shanks are finished cooking—and fork-tender—remove them to a platter. Discard bay leaf.

- Put the pot on a burner. Skim the fat and bring to a boil.

- Reduce the heat and simmer until reduced by about a third. Adjust the salt and pepper.

- Return the lamb shanks to the pan, just until heated through; serve over polenta, sprinkled with parsley, if you like.

Make the Polenta

- Bring 5 cups water to a simmer in a large saucepan. Gradually whisk in the polenta (to avoid lumps), then stir until water returns to a simmer.

- Reduce heat to low and cook uncovered for 30 minutes, whisking occasionally,

until thick but still fluid. If polenta becomes too thick, add a little extra water.

- Add salt to taste and, if desired, a chunk of butter. To keep warm, transfer to a double boiler, cover tightly and let rest 30 minutes or longer.

LAMB CHOPS WITH MINT

Meaty chops are bathed in a fresh mint vinaigrette and served over a bed of greens

This recipe comes courtesy of meat maven Bruce Aidells, author of *The Complete Meat Cookbook*. Since lamb and mint are a classic pairing, these chops are treated to a fresh mint vinaigrette and served over a platter of bitter greens, to offset the lamb's richness.

Take note of the type of lamb chops you are buying: Smaller loin and rib chops can be very pricey, as they are the most tender. For this dish we recommend the less-expensive sirloin (from the leg) or shoulder chops, both of which have a slightly chewier meat, but give back in flavor what they lack in buttery tenderness. *Yield: 4 servings*

Ingredients

4 ³/₄–1-inch-thick lamb shoulder or sirloin chops

Salt and pepper to taste

¹/₄ cup olive oil, plus more if needed, divided

¹/₃ cup beef or chicken broth

2 tablespoons balsamic vinegar

¹/₄ cup packed fresh mint leaves, keeping small leaves whole

8 cups washed and dried salad greens, ideally arugula or curly endive

Lamb Chops with Mint

- Salt and pepper the chops. Put 1 tablespoon oil in a large skillet over high heat. Cook the chops (in batches, adding more oil if pan doesn't fit all of them).

- Cook about 5 minutes per side, until nicely browned. Remove and cover with foil.

- Make a vinaigrette with the pan juices, pour over mint leaves, and steep 3 minutes.

- Spread the greens on a platter, put chops on top and pour vinaigrette and mint leaves over everything.

Baked Lamb Chops with Seasoned Bread Crumbs:
When a rack of lamb isn't in your budget, you can opt for this easy alternative that uses sirloin chops. Preheat the oven to 400°F. Pat dry 4 1-inch lamb sirloin chops and set in an oiled ovenproof baking dish. Brush the top of each chop with 1 teaspoon Dijon mustard. Combine ½ cup fresh bread crumbs (see recipe, page 89); 2 tablespoons olive oil; ¼ cup chopped parsley; 1 garlic clove, minced; ½ teaspoon grated lemon zest; ½ teaspoon salt; and some ground pepper. Pack this bread crumb mixture evenly on top of the chops. Bake until lamb is 125°F and the crust golden, about 20 minutes.

BEEF & LAMB

Make the Vinaigrette

- After the chops have cooked, spoon off all fat from the pan, leaving behind any juices.

- Add broth and scrape browned bits from the bottom of the pan. Boil until reduced to about 1 tablespoon.

- Add vinegar and remove pan from heat. Whisk in 3 tablespoons olive oil to make a vinaigrette. Taste and adjust salt and pepper.

- Put mint leaves in a small bowl and pour vinaigrette on top. Steep 3 minutes.

Choosing the Lamb Chops

- This dish can also be made with the very tender—and expensive—rib or loin chops.

- But chops cut from the shoulder or leg are also delicious and much cheaper.

- Sirloin chops, from the leg, have the least bone and are reliably tender.

- Shoulder chops have a fair bit of bone but are the least expensive option. Just be sure to buy chops cut near the rib, which are the most tender. They will have a bit of the rib bone attached.

MEAT LOAF WITH TOMATO JAM

Meat loaf is taken to a new level when served with a red wine–tomato gravy

This showstopper meat loaf, courtesy of Jenni Barnett, is fit for entertaining company on a budget. More than a few things set it apart from Mom's meat loaf. First, fresh mint, shredded zucchini, and chopped bell peppers are mixed with the ground meat to add a whole new dimension of flavor.

And to truly make this meat loaf fit for special guests, a daisy-chain design is pressed onto the top of the meat loaf, created from pepper rings, olives, and fresh sage leaves. *Yield: 12–14 servings*

Ingredients

6 pounds ground beef

2 large onions, chopped fine

2 red or yellow bell peppers: 1 ³/₄ chopped and the other ¹/₄ cut into thin rings and reserved

1 tablespoon tomato paste or ketchup thinned with 1 tablespoon red wine

1 zucchini, chopped

Salt and pepper to taste

2 eggs

1 cup mint, chopped

1 bunch fresh thyme

Sage leaves (optional)

Olives (optional)

2 red onions, chopped

1 tablespoon butter or olive oil

4 tomatoes or a 15-ounce can whole tomatoes, quartered

1 cup red wine

Meat Loaf with Tomato Jam

- Preheat oven to 350°F.

- Mix together the beef, onions, chopped peppers, tomato paste mixture, zucchini, salt, and pepper. Lightly beat the eggs, add the mint and some salt and pepper. Bind meat with the egg mixture.

- Arrange the thyme branches down the center of a large roasting pan. Shape the meat on top into a long slender log. Decorate top.

- Bake for 1 hour, 5 minutes. Spoon tomato marmalade around meat loaf, cook 10 minutes more, and serve.

Make sure not to overmix the meat loaf ingredients; ground meat gets tougher the more you handle it. Mix ingredients with a wide slotted spoon and then gently with your hands bind in the egg mixture.

Mixing Meats: Meat loaf is traditionally made with a mixture of ground beef, pork, and veal. You can add any of those to this meat loaf recipe, keeping the proportions even (2 pounds each beef, pork, and veal). You can also substitute ground turkey for some or all of the ground meats. Just be sure to add 1½ cups dried bread crumbs to help hold its shape.

Decorate the Meat Loaf

- Part of what elevates this meat loaf from everyday ho-hum to truly spectacular is the optional decoration that runs across the top.

- After the loaf has been formed, press rings of bell pepper across the top, leaving a little space between them.

- Press an olive (black or green) in the center of each ring.

- Press a whole sage leaf in between each pepper for a daisy-chain pattern

Make the Tomato Jam

- In a medium skillet over medium heat, gently fry the red onions in the oil or butter; season with salt and pepper.

- Add the tomatoes and turn heat to the lowest setting.

- Cook 30 minutes and add the red wine. Continue cooking on low.

- Ten minutes before meat loaf is finished cooking, spoon the tomato marmalade around meat loaf.

JULIA CHILD BURGERS

The grande dame of French cooking takes on the classic American hamburger

There doesn't appear to be much room for improvement when it comes to the juicy hamburger, but leave it to Julia Child to know how to improve upon even the simplest dishes. Here ground beef is enhanced with sautéed shallots and fresh thyme and bound together with a little beaten egg, much like a mini meat loaf. The patties are cooked through,

then removed to make room for a red wine pan sauce, which bubbles up all the flavor from the browned patties left in the bottom of the pan. To soak up every drop of red wine gravy, serve these with a side of mashed potatoes, or as Julia might say, "pommes puree." *Yield: 4 servings*

Ingredients

4 tablespoons olive oil, divided

¹/₄ cup minced shallots, divided

¹/₂ teaspoon fresh thyme leaves

1¹/₃ pound ground beef

1 large egg, lightly beaten

¹/₂ teaspoon salt, plus more to taste

¹/₄ teaspoon pepper, plus more to taste

²/₃ cup red wine

1 teaspoon butter

Chopped parsley (optional)

Julia Child Burgers

- Heat 1 tablespoon olive oil in a large skillet over medium heat. Add half the shallots and the thyme and cook until soft.

- In a large bowl, combine shallot-thyme mixture with meat, egg, salt, and black pepper. Shape into four oblong patties, about 1-inch thick.

- Wipe skillet, add 2 tablespoons olive oil and brown patties on both sides (about 8 minutes for medium doneness).

- Make deglaze sauce with remaining ingredients, pour over patties, and serve.

Burgers with Mushroom Sauce: Slice a pint of brown mushrooms. Heat 3 tablespoons butter in a large skillet. Cook 2 sliced shallots until soft. Add the mushrooms and cook until browned, 6 minutes. Then remove and cook burgers in this pan. Remove burgers and deglaze pan with ²/₃ cup red wine, reduce by half. Add mushrooms, heat through, and serve over burgers.

Uncooked burgers make excellent freezer food and thaw more quickly than unground meat. Instead of buying those prepackaged flat burger disks (often lousy quality and more expensive than plain ground beef), make your own frozen patties. Wrap each burger individually in plastic wrap then place into a large freezer bag to add another layer of insulation against pesky freezer burn.

Make the Red Wine Gravy

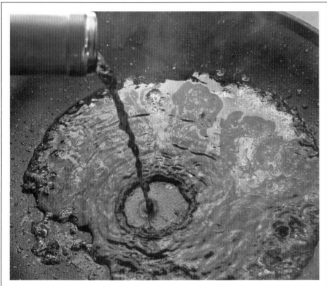

- When patties are cooked, set them on a warm covered plate and pour grease out of the pan.

- Add 1 tablespoon oil and remaining shallots and cook until soft.

- Add wine and turn up heat, scraping browned bits from the bottom of the pan. Cook until reduced by half and slightly thickened. Remove from heat and, if you like, swirl in the butter, broken into bits.

- Season with salt and pepper, and pour sauce over patties. Garnish with chopped parsley.

The Most Tender Patties

- The less you handle ground meat, the better—overwork it, and you'll end up with a tough burger, meatballs, or meat loaf.

- Start with the ground meat in the bowl, broken into chunks. Sprinkle the ingredients over the top to start distributing them.

- Then toss everything together gently—ideally you want to use your fingertips.

- When you form the patties, be careful to just shape the meat, not compress it.

GROUND MEAT

SARDINIAN MEATBALLS

Tender meatballs are seasoned with sharp pecorino cheese and simmered in an onion-tomato sauce

Thank you Joyce Goldstein, author of *Italian Slow and Savory*, for these savory meatballs.

Spaghetti and meatballs is wonderful economy food, but when you season the meatballs well, it won't seem as though you skimped on taste. Using ground pork in lieu of beef adds richness, and pecorino—a sharp sheep's milk—adds a sharp,

salty tang. Handle meatballs gently so they don't toughen while you shape them. If you can, use fresh bread crumbs; they create meatballs with a lighter texture than those made with dried bread crumbs. *Yield: 4–6 servings*

Ingredients

1 pound ground pork

¹/₄ cup dried bread crumbs (or ¹/₂ cup fresh bread crumbs)

2 large eggs

6 tablespoons grated pecorino cheese

2 cloves garlic, minced

¹/₄ cup chopped flat-leaf parsley

¹/₂ teaspoon salt, plus more to season

¹/₈ teaspoon black pepper, plus more to season

2–3 tablespoons olive oil

1 small yellow onion, chopped

1³/₄ cups canned tomatoes, seeded and chopped

¹/₂ cup water

Sardinian Meatballs

- Combine pork, bread crumbs, eggs, cheese, garlic, parsley, salt, and pepper. Form into 1-inch balls.

- Heat the olive oil in a skillet over medium heat. Sauté onion until soft. Add tomatoes and water, mix well, and add the meatballs.

- Bring to a gentle boil, reduce heat, and simmer, covered, until the meatballs are cooked through and tender, about 45 minutes. Season with salt and pepper.

- Serve over pasta or polenta.

Meatballs Parmesan: Heat olive oil in a pan over medium heat. Add meatballs and brown 2 minutes on each side. Add 2 sliced garlic cloves, 1 15-ounce can crushed tomatoes, and a few basil leaves. Cover and simmer until meatballs are cooked through, 10 minutes. Lay thin slices fresh mozzarella cheese over meatballs, cover, and cook until melted. Serve over pasta or bread.

Italian Hamburgers: Combine 1 pound ground pork; 3 tablespoons grated pecorino cheese; pinch of dried oregano; 4 basil leaves, sliced; 2 minced garlic cloves; and ½ teaspoon salt. Shape into 4 patties. Grill and top with a slice of fresh mozzarella cheese; melt. Serve on crusty buns with a slice of fresh tomato.

Chopping Onions

Old Bread to Bread Crumbs

- Peel the onion and cut it in half, from the top to the root. Set the flat side on the cutting board and trim off the top.

- Make a series of thick or thin slices—depending on how big you want the pieces— through the top of the onion. Don't cut through the root.

- Then make two or three horizontal slices. Again, don't cut the through root.

- Slice the onion crosswise and even pieces will fall away.

- To make fresh bread crumbs from slightly stale or fresh bread, remove the crusts (if you don't mind a rougher crumb, leave them on) and tear the bread into 1-inch pieces.

- Pulse in a food processor until crumbs are the size you want.

- For dry bread crumbs, put slices on a baking sheet in a single layer and bake at 300°F degrees until dry and barely brown.

- Break into 1-inch pieces and process until the crumbs are the size you want.

LAMB BURGERS

Fragrant lamb patties are served with a cooling tomato-cucumber salad and spicy cilantro sauce

Using ground lamb affords you all the luxurious flavor of lamb without spending a lot of money. Ground lamb is made from the lamb's tougher (but more flavorful) cuts, which are rendered more tender by the grinding process. Lamb is traditionally paired with fresh flavors, which brighten its mild gamey flavor.

In these burgers, adapted from Chef Suvir Saran's recipe, more than a few ingredients are on hand to bring out the best of lamb's flavor: fresh cilantro and mint, fresh scallions, and sweet lemon zest. Then the finished burgers are paired with a cooling cilantro-yogurt sauce and topped with a fresh tomato and cucumber salad. *Yield: 6 servings*

Ingredients

2 1/2 pounds ground lamb

4 jalapeños, seeded and minced, divided

6 scallions, white and light green only, finely chopped

1/2 cup finely chopped fresh mint

Zest of 2 lemons

5 tablespoons lemon juice, divided

4 teaspoons salt, divided

3/4 teaspoon black pepper, divided

1/4 teaspoon cayenne pepper

2 cups cilantro, roughly chopped

1 2-inch piece fresh ginger, roughly chopped

1 tablespoon sugar

1 small red onion, finely chopped, divided

3/4 cup plain yogurt

1 tomato, thinly sliced

1 small cucumber, halved, seeded, thinly sliced

6 rolls, split and grilled or toasted

Lamb Burgers

- Preheat a grill or broiler to medium high.

- Combine lamb with half the jalapeños, scallions, mint, lemon zest, and 2 teaspoons lemon juice. Mix in 2 teaspoons salt, 1/2 teaspoon pepper, and cayenne.

- Pat mixture into 6 burgers. Grill or broil until charred on the outside and pink within, 5 to 8 minutes per side.

- Spread some Cilantro-Yogurt Sauce on the top and bottom of each roll. Top with a burger, another dollop of sauce, and some tomato-cucumber salad.

Greek Lamb Burgers: Lamb is well enjoyed when paired with the flavors of Greece, where the meat is beloved. Combine 2½ pounds ground lamb; ⅓ cup crumbled feta cheese; ¼ cup chopped fresh mint; 1 garlic clove, finely minced; zest of 1 lemon; 2 tablespoons lemon juice; pinch of cayenne pepper; and 1 teaspoon salt. Form into 6 patties and cook as directed.

Serve with the cilantro-yogurt sauce and the tomato-cucumber salad, adding ¼ cup chopped black Kalamata olives to the salad. Serve with toasted pocketless pita bread on the side.

Cilantro-Yogurt Sauce

- In a food processor or blender, combine 3 tablespoons lemon juice, the remaining jalapeños, the cilantro, ginger, sugar, half the red onion, and 1 teaspoon salt.

- Process until fine, scraping down the sides to be sure the sauce is evenly mixed.

- Transfer to a small bowl, cover with plastic wrap, and refrigerate.

- Just before serving, fold in the yogurt.

Tomato-Cucumber Salad

- In a medium bowl, toss together the tomato, cucumber, and remaining red onion.

- Add 1 tablespoon plus 1 teaspoon lemon juice, 1 teaspoon salt, and ¼ teaspoon black pepper.

- Toss again to combine; set aside until burgers are ready.

THAI CHICKEN SALAD

Crispy lettuce leaves behold a chicken salad that is hot, sour, salty, and sweet

This traditional Thai chicken salad (called *laab*) is packed with flavor. You may need a trip to the Asian market to pick up fresh lemongrass, although many larger supermarkets are carrying it now due to the popularity of Southeast Asian cooking. It is often available dried in the spice aisle, but in a pinch, you can substitute ¼ teaspoon grated fresh lemon per stalk.

Fish sauce (called *nam pla*) can be found in the Asian aisle and is used in Thai cooking the same way soy sauce is used in Chinese and Japanese food, as a salt substitute. It has a rich saltiness that adds a distinct flavor that will be lacking if you omit it. Serve with steamed jasmine rice for a complete meal. *Yield: 4 servings*

Ingredients

1 tablespoon vegetable oil

1 tablespoon chopped fresh ginger

1 stalk lemongrass, chopped

3 fresh red chiles (or to taste), chopped

1 pound ground (or minced) chicken

¼ cup fresh lemon juice

1 tablespoon fish sauce (nam pla)

2 teaspoons sugar

1 red onion, thinly sliced

1 cup cilantro leaves

2 tablespoons basil leaves, cut into ribbons

Lettuce, for serving

Thai Chicken Salad

- In a large skillet over high heat, heat the oil and cook the ginger, lemongrass, and chiles for about 1 minute.

- Add the chicken and cook, stirring continuously, until chicken is cooked, about 5 minutes Remove chicken to a bowl.

- Mix together the lemon juice, fish sauce, and sugar until sugar is dissolved. Add to the chicken along with the onion, cilantro, and basil.

- Toss together and serve over crisp lettuce.

Cooking the Chicken

Serving the Salad

GROUND MEAT

- It's important to stir the chicken constantly as it cooks so that it doesn't form clumps.

- This will give you a finer texture for this salad—and more surfaces for the sauce to flavor.

- You can buy ground chicken, or you can easily make it yourself from skinless breasts or thighs.

- Just mince them finely, or pulse them in a food processor until they are roughly ground.

- You can present the finished salad a number of ways.

- Try laying crisp lettuce leaves such as romaine or iceberg at the bottom of a plate and tumbling the chicken on top.

- Or serve a stack of leaves on the side, for scooping.

- Or, use butter lettuce cups—just fill them with spoonfuls of salad and eat with your hands.

JUICY TURKEY BURGERS

Guild the lily by topping these burgers with avocado, melted Swiss, and sautéed mushrooms

This recipe comes from Chef Andrew Kirschner at Wilshire Restaurant in Santa Monica. It is a popular item on the bar menu there and unlike most turkey burgers, it doesn't use any fillers to hold it together. He grinds his turkey daily with 70 percent white meat and 30 percent dark. The key to this moist burger is its thickness (don't press into a flat disk). Keep a close eye on the burgers and the moment the juices run clear, remove them from the pan.

The burgers are served with a mayonnaise spiked with piquillo peppers, a spicy-sweet roasted red pepper from Spain, sold in jars. Any roasted red pepper (spiked with a little cayenne for heat) can be substituted. *Yield: 4 servings*

Ingredients

2 pounds ground turkey

³/₄ teaspoon salt

¹/₂ teaspoon freshly ground black pepper

1 tablespoon olive oil, plus more for brushing

4 thin slices Swiss cheese

1–2 jarred piquillo peppers or roasted red peppers

6 tablespoons mayonnaise

1 teaspoon lemon juice

4 rustic rolls, split, buttered and toasted

1 avocado, sliced thin

1 tablespoon butter

1 clove garlic, minced

1 shallot, diced

1 pint white mushrooms, washed and sliced

¹/₄ teaspoon thyme

1 tablespoon wine vinegar

Juicy Turkey Burgers

- Lightly mix salt, pepper, and turkey, and shape into 4 ¾-inch-thick patties. Brush with olive oil and cook on a hot grill, indoor grill pan, or nonstick skillet. Turn patties and top with Swiss cheese.

- The moment juices run clear, remove patties from heat.

- Spread Piquillo Mayonnaise on the bottom halves of the toasted rolls. Top each with a patty, then sliced avocado and sautéed mushrooms.

- Spread mayonnaise on the bun tops, cover the burger, and serve.

Sauté the Mushrooms

Piquillo Mayonnaise

GROUND MEAT

- Put 1 tablespoon olive oil and 1 tablespoon butter in a sauté pan over medium heat.

- Sauté garlic and shallot until they begin to soften, then add mushrooms and thyme.

- Cook until mushrooms are tender and juices have evaporated, 7 minutes.

- Deglaze pan with a tablespoon of wine vinegar.

- Drain piquillo peppers and puree in a food processor or blender.

- Measure out 2 tablespoons puree and mix with mayonnaise. Add lemon juice.

- Taste. You may want to adjust salt.

- If you can't find jarred piquillo peppers from Spain, substitute jarred roasted red peppers and a pinch of cayenne pepper to approximate their heat.

BRAISED PORK CHOPS

Prunes and red wine infuse meaty pork chops with sweet-and-sour goodness

Meaty pork chops benefit from being cooked in a two-step process called brown braising. First, the chops are browned to create a caramelized crust, which adds sweetness and a visually pleasing exterior. Then the chops are finished by braising them in a rich red wine and prune gravy, which adds moisture to the chops. Because of the sweetness of the prunes, the chops are well paired with a side of slightly bitter turnips.

Another side suggestion to soak up all the prune gravy is turnip mashed potatoes (see Recipe Variation, right). *Yield: 4 servings*

Ingredients

1 cup red wine

8 prunes

Pinch of cinnamon

4 thick-cut pork chops

Salt and pepper to taste

3 tablespoons olive oil, divided

$^1/_2$ medium yellow onion, chopped

1 teaspoon thyme, divided

3 medium turnips

1 tablespoon butter

1 clove garlic, minced

Braised Pork Chops

- In a small saucepan over medium heat, warm the wine but do not boil. Add prunes and cinnamon. Set aside.

- Salt and pepper pork chops. Heat 2 tablespoons olive oil in a skillet over medium-high heat. Brown pork chops on both sides and remove to a plate.

- Build the pan sauce with onion, ½ teaspoon thyme, and wine (but not the prunes). Add chops and prunes and cover to finish cooking, 6 to 8 minutes.

- Serve chops with pan juices, prunes, and sautéed turnips.

Pork Chops with Apples, Orange Zest, and Honey: Sauté half a chopped onion until soft. Add 1 peeled and cubed apple and cook until browned, 5 minutes. Stir in ¼ cup white wine, ½ cup chicken broth, ½ teaspoon orange zest, and 1 tablespoon honey. Bring to a simmer and return browned pork chops to the pan. Cover and cook just until the pork chops are tender, 6 to 8 minutes. Season with salt.

Turnip Mashed Potatoes: Peel and cube 1 pound each russet potatoes and turnips. Boil in salted water until tender. Drain, reserving ½ cup cooking water. Mash vegetables, adding 3 tablespoons butter and a little cooking water to moisten. Season with salt and plenty of pepper.

Building the Pan Sauce

- Once the chops are browned, remove them from the pan and use the drippings and browned bits to create a sauce.

- Add the chopped onion and ½ teaspoon thyme to pan and cook until soft.

- Add red wine from prunes (but not prunes), and cook until reduced by a third, scraping browned bits.

- Return pork chops to pan and add prunes. Cover and cook 6 to 8 minutes, until chops are just cooked through. Serve with pan juices and prunes and sautéed turnips on the side.

Accent with Sautéed Turnips

- Peel turnips, cut in half, and slice into ¼-inch-thick crescents.

- Heat 1 tablespoon olive oil and 1 tablespoon butter in a skillet over medium heat.

- Cook turnips, stirring occasionally, until browned and almost tender.

- Add garlic, ½ teaspoon thyme, salt, and pepper and cook, stirring, until tender.

PORK

PORCHETTA

Slow-roasted and richly seasoned pork makes for terrifically moist and delicious meat

Dotting the highways and back roads of Italy are the beloved porchetta trucks, where vendors thinly slice highly seasoned meat off whole, slow-roasted pigs and pile it high inside split crusty rolls with a sprinkling of coarse salt.

The sandwiches are addictive, and while it is hard to beat the flavor of the whole hog, you can approximate the flavor and texture at home with a boneless (or bone-in) pork shoulder and plenty of herbs. The meat can be served shredded, as a sandwich filling, or thickly sliced as an entree with a side of bitter greens (escarole, broccoli rabe) and mashed potatoes.
Yield: 8–10 servings

Ingredients

1 6-7-pound boneless pork shoulder butt

10 cloves garlic, peeled

$^1/_2$ cup fennel seeds

5-6 small dried red chiles, crumbled with seeds, or 1 tablespoon chopped rosemary

2 tablespoons coarse salt

$^1/_2$ teaspoon pepper

4 tablespoons olive oil, divided

$^1/_2$ cup hot water

Juice of 1 lemon

$^1/_2$ cup chicken broth

Porchetta

- Preheat oven to 450°F. Season the pork. Heat 2 tablespoons oil in a large Dutch oven over medium-low heat. Brown meat on all sides; don't let garlic burn.

- Remove pork, add ½ cup hot water, scraping browned bits, return meat to pan on a rack.

- Roast 30 minutes, add lemon juice and broth, and brush with remaining oil. Cover and roast 8 to 10 hours at 250°F.

- Remove to a serving platter. Skim fat and serve juices on the side or over the meat.

Porchetta Sandwich with Roasted Pepper Aioli: To make the aioli, combine 1 roasted red pepper (homemade or jarred), 1 egg yolk, 1 garlic clove, 1 tablespoon fresh lemon juice, and 1 tablespoon capers and blend until smooth. With the blender running, slowly drizzle in ¾ cup olive oil until thick and creamy. Season with salt and pepper. Slather the aioli on slices of thick crusty bread and top with shredded leftover porchetta.

Roasted Garlic Mayonnaise: To make mayo, roast garlic, cut ¼ inch off the top of a garlic head. Drizzle cut edges with olive oil and wrap head in aluminum foil. Roast at 400°F degrees until soft, about 45 minutes. Squeeze out soft garlic and mix with ¼ cup mayonnaise.

Seasoning the Pork

- Crush together the garlic and fennel seeds in a mortar and pestle (or put them in a small bowl and mash together with the back of a wooden spoon).

- Mix garlic-fennel paste with the crumbled chiles or rosemary, 2 tablespoons coarse salt, and ½ teaspoon pepper.

- Cut 1-inch slits over the entire surface of the pork.

- Rub the garlic and seasonings mixture into the slits.

Slow-Roasting the Pork

- After the hot water has been added to the browning pot, put a rack in the bottom of the pot and return the meat to pot, fat side up. Roast uncovered 30 minutes.

- Pour the lemon juice and chicken broth on meat and brush the surface with 2 tablespoons olive oil.

- Reduce heat to 250°F. Cover pan and roast 8 to 10 hours, basting occasionally.

- Meat is done when it's falling-apart tender.

PORK

PORK CHILI

Long-simmered pork butt makes a chili fit for company.

This recipe uses one of the most flavorful and inexpensive cuts of pork: the butt—an economical and somewhat rectangular cut of meat that also goes by the name pork shoulder, from the region where it is cut. It is rich in flavor and produces tender meat when subjected to a long, slow simmer, as in this recipe, a version of chili Colorado. This chili has character enough to serve for guests.

Make sure you use ground *chile* powder, which refers to spice that contains just ground dried chiles. *Chili* powder also contains ground chiles but also includes a whole host of other dried herbs and spices that give it a bit of a generic taste. Better to add your own additional spices. *Yield: 4 servings*

Ingredients

¹/₄ cup vegetable oil, divided

2 onions, chopped

6 cloves garlic, minced

3¹/₂ pounds boneless pork shoulder butt, fat trimmed and cut into ¹/₂-inch cubes

¹/₃ cup ground New Mexico chile, or other mild chile (not chili powder)

1¹/₂ tablespoons cumin

1¹/₂ tablespoons oregano

¹/₂ teaspoon cayenne pepper, or to taste

1 teaspoon salt

3¹/₂ cups chicken broth

1 15-ounce can Italian plum tomatoes, undrained

1 15-ounce can black beans, rinsed and drained

Cooked white rice

Sour cream

Minced fresh cilantro leaves

Pork Chili

- Heat 2 tablespoons oil in a large pot over medium heat. Cook onions and garlic, covered, stirring occasionally, until soft. Remove and add 2 tablespoons oil.

- Cook pork until lightly browned. Add onions and garlic, spices, and salt. Cook 5 minutes; add broth and tomatoes, breaking up with a spoon.

- Bring to boil, reduce heat, and simmer uncovered for 2 hours, until chili is thick and pork tender.

- Stir in beans and serve with garnishes.

There are so many dried chiles on the market, and each has its own unique flavor. Chiles are available fresh (like jalapeños and poblanos), dried whole (like anchos and guajillos), and dried ground (think cayenne). Some are smoked before they are dried, as in chipotles, which are smoked jalapeños.

Often recipes will call for more than one kind of chile (as in mole sauce), because it deepens the flavor of the finished dish. Dried chiles must be soaked in hot water to soften them, before being deseeded and pureed (with some soaking water) to make chile sauce. Cellophane bags of dried chiles and glass jars of ground chiles can be found in any Spanish foods store or in most large supermarkets.

Preparing the Pork Butt

- *Pork butt* is a loose term for several cuts of pork. When you buy, be sure to get Boston butt, which is deeply flavored and has relatively little waste.

- Ask your butcher to bone the meat, and if he or she is willing, cut it into cubes.

- If you do it yourself, trim off all visible fat and use a sharp knife to cut up the meat.

- Don't worry about making the pieces perfectly uniform. It's impossible with the irregular shoulder cut.

Layering the Garnishes

- This is a delicious chili served straight from the pot—but if you take care with the plating, it is elevated to a dinner party dish.

- Spread a thin layer of rice at the bottom of a shallow soup bowl.

- Spoon on a generous helping of chili, making sure to leave a rim of rice visible along the edges.

- Top the chili with a dollop of sour cream and sprinkle chopped cilantro over the top.

SPICY PORK TENDERLOIN
Slices of smoky chipotle-rubbed tenderloins are cooled by a bright mango salsa

The ingredients used to season this pork dish are classic Mexican fare: chipotles, mangoes, limes, jalapeños, and cilantro. And it is no wonder, since they all marry beautifully, both on the tongue and to the eye, creating a brightly colored plate of food. They are served with a side of quick black beans and rice, simplified by stirring drained canned beans into cooked garlic-infused rice. Chipotle peppers in adobo are smoked jalapeños packed in a rich tomato sauce. The sauce itself takes on a great deal of the chipotle's heat, so it can be used on its own to flavor food.

Consider a side of garlicky sautéed spinach to complete the meal. *Yield: 6 servings*

Ingredients

1 7-ounce can chipotle chiles in adobo

2 pork tenderloins (about 2 pounds total)

1 tablespoon vegetable oil

1 1/2 cups white rice

1 small white onion, diced

5 cloves garlic, diced

Salt to taste

1 15-ounce can black beans, rinsed and drained

1 mango, diced

1/2 small red onion, diced

1 jalapeño, seeded and minced

1/4 cup chopped cilantro leaves

1/2 red bell pepper, diced (optional)

3 tablespoons lime juice

Spicy Pork Tenderloin

- Puree the chiles in adobo in a blender until smooth. Trim the silver skin off the tenderloins. Scrape puree over tenderloins and turn until all surfaces are covered.

- Cover and marinate 1 hour at room temperature or overnight in the refrigerator.

- Heat a grill, indoor grill pan, or skillet until hot. Cook tenderloins, turning, until cooked through but still pink in the center.

- Slice thinly and serve with Mango Salsa and Back Bean Rice.

Mangoes are notoriously difficult to cut. To avoid frustration, stand the pit on its short side and position your knife directly in the middle, lengthwise. Move the knife over ½ inch (to avoid pit) and cut off one "cheek." Repeat on other side. Score the flesh in a crisscross pattern (don't cut through skin) and then press up on the underside to "pop-up" the mango cubes. Cut out with a small knife.

Chipotle Pork Burritos: Leftover chipotle pork, rice and beans, and accompanying salsa make excellent burritos fillings. Shred the pork or cut it into small dice. Lay out a burrito-size tortilla and mound the chopped pork, rice and beans, mango salsa (or any salsa), shredded lettuce, hot sauce, and sour cream in the middle. Fold in the sides, roll up, and enjoy.

Black Bean Rice

Mango Salsa

- Heat the oil in a saucepan over medium heat. Add the rice and white onion and cook until the onion is soft. Add the garlic and cook a minute more.

- Stir in 3 cups water and salt. Bring to a boil, reduce heat, cover and cook over medium-low, about 15 minutes.

- Add drained black beans, stir through, cover, and let warm through, about 2 minutes.

- Fluff and serve.

- In a large bowl, add the mango, red onion, jalapeño, cilantro, and, if using, bell pepper.

- Pour in lime juice and toss gently, evenly distributing the ingredients. Add salt, if you like.

- Serve with the chipotle pork loin or with other grilled meats.

- The salsa is also very good with fish. Try adding a cucumber—peeled, seeded, and diced—or half an avocado, diced.

ITALIAN SAUSAGE & PEPPERS

Simplicity is a pan of perfectly roasted sausages, potatoes, and peppers

This is not only perfect economy food but it is one of the simplest dishes to prepare. The ingredients are cooked together, so their flavors can season each other making a perfect one-pan dinner.

Use uncooked sausages for this dish because it is the juices that are released from the roasting sausages that season and

add moisture to the bed of sliced potatoes and peppers they are resting on. The sausages must be pierced before cooking so their flavorful liquid has a place to escape.

Green peppers are much less expensive than ripe red and yellow bell peppers and add a nice sharp brightness to the rich sausage and potatoes. *Yield: 4 servings*

Ingredients

3 medium russet potatoes, peeled and quartered

Salt and pepper to taste

2 cloves garlic, minced, divided

2–3 bell peppers, cut into wide strips

1 pound Italian sausages, hot or sweet

3 tablespoons olive oil

Italian Sausage and Peppers

- Preheat oven to 350°F.

- Arrange potatoes at the bottom of a large baking dish or casserole. Salt and pepper the potatoes and sprinkle with half the garlic.

- Layer the peppers on top; salt and pepper and sprinkle with remaining garlic.

- Set sausages on top of the peppers, drizzle everything with olive oil and cover tightly with foil or a lid.

- Bake 1 hour, remove foil or lid, and continue baking until potatoes are browned and cooked through, about 25 minutes. Serve with crusty bread and a salad.

Roasted Sausages with Grapes: This is another sausage pleaser, based on a dish at Al Forno restaurant in Providence, RI. Melt 2 tablespoons butter in a skillet. Toss 1½ pounds red seedless grapes with the melted butter and bury 1½ pounds uncooked pork sausages (hot or sweet) under the grapes. Roast at 425°F until the sausages are well browned and the grapes are very soft, 25 minutes, turning sausages once for even browning. Transfer the grapes and sausages to a platter and set skillet (with pan juices) over medium high heat. Add 2 tablespoons balsamic vinegar and scrape the browned on bits off the bottom of the skillet. Cook until the mixture is syrupy. Immediately pour over the sausages and grapes and serve.

Piercing the Sausages

Cutting the Vegetables

- The flavor of the sausage seasons the entire dish.

- To capture the most of it, prick each sausage with a fork three times before you layer them on the peppers.

- This will allow the spicy drippings to baste the potatoes and vegetables as they cook and will release much of the fat, making the sausages less greasy.

- Either hot or sweet sausages are good in this recipe. And of course you can always use a combination.

- This is a rustic dish, but paying attention to the details gives it polish.

- Cut the vegetables into long shapes that echo the shape of the sausages. The potatoes should be peeled and quartered lengthwise, not cut into 4 chunks.

- Similarly, the peppers should be cored, seeded, and cut into wide strips, about 1 to 1½ inches wide.

- Be sure to arrange the ingredients in layers to ensure even cooking and seasoning.

PORK

105

PORK CUTLETS WITH SAGE

Thin slices of pork are crisped until brown in a lemony sage oil

It is good practice, when cooking pork chops in a pan, to buy them as thin as possible. They cook more quickly that way and you can avoid drying with the prolonged cooking time necessary to cook thicker chops through to the middle (they fare much better in an oven).

If they are not available thin, just take cutlets and place between 2 sheets of waxed paper and pound lightly with a rolling pan until it is sufficiently thin.

The cutlets are then browned and seasoned in oil that has been infused with lemon zest and sage leaves. The seasonings are removed before the cutlets are added to avoid burning them. The crisp zest and sage are then used as garnish for the finished dish. *Yield 4 servings*

Ingredients

5 tablespoons olive oil, divided

2 tablespoons fresh sage leaves

Zest of 1 lemon

Freshly ground black pepper to taste

8 ¹/₂-inch-thick pork cutlets or pork chops

Salt to taste

1 small kabocha squash or sweet pumpkin, cut into 12 wedges

Pork Cutlets with Sage

- Heat 3 tablespoons olive oil in a large skillet over medium-high heat. Add the sage, lemon zest, and cracked black pepper.

- Cook until the sage is crisp, about 2 minutes. Remove sage and as much lemon zest as possible from pan. Set aside.

- Salt the cutlets and sauté in the pan until browned and cooked through, about 4 minutes per side.

- Remove to a serving plate, top with crisp sage leaves and zest and serve with roasted squash.

Winter squashes store well so they are available year-round. They generally have a leathery, inedible skin and brilliant orange or yellow flesh, which has a sweet flavor when cooked. The Japanese variety has a distinctly drier flesh when cooked and a deep, rich flavor (less water to dilute the taste).

You can use winter squashes interchangeably in recipes, keeping in mind that some are better suited to roasting (acorn, hubbard). Butternut squash is the most readily available of the winter squashes.

Roast the Squash

- Preheat oven to 425°F.

- Toss the squash or pumpkin wedges—no need to peel them—with 2 tablespoons olive oil, salt, and pepper to taste.

- Set wedges on a baking sheet or large roasting pan in a single layer.

- Roast for 30 minutes, until tender and golden.

Zesting the Lemon

- There are numerous ways to remove the flavorful skin of a lemon or any other citrus: box graters, hand graters, nifty little zesting tools, a paring knife.

- By far the best implement is a microplane zester, which grabs the zest at just the right depth and leaves the lemon completely bare.

- It's a few dollars very well spent—the microplane is also an excellent way to grate cheese or chocolate.

FISH STEAMED IN PARCHMENT

Steaming fish in small packages protects the delicate fillets from drying out in the oven

Steaming is an ideal method for cooking fish. By enclosing fish fillets with their seasonings (in parchment paper or aluminum foil), they can cook without losing precious juices. The fish is essentially steamed in its own aromatic liquid. You can vary the fish and the seasonings to make this a dish that you will never tire of.

This method is derived from the French *en papillote*, where a puffed parchment paper package is presented to a dinner guest on a plate, then snipped open with scissors so he or she can enjoy the heady aroma of the steam that first escapes. This is a bit less dramatic, but every bit as delicious. *Yield: 2 servings*

Ingredients

2 pieces any firm fish, about 6 ounces each

Salt and pepper to taste

¹/₂ teaspoon minced fresh ginger

1 lemon, sliced very thin

2 scallions, cut into 3-inch matchsticks, including most green

Fish Steamed in Parchment

- Preheat the oven to 350°F.

- Place each piece of fish on a sheet of parchment paper or aluminum foil. Sprinkle with salt, pepper, and ginger.

- Cover with lemon slices, slightly overlapping, so

  that the surface of the fish is almost entirely covered. Top with a scattering of scallions.

- Seal the packet and bake fish 10 to 20 minutes, depending on thickness. Remove from packet and serve.

Try these flavor combinations: Cod fillets topped with ½ teaspoon chopped tarragon leaves or crushed fennel seeds, 1 teaspoon butter, and orange slices; skinless salmon fillets topped with 1 teaspoon capers, 1 teaspoon butter, lemon slices, and 1 tablespoon white wine; tilapia fillets topped with sautéed mushrooms, thinly sliced tomatoes, and 1 tablespoon white wine.

YELLOW ⬤ LIGHT

There are some instances when parchment paper is a better choice than aluminum foil when steaming your fish. Aluminum foil (like cast-iron and aluminum pans) tends to leech a bit of its metallic taste into food when an acid is present. If you are using aluminum foil, take care to lay any lemon slices or tomatoes on top of the fish so it isn't resting on the foil, or use parchment paper.

Preparing the Parchment Packet

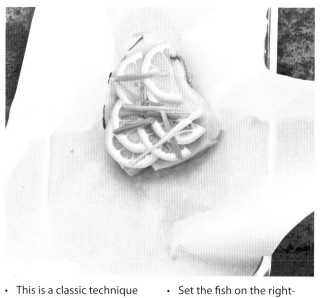

Is It Done Yet?

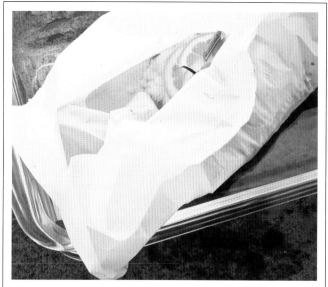

- This is a classic technique using parchment baking paper. You can also use aluminum foil, which is often easier to find and works just as well.

- Cut a large square of paper, fold it in half to crease it and unfold.

- Set the fish on the right-hand side. Add other ingredients and fold the paper over the top.

- Seal edges by making a series of small, overlapping folds. Press firmly to seal each—this will keep in the flavorful steam and liquid.

- Since you can't just prod the fish to see if it is done and flaking, this technique can make cooks a little nervous.

- Remember: This fish cooks at the same rate as it does with most methods, about 10 minutes per inch of thickness.

- And you can test to see if it is ready. Just unfold an edge—carefully, so you don't get burned by the steam. If it's not ready, fold it back up and continue baking.

WHOLE ROASTED FISH

Talk about presentation! Roasting fish on the bone is both impressive and delicious

In many parts of the world, you will see whole fish only being sold at the marketplace. That's because only the whole fish, with head and scales intact, will tell you the whole story when it comes to freshness (see YELLOW LIGHT). It is also the least expensive way to buy fish, since you are cutting down on the fishmonger's labor by filleting it yourself once it is cooked.

The bones, skin, and head offer both flavor and moisture to the fish while it is roasting, creating a tender and juicy meat.

Ask the fishmonger to gut and scale the fish for you, leaving the head and tail on. Some of the most common whole fish available are red snapper, tilapia, bass, and porgies. *Yield: 4 servings*

Ingredients

1 lemon

1 orange

1 lime

Salt and pepper to taste

1 whole firm-fleshed white fish, 3^1/$_2$–4 pounds

1^1/$_2$ medium onions, peeled, halved, and sliced thin

1 bunch fresh thyme

^{1}/$_2$ bunch fresh parsley

1 tablespoon olive oil, plus extra for serving (optional)

Whole Roasted Fish

- Preheat oven to 400°F. Cut half of the lemon, orange, and lime into thin slices. Cut the other halves into wedges.

- Salt and pepper the inside of the fish. Fill the cavity with ¼ of the onion slices, 3 branches thyme, the parsley, and some sliced citrus.

- Oil a roasting pan; add the fish, salt and pepper the top, and scatter the remaining citrus slices, onions, and thyme.

- Roast, then carve and serve with citrus wedges.

When is it done? Count on 10 minutes per 1 inch of fish, measured at the thickest part of the fish. To check for doneness, poke a chopstick (the blunt end is more telling than a sharp knife tip) into the flesh at the thickest part (near the spine). It should easily pierce through the fish all the way to the bone. Any sign of resistance or pinkness near the bone means the fish is not fully cooked.

How to Buy the Freshest Fish: Make sure to look for these signs of freshness: Bright red gills under the collar, moist tail (not dried or shriveled), clear bulging eyes (no signs of milky whiteness or sunken eyes), tight scales and taught skin. It should smell briny and fresh like the ocean, and not at all "fishy." Count on 1 to 1½ pounds of whole fish (weighed before it is gutted) per person.

Roast the Fish

Carve the Fish

- Choose the smallest roasting pan that will fit the fish and other ingredients.

- Spread 1 tablespoon olive oil on the bottom of the pan. Add the fish (with the aromatics inside). Scatter the remaining citrus slices, onions, and thyme on and around the fish—mostly on it.

- Roast 35 to 40 minutes, until fish is cooked through.

- Carve and serve with wedges of lemon, lime, and orange. Pass olive oil at the table to drizzle, if you like.

- Insert a knife along the top fin and make a gill-to-tail cut.

- Insert the knife just behind the gills until it hits bone; make a vertical cut behind the gills.

- Cut down the center of the fish, along the spine. Lift away the top half of the fillet in two portions. Cut along the bottom of the fish and lift away the rest of the fillet.

- Slide knife under the backbone and remove. Cut bottom fillet into four similar pieces.

FISH & SEAFOOD

FRITTO MISTO

Tender squid is lightly fried with fresh fennel and lemon slices

This recipe could very well be called Cheap-o Fritto Misto, because inexpensive squid is used in place of this dish's more traditional (and pricier) seafood, like sea scallops and oysters, which you can splurge on when the moment arises.

Other seafood ideas, which would complement the squid (after all, *misto* means "mixed"), are whole (cleaned and boned) anchovies, sardines, and shrimp. In addition to frying lemon and fennel slices, you can also try slices of zucchini and bell peppers to round out the dish. Make sure the oil is the right temperature before adding ingredients. The frying food will soak up more oil if it is not hot enough. Invest in a deep-frying thermometer before you start. *Yield: 8 servings*

Ingredients

Vegetable oil for deep-frying

1¹⁄₂ cups flour (Wondra, if you have it)

1 cup cornstarch

Pinch of sugar

Pinch of cayenne pepper

2 teaspoons salt

2 teaspoons black pepper

1 pound squid, cleaned and cut into 1¹⁄₂-inch pieces

1 pound other seafood (or a second pound of squid), cut into bite-size pieces if necessary

2 lemons: 1 thinly sliced, 1 cut into wedges

1 bulb fresh fennel, cleaned, trimmed, and thinly sliced

Fritto Misto

- Fill a narrow, deep sauce-pan with at least 2 inches oil and place over medium heat; bring to 375°F.

- Combine flour, cornstarch, sugar, cayenne, 2 teaspoons salt, and 2 teaspoons pepper.

- Dredge the fish, lemon slices, and fennel slices, shake off excess, and fry in batches until golden, about 3 minutes.

- Season with salt and pepper and serve on a platter with lemon wedges.

Crispy Fried Calamari: Bring 2 inches vegetable oil to 375°F in a narrow, deep saucepan. Cut 1 pound squid into 2-inch rings and separate out the tentacles. In a wide bowl toss together 1 cup flour (and/or fine cornmeal, rice flour, or Wondra, all of which are lighter than all-purpose flour and will create a thinner crust) with sufficient salt and pepper to season it. When the oil is hot enough, dredge the squid (in batches) until lightly coated. Tap off excess and add to the hot oil. Cook until golden brown, about 3 minutes. Serve with fresh lemon wedges or your favorite marinara sauce.

The Seafood Mix

- Fritto Misto is usually made with luxury ingredients like shrimp and shucked oysters.

- But it is still a fabulous dish made with a mix of any fish that's fresh and affordable.

- Consider bay scallops, inexpensive white fish, or smelt. Or just use all squid.

- Cut larger fish into bite-size pieces before dredging them.

Fry the Fish

- Dredge the fish, lemon, and fennel just before you drop it into the oil—don't let it sit, or the flour will get pasty. Cook 4 to 6 pieces at a time.

- Shake off excess flour and lower into the hot oil with a slotted spoon. Oil should bubble and sizzle but not spatter. Adjust heat if needed.

- When golden and crisp, after about 3 minutes, remove with a slotted spoon to a paper towel to drain; immediately sprinkle with salt and pepper.

CEVICHE

Lime-cured fresh seafood gets a kick from hot peppers, cilantro, and tomatillos

This recipe comes courtesy of Thomas Schnetz and Dona Savitsky of Doña Tomás restaurant in Oakland, California.

Their take on traditional ceviche—seafood that is lightly "cooked" in the acid of fresh citrus juice—includes the unusual addition of fresh tomatillos. These slightly tart green tomatoes, sold in a papery husk, have just the right amount

of sourness to offset the sweet tomatoes and avocados.

You can substitute any white fish fillets for the snapper; choose whatever looks freshest in the market and is on sale that day. Sole, sea bass, tilapia, and small bay scallops all make an excellent ceviche. You can also add cubes of fresh mango or papaya to this dish. *Yield: 6 servings*

Ingredients

³/₄ pound fresh skinless white fish fillets, such as snapper

¹/₄ cup fresh lime juice

Pinch of salt

2 avocados, diced

2 tomatoes, diced

2 jalapeños, seeded and minced, divided

¹/₂ red onion, minced

1 bunch cilantro, leaves only

³/₄ pound tomatillos, husks removed

¹/₂ cup water

1 clove garlic

¹/₂ teaspoon salt

Tortilla chips

Ceviche

- In a large bowl, toss together prepared fish with the lime juice, a large pinch of salt, avocados, tomatoes, 1½ jalapeños, onion, ⅔ of the cilantro leaves, and about ½ the prepared Tomatillo Salsa.

- Toss the mixture well, adjust the consistency with

more salsa and add salt if needed. Toss 2 or 3 more times.

- Let the ceviche "cure" in the refrigerator for at least 2 hours, up to 8 hours. Serve on a platter and line the edges with a pointy row of tortilla chips.

In Ecuador, ceviche is served with a side of crispy corn nuts or popcorn, either in a small dish or sprinkled around the plate, which not only complements the flavor but also adds a nice crunch to the otherwise soft ceviche. You can also use fried plantain chips (look for them near the potato chips in the supermarket) in place of the tortilla chips for a more authentic scooper.

• • • • RECIPE VARIATION • • • •

Quick Citrus Shrimp Ceviche: Lightly steam 1 pound medium peeled shrimp, 2 minutes. Cool and cut into ½-inch pieces. Toss with juice of 1 each lemon, lime, and orange; 1 cup each diced cucumber, tomato, and avocado; 2 tablespoons each cilantro leaves and minced jalapeño; and ¼ cup each chopped red onion and olive oil. Season with salt and let sit 30 minutes.

Prepare the Fish

- Choose only the freshest fish from a good fishmonger. Remove any bits of skin or pin bones.

- Cut the fillets into 1 x ½-inch strips, then cut each strip into ⅛-inch-thin slices on the bias.

- Toss the fish with the lime juice and a large pinch of salt.

Tomatillo Salsa

- Soak the tomatillos in cold water and peel off their husks. Cut away any brown spots and drop into a blender.

- Add water, ⅓ of the cilantro leaves, garlic, ½ a jalapeño, and ½ teaspoon salt.

- Puree until smooth.

- Adjust salt and chill until needed. This can be made 2 days ahead.

ULTIMATE FISH SAUCE
This orange-ginger vinaigrette complements any grilled or pan-cooked fish

This recipe is straight from Chef Rick Moonen formerly of Oceana restaurant in New York City. This universal sauce is just the right accompaniment for any fish preparation.

Since fish is not cooked long enough to make a good pan sauce from, a side sauce is often your only option, aside from a squeeze of fresh lime or lemon juice (no shame in that!).

The beauty of this recipe is that you can make several batches of it and freeze any leftovers for your next fish dinner. The key to the delicious flavor of this sauce is the reduction of the broth and orange juice to concentrate their flavors. Ginger, soy sauce, and rosemary each adds its own notes, which combine to make an addictive sauce. *Yield: 6 servings*

Ingredients

¾ cup unsalted chicken broth

2 tablespoons olive oil, plus more for cooking fish

1 ounce fresh ginger, cut in ¼-inch slices

1 large shallot, peeled, trimmed, and cut into ¼-inch slices

2 cloves garlic, peeled and sliced

1¼ cups orange juice, divided

¼ cup white wine

2 tablespoons soy sauce

2 tablespoons wine vinegar

1 orange, cut in half

1¼ teaspoons rosemary

1 cup grape seed oil

Lemon juice

Salt and pepper to taste

Any fish, up to 6 portions

Ultimate Fish Sauce

- In a small pan over medium heat, reduce broth to ¼ cup.

- Heat olive oil and ginger in a skillet over high heat. Stir in shallot and garlic. Add 1 cup orange juice, wine, soy sauce, and vinegar. Squeeze in juice from orange halves and add orange halves.

- Boil 15 minutes, add remaining orange juice and reduce to ½ cup. Turn off heat and stir in rosemary and reduced broth. Steep 5 minutes.

- Pour through a strainer, emulsify with grape seed oil, and serve with fish.

Orange-Olive Relish for Fish: Here is yet another great sauce for fish, particularly excellent with salmon, tuna, swordfish, bluefish, or any other strong-flavored fish (the sauce's sharp flavors are wonderful for cutting their rich flavor). Allow the sauce to sit for at least 30 minutes at room temperature before serving to allow the flavors to meld. Combine ⅓ cup chopped Kalamata olives; 2 garlic cloves, very finely minced (or put through a garlic press); 2 large navel oranges, segmented and cut into ½-inch pieces; 2 tablespoons chopped fresh parsley; juice of ½ lemon; 1 tablespoon red wine vinegar; 2 tablespoons capers; 2 tablespoons dried currants or minced raisins; ¼ cup extra-virgin olive oil; and ½ teaspoon salt. Toss to combine.

Emulsify the Sauce

- Put the orange-ginger reduction into a blender.

- With the blender at medium-low speed, slowly add the grape seed oil, blending until the sauce is emulsified. Adjust the seasonings, adding lemon juice, salt, and pepper to taste.

- Serve with any fish—simply prepared or complex.

- If preparation is simple, surround fish with about ¼ cup sauce per serving. If preparation is more complex, include just a little sauce on the plate as an accent.

Panfry the Fish

- Choose any fish that is fresh and affordable, either steaks or fillets.

- Salt and pepper the fish. Heat a tablespoon or two of oil in a skillet over medium-high heat.

- Place fish in the pan (if there is skin, skin side down—and press fish a little to be sure all the skin makes contact with the pan).

- Cook about 4 minutes, until skin is crisp and brown; turn and cook until fish is cooked through. Serve with sauce.

FISH & SEAFOOD

LINGUINI WITH CLAMS

Comfort is a bowl full of soupy clams

The beauty of clams is that they cook so quickly and offer up their own delicious liquid when steamed open. Their briny tang is a perfect complement to wine, garlic, and fresh herbs, with which they are traditionally cooked.

Cooked linguine absorbs their flavorful sauce, so you get more clam goodness in each bite.

You don't want to use any clams that are slightly opened before cooking. If they are open, tap the bottom of their shells firmly on the countertop. If the clam tightens its shell to close it, it is still alive; if not, discard it. In a pinch, you can substitute canned clams (with juice) for the fresh ones. *Yield: 4 servings*

Ingredients

3 tablespoons olive oil

2 tablespoons butter

6 garlic cloves, minced

¼ teaspoon red pepper flakes

2 pounds Manila or small littleneck clams, scrubbed

¼ cup chopped parsley, plus 2 tablespoons for sprinkling

½ cup dry white wine

¼ cup lemon juice

¾ pound linguini

Salt and pepper to taste

Linguini with Clams

- Heat oil and butter in a large pot over medium-high heat. Sauté garlic and red pepper flakes until soft.

- Add scrubbed clams and ¼ cup chopped parsley. Stir 2 minutes. Add wine and simmer 2 minutes more. Add lemon juice, cover, and simmer until clams open,

about 6 minutes. Discard unopened clams.

- Cook pasta in a large pot of boiling salted water. Drain and toss with clams.

- Season to taste with salt and pepper. Serve in shallow bowls, sprinkled with parsley.

YELLOW LIGHT

Count on 1 pound clams per person for a main course and ½ pound per person for an appetizer (or when served with pasta). If you buy wild (not farm-raised) clams, soak them in salted water with a bit of coarse cornmeal to help them purge their sandy grit. Any clams that don't open after sufficient steaming should be thrown away (it indicates that the clam expired before cooking).

• • • • RECIPE VARIATION • • • •

Linguine with Red Clam Sauce: In a large skillet heat 2 tablespoons oil over medium heat. Add 2 thinly sliced garlic cloves and a pinch of crushed red pepper flakes; cook 1 minute. Add 2 cups chopped fresh or canned tomatoes (with juice) and ¼ cup white wine; simmer 10 minutes. Add 2 pounds scrubbed clams, cover, and cook until opened. Serve over linguini.

Scrub the Clams

- Fill a large bowl with cold water.

- Rinse clams and drop into the bowl of water. Let stand 20 minutes.

- Remove with a strainer or a slotted spoon, being careful not to disturb any sand that has settled at the bottom of the bowl.

- Scrub shells with a vegetable brush.

Steam the Clams

- Steamed clams are one of the great luxury foods— and one that doesn't cost a lot of money and couldn't be simpler to make.

- Buy the smallest clams you can find.

- Since they are almost always farm raised, there is usually very little fuss with cleaning.

- If you want to enjoy just a bucket of "steamers" with some crusty bread to soak up the juices, follow this recipe but omit the pasta and boost the wine to 1 cup.

FISH & SEAFOOD

STUFFED ARTICHOKES

Sweet artichokes are steamed until tender with a garlic-herb stuffing

This is a traditional Southern Italian preparation for artichokes, turning this spiny vegetable into a hearty appetizer or light meal. Choose artichokes that are wide and heavy and brightly green. The pointy tips should be fresh and not at all shriveled, which is just a sign of age.

Like apples and pears, artichokes turn brown where they are cut. After you have trimmed off the sharp tips and removed the stem, make sure to keep it in a bowl of "acidulated water," which is water with lemon juice added, to prevent discoloration. There is tasty meat inside the stem too, so peel off the tough green outer skin and add the tender stems to the stuffing. *Yield: 4 servings*

Ingredients

4 large artichokes

Lemon juice or white vinegar

8 cloves garlic: 6 finely minced and 2 whole

Salt and pepper to taste

5 tablespoons olive oil, divided

9 slices sturdy white bread, crust trimmed and cut into coarse bread crumbs

1/2 bunch parsley, chopped fine

Stuffed Artichokes

- Trim the artichokes and fill the center of each with the stuffing, packing lightly.

- Fill a large pot with water so that it will reach about a third of the way up the artichokes. Arrange the artichokes tightly in the pan. Drop the whole garlic into the water, sprinkle with salt and pepper.

- Drizzle 2 tablespoons olive oil over the artichokes and into the water.

- Bring to a boil, reduce heat, and simmer, covered, 45 minutes to 1 hour, until chokes are tender when pierced with a fork.

•••• RECIPE VARIATIONS ••••

Unstuffed Artichokes: If you plan on steaming artichokes without a stuffing, you can avoid having to dig out the furry choke beforehand, further simplifying the recipe. Instead, trim off the spiky leaves and stem, and steam the choke until tender. Once you have enjoyed the sweet meat at the base of each leaf, use a small spoon to dig out the spiky interior leaves and the fuzzy choke. Then slice the artichoke into wedges and eat!

Browned Butter for Dipping: Melt 4 tablespoons butter in light-colored skillet over medium heat until foamy. Once little brown flecks start to appear in the butter (the milk solids starting to toast), remove from heat and swirl the pan a few times to cool the butter.

Trim the Artichokes

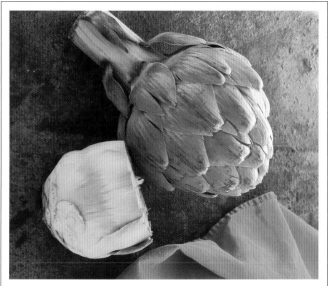

- Fill a large bowl with cool water and add a little lemon juice or vinegar.

- Rinse the artichokes. Cut off the stem at the base; then take the stems and cut off the tough outer layer and finely mince the core. Reserve for stuffing.

- Snip off the spiny leaf tips. Cut off the top ½ inch of the artichoke and scoop out the inner leaves and the furry core to expose the smooth heart.

- Drop into acidulated water until ready to stuff.

Make the Stuffing

- In a large bowl, using a fluffing motion, toss the bread crumbs with the minced garlic, parsley, minced stem core, salt, and pepper.

- When everything is mixed through, drizzle with 3 tablespoons olive oil and toss again to distribute.

- If you have a food processor, it makes this recipe extremely efficient. Simply mince the stem cores, garlic, parsley, and bread in the processor, one at a time, finishing with the bread so the resulting crumbs absorb every bit of flavor.

ROASTED TOMATOES

Maximize the delicious flavor of tomatoes so you can enjoy them year-round

Nothing will prepare you for what happens when you roast tomatoes with garlic until both are soft and melting—the flavors mingle and intensify. To boot, roasting tomatoes with whole garlic also delivers two extra ingredients: the roasted garlic itself and an intense tomato "stock" to use in risotto or soup, or as a dip for crusty garlic bread.

Make large batches of it in the summer, when tomatoes are bountiful and cheap. Freeze the leftovers for a time when you crave the sweet tomato taste of summertime. This recipe is adapted from chef Tom Colicchio. *Yield: 20 roasted tomatoes*

Ingredients

20 tomatoes, or more

1 head garlic

Salt and pepper to taste

3 tablespoons olive oil

4 branches fresh thyme

Roasted Tomatoes

- Preheat oven to 350°F.

- Cut tomatoes in half horizontally; put in a large bowl. Separate the garlic into cloves, leaving the papery skin on; add to the bowl.

- Season with salt and pepper and drizzle with olive oil. Toss until coated.

- Line a rimmed baking sheet or large roasting pan with parchment (do not let tomatoes touch metal). Put the garlic and tomatoes, skin side down, in pan. Add the thyme.

- Roast 1½ hours, pouring off and reserving juices.

• • • • RECIPE VARIATION • • • •

Roasted Tomato Risotto: Heat 7 cups chicken broth until hot. In another saucepan, sauté 1 diced shallot in 2 tablespoons olive oil. Add 2 cups arborio rice, stir to coat. Add 1 cup reserved tomato "stock" from recipe and stir until absorbed. Add hot chicken broth 1 cup at a time, stirring until it is almost absorbed before adding another cup, until the rice is tender, 15 minutes. Add 1 cup chopped roasted tomatoes and 6 cloves roasted garlic, smashed, cook 1 minute more, stirring. Remove from heat and stir in 2 tablespoons butter and ½ cup grated Parmesan cheese. Thin with enough broth to make it the consistency of thick soup. Top with snipped basil and extra grated cheese.

Roast the Tomatoes

- After 30 minutes of roasting, remove the tomatoes from the oven and carefully remove and discard the skins.

- Pour off juices into a bowl and reserve.

- Return the tomatoes to the oven and roast for 1 hour more, pouring off juices every 15 to 20 minutes into the bowl of reserved juice.

- Remove tomatoes from oven; let cool.

Store the Tomatoes

- You can use the roasted tomatoes, roasted garlic, and tomato juices immediately, or you can store them to enjoy long after tomato season is over.

- Store tomatoes up to 3 weeks, spooned into a clean glass jar with garlic and some juices. Store remaining juice in a separate glass jar.

- Store tomatoes for several months in the freezer, in an airtight container.

- The tomato juices and garlic can be frozen with the tomatoes or separately.

123

FRIED EGGPLANT & ZUCCHINI

The creamy texture of eggplant and zucchini are best appreciated in a crunchy coating

Zucchini and eggplant grow in abundance in the summertime and are available year-round in every supermarket. If you are lucky enough to grow zucchini yourself, you can use this same preparation for frying zucchini flowers, the prized part of the plant. You can avoid having to salt the eggplant slices altogether (which is meant to draw out some of its bitter juices) if you use smaller Italian or Japanese eggplants, with fewer seeds. Put them right into the hot pan after you coat them to keep them from becoming soggy.

These crispy vegetables also make great leftovers, cold in a sandwich or reused in eggplant parmigiana. *Yield: 8 servings*

Ingredients

1 eggplant, peeled and sliced into $1/4$-inch-thick rounds

4 medium zucchini, sliced $1/4$-inch thick lengthwise

1 cup flour, plus more if needed

6 eggs

Salt and pepper to taste

$3/4$ cup grated Parmesan cheese

$1/2$ cup finely chopped parsley

Vegetable oil for frying

Fried Eggplant and Zucchini

- Salt eggplant and place in a colander under a weighted plate. Let stand 30 minutes. Wipe dry with paper towels. Pat zucchini slices dry, too.

- Put flour on a rimmed plate. In a shallow bowl, beat together eggs, salt, pepper, Parmesan, and parsley.

- Fill your largest skillet with oil to about 1-inch deep. Heat over medium-high, until oil sizzles when you drop a little egg into it.

- Coat slices in flour, then egg batter, and fry until golden.

•••• RECIPE VARIATIONS ••••

Cold Zucchini Sandwiches: Use crusty white or sour-dough bread and use plenty of slices of fried zucchini. Top the zucchini with slices of provolone or fresh mozzarella, or spread goat cheese on the bread. Add a few slices of juicy tomato or roasted red pepper.

Eggplant Parmigiana: In a large baking dish, spread a layer of good-quality jarred tomato sauce. Top with a layer of leftover fried eggplant, then slices of fresh mozzarella cheese. Top with spoonfuls of fresh ricotta cheese and cover with a generous amount of sauce. Repeat, ending with a layer of mozzarella on top. Sprinkle with a heavy layer of grated Parmesan and bake at 350°F until hot and bubbling.

Coat the Zucchini and Eggplant

- Be sure to start with dry slices of eggplant and zucchini.

- Shake off any excess flour. You want only a light coating.

- Set up an "assembly line" beside the stove: sliced vegetables, rimmed plate of flour, and shallow bowl of egg batter nearest to the pan.

- You can't dip the vegetables in the egg in advance, they have to go directly into the oil.

Fry Until Golden

- Carefully slip the coated vegetables into the oil. Be sure it is hot enough to sizzle or the vegetables will be limp and greasy.

- Fry them in a single layer, until they are golden brown on both sides. Don't overlap; they will stick together.

- You'll have to do several batches; you may want to use two frying pans to get things done quicker.

- Instead of paper towels, drain the vegetables on a brown paper bag, cut open and laid flat.

ROASTED VEGETABLES
Root vegetables turn crispy and tender after a roast in the oven

Root vegetables were made for roasting; their tough interiors turn creamy and soft, while their skins crisp up to a golden brown. Any root vegetable, cut into bite sizes and tossed with oil, will work—carrots, beets, celery root, parsnips, turnips, rutabaga.

A few key things to remember: Cut all the vegetables the same size so they all cook at the same time. They should not overlap during cooking, or they will steam instead of brown; better to use two baking sheets and have a little space between the vegetables. Also, season the vegetables with salt and pepper once they are laying flat on the sheet, which coats them more evenly than tossing them with seasonings.
Yield: 6 servings

Ingredients

1 pound new potatoes

1 pound mixed root vegetables (carrots, sweet potatoes, parsnips, or turnips)

2 onions, peeled and cut into wedges

2 branches fresh rosemary or thyme (or 1 tablespoon dried rosemary or thyme)

3–4 tablespoons olive oil

Salt and pepper to taste

Roasted Vegetables

- Preheat oven to 425°F.

- Scrub potatoes but don't peel. Cut in halves or quarters if they are large, otherwise leave whole. Wash and peel the other root vegetables and cut into chunks the size of the small potatoes.

- In a large roasting pan, toss vegetables, onions, herb branches, and olive oil to coat. Distribute evenly, season with salt and pepper, and roast until tender, about 1 hour. Serve.

• • • • RECIPE VARIATION • • • •

Roasted Potatoes and Fennel: Choose potatoes that are small enough so you only need cut them in half to make them bite-size. That way the cut sides will brown on the bottom of the pan and their flesh will steam gently inside their skins, making the perfect roasted potatoes. Trim fennel bulb and cut into 16 wedges. Toss 1 pound halved small potatoes and the fennel wedges with about 3 tablespoons olive oil, or enough just to coat. Lay in an even layer on two baking sheets (separate the fennel and potatoes in case one browns more quickly). Sprinkle with salt and pepper. Roast at 400°F for 25 minutes, until golden and tender. Let cool on sheets for 3 minutes (so they loosen) and toss together.

Get Them Crisp

- One of the most appealing things about roasted vegetable is their crispy surface.

- You can help that along by starting with the driest possible vegetables.

- Set them, washed and cut, on a dish towel for up to an hour before roasting (don't do this with the potatoes if you needed to cut them).

- Although you would think more oil would help, it doesn't. Just use enough to coat the raw vegetables.

Roast Them Evenly

- Perfect roasted vegetables rely on even cooking. Be sure to start with vegetables cut to the same size.

- Then distribute them evenly in the pan—always in a single layer.

- It's important to turn them every 15 minutes or so while they roast so they get evenly browned and crisp.

- You can use softer vegetables, too—such as zucchini—but add them, tossed with oil and salt and pepper, about halfway through the cooking.

LUXURIOUS MASHED POTATOES

A few simple tips stand between you and perfect mashed potatoes

Mashed potatoes are the ultimate blank canvas and can be enjoyed simply on their own or doctored up with all kinds of flavors. Substitute some of the potatoes for different root vegetables (carrots, parsnips, and celery root are excellent) for a root vegetable mash. Or you can season melted butter (a better flavor carrier than milk) with roasted garlic cloves, thin slivers of raw garlic cloves (for a stronger flavor), or chopped fresh herbs like rosemary and thyme. Consider using warm extra-virgin olive oil in place of the butter for a lighter mash, which is particularly great with fish.

Boiling the potatoes in their "jackets" prevents them from absorbing water while they boil, allowing them to soak up more butter and milk when mashing for the fluffiest mash. *Yield: 4 servings*

Ingredients

1 1/2 pounds potatoes (Yukon Golds or russets), scrubbed but not peeled

Salt

3/4 cup half-and-half (or milk or buttermilk)

4–5 tablespoons butter

Grating of nutmeg, optional

Luxurious Mashed Potatoes

- Put potatoes in a large saucepan, cover with water by about an inch, and salt until the water tastes like the sea.

- Bring to a boil, reduce heat, and cook on a low boil 20 to 30 minutes, until tender when pierced with a knife.

- Bring the half-and-half or milk to a simmer in a small pan. Turn heat to very low.

- Peel the potatoes and mash or rice with the butter and half-and-half or milk. Season with salt and serve, with a grating of nutmeg if you like.

Never use a food processor, blender, or hand mixer to mash potatoes—it'll make them gluey. The best tool for the job is a ricer—a kind of giant garlic press that extrudes the finest mash. Keep an eye out at yard sales, they tend to turn up. The paddle attachment of a standing mixer also makes a nice, smooth puree. And of course, there is always the potato masher!

No-Milk Mashed Potatoes: The restaurant secret to great mashed potatoes is lots of butter and no milk, which masks potato's delicate flavor. Before draining the potatoes, set aside 1 cup of the cooking water. Use that in place of milk or cream when mashing, upping the butter by a few tablespoons. Season with plenty of salt and pepper.

Boil the Potatoes

- The dryer the potato, the lighter the mash.

- That's why it's best to boil the potatoes with their skins still on, rather than cutting them into chunks.

- They may cook faster cut into smaller pieces, but they will also absorb more of the cooking water.

- Another benefit: The peels just slip off after they are cooked. No messing with a potato peeler!

Mash the Potatoes

- To mash, clean the boiling pan and place it over low heat.

- Using a ricer, press the peeled potatoes into the pan. Using a masher, drop the peeled potatoes into the pan and quickly mash fine.

- Add half of the warm half-and-half or milk and stir. Add butter a few bits at a time, stirring and alternating with the rest of the half-and-half or milk.

- Season with salt and serve immediately (grate some nutmeg over the top if you like).

TUNISIAN CARROT SALAD

Caraway, olives, and feta combine to make a uniquely delicious salad

Carrots, one of the market's most affordable vegetables, is often a supporting player but rarely the star. That is a shame, because they are sweet and delicious and their orange color makes a stunning presentation. Here, in a recipe from Paula Wolfert (doyenne of Middle Eastern cooking), cooked sweet carrots are gently mashed with hot spices, salty olives, and creamy feta cheese. The combination is enough to serve with hummus and pita bread and call it a light meal, but it is also delicious as a side dish served alongside grilled meats and fish. Pair it with roasted beets on top of salad greens for a beautiful vegetarian dinner. *Yield: 6 servings*

Ingredients

2 pounds carrots, trimmed and peeled

3 large garlic cloves, unpeeled

1 teaspoon harissa, or more to taste

2 teaspoons ground caraway seed

7 teaspoons mild vinegar, such as malt or cider vinegar

2–3 tablespoons olive oil

Salt to taste

2 dozen small black olives, ideally niçoise, drained

4 ounces feta, cubed

Tunisian Carrot Salad

- Cook the carrots and garlic, reserving 1 tablespoon cooking liquid. Let carrots cool, then crush with a fork or pulse in a food processor.

- Blend the harissa with the reserved cooking liquid. Add caraway seed, cooked and peeled garlic, and vinegar, blending well.

Gradually beat in the oil. Toss dressing with crushed carrots; season with salt. Keep covered in the fridge, but return to room temperature before serving.

- To serve, mound the carrots on a serving dish and top with olives and feta.

•••• RECIPE VARIATIONS ••••

Ginger-Glazed Carrots: In a large skillet, bring ½ cup chicken broth, ½ cup water, 1 teaspoon grated fresh ginger, 1 tablespoon each sugar and butter to a boil. Add 1 pound sliced carrots; simmer, covered, until tender, 5 minutes. Remove, boiling liquid down to 3 tablespoons. Return carrots, heat through and coat with glaze. Stir in 1 tablespoon lime juice and season with salt.

Curried Carrot Slaw: Grate 1 pound carrots and add 1 sliced bell pepper; ⅓ cup toasted sunflower seeds; and ¼ cup currants or chopped raisins. In a small jar, shake together 2 tablespoons wine vinegar; 1 garlic clove, minced; ¼ teaspoon each curry powder and salt; and ¼ cup olive oil. Toss with salad.

Cook the Carrots and Garlic

- Cut the carrots into thin rounds.

- Arrange the rounds in layers in a steamer, pot, or covered glass dish. Add 3 tablespoons water, the garlic, and a pinch of salt.

- Cover and cook on the stove or in the microwave until the carrots are tender. Remove the garlic and peel it; set aside.

- Drain the carrots, reserving 1 tablespoon cooking liquid.

Reserve the Cooking Liquid

- Using a bit of the cooking liquid in the finished dish is an economical way to boost the flavor or loosen the texture—and get the most from your ingredients.

- In this dish the seasoned carrot cooking liquid becomes a kind of broth that helps unify the texture of the salad and adds extra notes of garlic and carrot.

ESCAROLE: SOUP & SALAD
Get the most out of two heads of crisp escarole

When buying escarole, it's always good to buy two heads at a time. That will give you enough tough outer leaves—the ones you usually strip off and throw away—to sauté for a side dish. Or use them in a recipe of beans and greens or—as we do—use them in a quick, wholesome soup. Use the tender center leaves to make a terrific, simple salad, dressed with a sweet vinegar like balsamic to offset its bitter punch. The

salad makes a great side dish to just about anything and is a good way to end a heavy meal.

Don't serve the soup and salad on the same night—you'll want the delicately bitter flavor of the escarole to contrast with something else to really appreciate it. *Yield: 4 servings*

Ingredients

2 large heads escarole

For the soup:

6 cups chicken broth

3 medium carrots, sliced or diced

3 stalks celery, sliced or diced

1 cup cooked chicken, turkey, or crumbled cooked sausage

1 cup cooked rice, or ½ cup dried tiny pasta (such as orzo)

Finely chopped parsley, for serving

Grated Parmesan, for serving

For the salad:

3 tablespoons olive oil

2 tablespoons balsamic vinegar

1 clove garlic, diced fine

Salt and pepper to taste

Escarole: Soup and Salad

- Remove dark green, tough outer leaves; make the soup by slicing the leaves and adding them to the chicken broth with the carrots and celery, and then add the cooked meat.

- Add cooked rice and heat through, or add dried pasta and cook until tender. Serve topped with parsley and a grating of Parmesan.

- Make a simple salad dressing by whisking together the olive oil, vinegar, garlic, salt, and pepper.

- Tear tender inner leaves into bite-size pieces; toss with dressing and serve.

• • • • RECIPE VARIATION • • • •

Curly Endive: Since escarole is a member of the endive family, you can use curly endive as a substitute for the escarole. Make sure to choose the very large heads of curly endive and not the small dainty heads called *frisée* used exclusively for salads. Like the escarole, the outer prickly leaves for the endive must be cooked, but the soft inner leaves can be enjoyed raw.

Make the Soup

- Stack the outer leaves and slice in half lengthwise. Stack again and cut across into 1-inch ribbons.

- Heat broth in a large pot over medium-high heat. Add the greens, cook 5 minutes. Add the carrots and celery; cook until tender, 10 to 15 minutes.

- Stir in cooked meat. Stir in cooked rice or dried pasta; cook until pasta is done or rice is heated through.

- Serve topped with parsley and a grating of Parmesan.

Make the Salad

- Rinse the tender inner leaves, drain them well, and tear into bite-size pieces.

- Make the salad dressing by whisking together the vinegar, garlic, salt, and pepper.

- Taste and adjust seasonings.

- Place inner leaves into a large bowl; toss with dressing and serve.

BEETS, TOP TO BOTTOM
A fresh bunch of beets gives you two wonderful ingredients for the price of one

What is more economical than a bunch of beets? You get the bright sweet roots, perfect for roasting, plus a head of leafy greens which are very similar in flavor to red chard.

Always opt for a fresh bunch over cold-storage beets sold without their greens; they are fresher and, of course, come with a free bunch of greens.

The pasta recipe here is based on one from Chez Panisse restaurant in Berkeley, California. The sweet currants and mint are perfect with the earthy beet greens. The roasted beet salad could be served alongside it or saved for another meal. Roasted beets will keep for up to 5 days in your refrigerator. *Yield: 4 servings pasta, 6–8 servings salad*

Ingredients

3–4 bunches beets

For the beet-greens pasta:

$^1/_2$ cup currants

$^1/_4$ cup olive oil, plus more if needed

2 red onions, chopped fine

2 garlic cloves, chopped fine

1 pound dried fedelini or other long, thin pasta

1 small bunch fresh mint leaves, cut into chiffonade

Salt and black pepper to taste

Pinch cayenne pepper (optional)

For the beet salad:

$1^1/_2$ tablespoons balsamic vinegar, plus more if needed

Salt and pepper to taste

Pinch sugar, if needed

4 tablespoons olive oil, plus more if needed

2 shallots, diced fine

$^1/_3$ cup walnuts, toasted and chopped

Lettuces, washed, torn, and dressed in a light vinaigrette (optional), for serving

Beets, Top to Bottom

- Separate the beet greens from the beets. Scrub the beets and wash the greens.

- Make the pasta: Plump the currants, then sauté the onions, garlic, and beet greens in olive oil. Add mint. Cook pasta and toss together with greens and cayenne, if desired.

- Make the salad: Roast the beets until tender, then toss with vinegar, salt, and pepper. Let rest 30 minutes; toss with olive oil, shallots, and walnuts. Serve over dressed lettuces, if desired.

Warm Beet Salad with Bacon and Mint: Separate beets and greens from one healthy bunch. Roast beets (see method below), cool, peel, and cut in ½-inch cubes. Thinly slice beet greens (not stems); set aside. In a large skillet over medium heat, cook 3 slices of bacon until crisp. Remove bacon, crumble, and set aside. Add 1 sliced shallot and 1 minced garlic clove to the hot bacon fat and cook until golden, 4 minutes. Add shredded greens and cook until wilted, about 3 minutes. Remove from heat and add roasted beets, 1 tablespoon red wine vinegar, and ¼ cup thinly sliced mint leaves. Toss to combine. Serve beets and greens topped with crumbled bacon.

Make the Beet-Greens Pasta

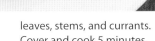

Make the Beet Salad

- Cover currants with boiling water, drain after 15 minutes. Wash beet greens; remove leaves from stems. Cut leaves into ribbons. Chop stems into 2-inch segments.

- Gently sauté onions and garlic in ¼ cup olive oil over medium heat. Add beet leaves, stems, and currants. Cover and cook 5 minutes.

- Meanwhile, cook pasta in boiling salted water.

- Add mint leaves, salt, pepper, and pinch of cayenne. Drain pasta; add to greens. Toss well, adding pasta water or olive oil if needed.

- Heat oven to 400°F. Line a baking pan with foil, add beets and a splash of water. Cover tightly with more foil and bake until tender, 45 minutes to 1 hour.

- Cool and peel beets; cut off stems and tails and cut in half or quarters. Sprinkle with vinegar, salt, and pepper (and a pinch of sugar, if bitter). Let rest 30 minutes; toss with olive oil, shallots, and walnuts.

- Adjust seasonings and serve on a bed of dressed lettuces, or on their own.

GARLICKY GREENS

Every meal is made more delicious and nutritious with a side of wilted greens

A head of greens provides you with a vitamin-rich and terrific side dish for any meal. And there are so many varieties to choose from: hearty kale and collards, sweet spinach and Swiss chard, bitter mustard greens or turnip greens. For greens with tough, inedible cores and stems (like curly kale and collards), slice them out and discard before shredding.

For tender-stemmed, not to mention colorful, chard, you can cut the stalk into ½-inch pieces and sauté for a few minutes before adding the greens.

You can make greens into a meal by stirring in a can of drained beans at the end (chickpeas or cannellini) and serving over pasta. *Yield: 4 servings*

Ingredients

2 bunches greens (kale, chard, spinach, mustard greens, collards)

3 tablespoons olive oil

2–3 garlic cloves, peeled and smashed

Pinch red pepper flakes, or more to taste

Salt and pepper to taste

1–2 tablespoons red wine vinegar (optional)

Garlicky Greens

- Wash and prepare the greens. Remove and discard the core and stems of the tougher greens, like kale and collards.

- For softer greens, such as spinach, use whole leaves.

- In a large skillet, heat the olive oil, garlic, and pepper flakes over medium-high heat until small bubbles form around the garlic.

- Add greens and sauté, stirring continuously, until tender.

- Season with salt and pepper and, if you like, a splash of vinegar.

Braised Collard Greens with Bacon and Onions: This is the classic Southern preparation. Braising tougher greens, like collards and kale, in broth softens them and makes them wilt into a tender heap. Remove cores from 1 bunch collards and cut leaves into ½-inch strips. In a large deep saucepan over medium heat, fry 4 slices chopped bacon until crisp and all the fat has rendered, about 8 minutes. Add 1 onion, minced, and cook until translucent, about 4 minutes. Add the collard greens, ½ cup chicken broth, dash of Worcestershire sauce, and 1 tablespoon cider or wine vinegar to the pot; bring the broth to a boil. Cover, reduce heat to low, and braise the collards until tender and dark green, about 20 minutes. Season with salt and serve.

Prepare the Greens

- If the leaves are big and coarse—such as kale or collards—remove the stems and tough cores and discard.

- Stack the leaves, roll them up, and slice into ¼-inch ribbons. Cutting them thin eliminates the need to blanch them before sautéing.

- For other greens, simply stack the leaves, roll them up, and slice into 2-inch ribbons.

- Very tender greens such as spinach can be cooked whole.

Cook the Greens

- Once the greens are in the pan, they'll need close attention. They cook fast, and you don't want to scorch them.

- Depending on the size of your skillet, you will probably have to add them in batches.

- Just let the first batch wilt down a bit, then add the next, turning continuously, and repeat until all the greens are in the pan.

- Finish cooking, turning all the while.

SPINACH SALAD FOR SUPPER

Leftover chicken makes a meal out of a bunch of spinach and arugula

This is a terrific way to make fresh raw greens the centerpiece of a meal. Baby spinach, arugula, and soft lettuces like Bibb, red leaf, and Boston all make a terrific base for a hearty dinner salad. By mixing lettuces, you will never tire of the salad's flavor, since every bite will be different. Try adding whole herb leaves too: basil, flat-leaf parsley, cilantro, and mint.

And what a great use for leftover chicken! If you don't have leftovers, you can buy a fresh rotisserie bird from the supermarket and use that. In lieu of chicken, try leftover slices of steak or pork or some freshly grilled shrimp (just omit the pecans). *Yield: 4 servings*

Ingredients

¹/₂ cup pecans

5 tablespoons olive oil, divided

¹/₂ teaspoon salt, plus more to taste

3 tablespoons sherry vinegar or other mellow vinegar

³/₄ teaspoon thyme

¹/₄ teaspoon oregano

Pepper to taste

2 teaspoons Dijon mustard

¹/₂ of a roasted chicken, white or dark meat

4 cups baby spinach or regular spinach

3 cups baby or regular arugula

3 cups bitter greens, such as dandelion or mustard, torn

¹/₄ red onion, thinly sliced

1 tablespoon capers, rinsed (optional)

¹/₄ cup Kalamata olives (optional)

¹/₄ pound fresh goat cheese

Spinach Salad for Supper

- Preheat oven to 350°F. Toss pecans with 1 tablespoon olive oil and a pinch of salt Toast about 7 minutes. Cool.

- Prepare the dressing. Discard chicken skin and bones and chop meat into bite-size cubes.

- In a large bowl, combine spinach, arugula, and bitter greens. Toss with red onion, and capers and olives if using, and half the dressing. Toss again with chicken and additional dressing.

- Divide salad among 6 plates. Top with pecans and a crumble of goat cheese.

These days you can find plastic boxes of baby spinach and arugula in the produce section. These are specifically designed for enjoying raw in salads, as they are picked well before their leaves turn tough, and their diminutive shape makes them perfectly bite size. Don't be tempted to cook with these leaves, though, as they will wilt into practically nothing. Save them for salads and sandwiches.

• • • • RECIPE VARIATION • • • •

Tuna Niçoise Salad for Supper: Lay a bed of mixed greens on a platter. Sprinkle with 1 can lightly drained olive-oil packed tuna; ¼ pound steamed string beans, cut; 1 cup halved cherry tomatoes; ⅓ cup pitted black olives; and 2 quartered hard-boiled eggs. Dress with 3 tablespoons olive oil, 1 tablespoon fresh lemon juice, and 1 teaspoon Dijon mustard, seasoned with salt.

Prepare the Dressing

- Pour the sherry vinegar into a medium bowl.

- Add thyme, oregano, about ½ teaspoon salt and black pepper to taste. Whisk until salt is dissolved.

- Add Dijon mustard; whisk until incorporated.

- Add 4 tablespoons olive oil, 1 tablespoon at a time, whisking until emulsified.

- Taste and adjust seasonings as needed.

Mix Your Greens

- Making a salad with different greens gives you a much more interesting result. That's why this "spinach" salad is actually made with three different greens.

- Mix peppery greens like arugula and watercress with sweeter greens such as spinach or red leaf lettuce. Accent with strongly flavored or bitter greens, such as dandelion, frisée, and mustard.

- And no matter what, a handful of fresh herbs will always improve the mix.

STIR-FRIED CHINESE GREENS
High heat and flavorful ingredients make these Asian greens sing

The key to making crisp, juicy Asian greens, like bok choy or Napa cabbage, is to subject them to high heat for a short amount of time. This maximizes the transfer of flavor from the seasonings to the greens, while retaining their pleasing crunch. Here, in a recipe courtesy of Jenni Barnett, toasted sesame oil, garlic, ginger, oyster sauce, and rice wine season the greens as they cook. You have the option of adding thinly sliced steak to make this pan of sautéed greens a hearty and delicious meal. Just serve over a bed of steamed white or brown rice.

To make the thinnest slices possible, freeze the steak for a few hours (not completely) before slicing. *Yield: 4 servings*

Ingredients

1 pound Asian greens, such as baby bok choy or Napa cabbage

1 tablespoon dark sesame oil

2 tablespoons minced ginger

2 cloves garlic, sliced

$1/2$ pound rump steak, sliced thin (optional)

2 tablespoons oyster sauce

$1/2$ cup rice wine or dry sherry

1 teaspoon cornstarch, mixed with water to form a smooth paste (optional)

$3/4$ cup sliced scallions

Cooked rice for serving

Stir-Fried Chinese Greens

- Cut baby bok choy or similar greens in half; slice Napa cabbage leaves crosswise into thin strips.

- Heat sesame oil in a skillet over high heat. Add ginger and garlic; cook 1 minute, just until soft. Add beef, if using, and stir-fry until browned, about 3 minutes.

- Add greens, oyster sauce, and rice wine or sherry; stir-fry 2 minutes. Add cornstarch paste to pan, if desired, and stir-fry until greens are tender and sauce has thickened. Sprinkle with scallions and serve over rice.

•••• RECIPE VARIATION ••••

Braised Baby Bok Choy: In a deep skillet bring ½ cup chicken broth, 1 tablespoon butter, and ½ teaspoon minced ginger to a simmer. Arrange 6 halved baby choys, cut side down on the bottom. Cover and simmer until tender, 4 minutes. Remove bok choy and reduce braising liquid to ½ cup, 5 minutes. Stir in 1 teaspoon each dark sesame oil and soy sauce. Pour over bok choy.

ZOOM

Cornstarch is commonly used in Asian stir-fries to thicken the sauce to the point that it clings to the vegetables and meats. It is a perfectly smooth thickener with a slightly viscous quality, almost gelling the sauce. To thicken any sauce use about 2 teaspoons per 1 cup liquid, first dissolving it in a bit of water before adding it to prevent clumping. The liquid will thicken when it reaches a boil.

Stir-Fry the Dish

- A good stir-fry requires high heat and speed.

- That means the cook must fearlessly crank up the flame beyond the usual sauté.

- And all the ingredients must be cut, measured, and ready to go before the cooking starts.

- The food must be tossed continually as it cooks so the maximum contact is made with the hot pan (and, of course, so nothing burns).

Wok versus Skillet

- There are advantages to stir-frying in a wok, as you might guess.

- The high sides let you cook a great deal of food very quickly. They help to contain it as you toss it about and give you a larger hot surface area for the food to come in contact with.

- You needn't spend money on a wok to make a good stir-fry, however. Just keep the heat high and the food in motion.

GRILLED CAESAR SALAD

The char from the grill makes this crispy salad unique

It is hard to improve upon the classic Caesar salad. But we think throwing the split head of romaine lettuce on the grill before serving adds a light touch of smokiness that marries well with the garlicky dressing. This is a terrific trick for summertime, when the grill is already on, and it makes an excellent accompaniment to juicy hamburgers and steaks. Or grill up some chicken breasts or shrimp and serve on top

of the salad for a delicious and filling main course.

If you don't want to eat raw egg, you can substitute a tablespoon of mayonnaise for the raw yolk in the dressing. If you can, splurge on real Parmigiana Reggiano for this dish. *Yield: 6 servings*

Ingredients

For the croutons:

3 tablespoons olive oil

1 clove crushed garlic

1 tablespoon finely chopped flat-leaf parsley

6 thick slices crusty white bread (not sourdough), cut into 1-inch cubes

For the dressing:

2 cloves garlic, finely minced

1 large egg yolk

1 tablespoon Dijon mustard

3 large anchovies

2 tablespoons lemon juice

$1/2$ teaspoon coarse salt

Freshly ground black pepper to taste

$1/3$ cup olive oil

For the salad:

6 romaine hearts

Olive oil for brushing

Parmesan cheese, grated or shaved

Grilled Caesar Salad

- Make the croutons and the dressing. Set aside.

- Wash the romaine and dry thoroughly. Trim off toughest outer leaves and trim base, but leave core intact. Cut each heart into halves lengthwise.

- Brush with olive oil and grill over medium-high heat until lettuce is slightly charred on all sides but still crisp at the center, about 5 minutes.

- Put two sections of romaine on each plate, drizzle with dressing, top with croutons and Parmesan, and serve.

ZOOM

There are many different qualities of Parmesan cheese on the market, with Parmigiana Reggiano from Italy topping the charts in quality and flavor. It is made from cow's milk and has been aged for two years under strict supervision. It bears a thick waxy rind emblazoned with its name (so you will always know you are getting the real thing). Its texture is crumbly and a bit crunchy (from calcium crystals) and is best enjoyed finely grated over food or cut into little chunks to be nibbled slowly. You can also use a vegetable peeler to create long thin slices of cheese that are terrific for dressing salads.

Make the Croutons

- Preheat oven to 350°F.

- In a large bowl, combine the olive oil, garlic and parsley. Add the bread cubes and toss thoroughly to combine.

- Transfer bread cubes to a baking sheet and bake until golden and crisp, about 10 minutes.

- Set aside to cool.

Make the Dressing

- In a large bowl, combine crushed garlic, egg yolk, and mustard.

- Add the anchovies and mash with the back of a fork until the mixture forms a paste.

- Add the lemon juice, ½ teaspoon coarse salt, and ground black pepper to taste.

- Whisking constantly, slowly drizzle in the olive oil, a bit at a time, until completely emulsified. Set aside.

WHITE BEAN & AVOCADO SALAD

Creamy beans and avocado are dressed with a parsley-lemon vinaigrette

This deceptively simple recipe is inspired by the sidewalk trattorias of Northern Italy, where rich and delicious vegetable salads abound.

Luckily this is a recipe that tastes just as good coming out of your own kitchen. You may be tempted to add more lemon juice to the beans and avocados, but try it first as is.

The ingredients couldn't be more rustic, but the layers of richness—the creamy beans, the buttery avocado, the fruity olive oil—are heavenly. The lemon juice brightens the flavors but subdues the luxuriousness. You might want to skip the lemon entirely! You can also add a bit of lemon zest to boost the lemon flavor but not the acidity. *Yield: 4 servings*

Ingredients

1 cup dried cannellini beans

1/2 bunch flat-leaf Italian parsley

1 ripe but firm avocado

3–4 tablespoons extra-virgin olive oil

1 teaspoon lemon juice, or to taste

Salt to taste

White Bean and Avocado Salad

- Make the beans; let cool completely to room temperature.

- Separate the parsley leaves from the stem and very roughly chop (or leave whole).

- Cut avocado into a dice roughly the size of the beans.

- Put beans, avocado, and parsley in a bowl and dress with olive oil, lemon juice, and salt to taste. Gently toss together and serve.

Tuna and White Bean Salad: Cannellini beans are also terrific served with olive-oil packed tuna fish for an excellent warm-weather lunch. In a bowl combine 1 6-ounce can tuna packed in olive oil (lightly drained); 2 cups cooked cannellini beans (or 1 15-ounce can, drained); ½ small red onion, diced; 1 tablespoon capers; 2 mashed anchovy fillets; 1 tablespoon red wine vinegar; 1 tablespoon extra-virgin olive oil; 2 tablespoons chopped fresh flat-leaf parsley; and the grated zest of 1 lemon. Toss together and season with salt and freshly ground black pepper. You can serve it atop a bed of greens or on top of toasted bread for an excellent open-face sandwich. Serve with a handful of sliced cherry tomatoes.

Make the Beans

- Inspect the beans, discarding any small stones or debris. Rinse and soak in a large bowl of water overnight.

- Or, put rinsed beans in a pot of water, bring to a boil, and boil for 3 minutes. Remove from heat, cover, and soak 1 hour.

- Drain the beans.

- Put them in a medium pot and cover with water by 2 inches. Bring to a boil, reduce heat, and simmer, partly covered, until tender, 1 to 2 hours.

Dried versus Canned

- While canned beans aren't exactly a luxury ingredient, they are more expensive than dried beans that you cook yourself.

- It's worth the effort to follow the method here for beans you use regularly, then drain and freeze the beans for when you need them.

- They'll easily keep a year in the freezer.

- And, not only are they cheaper, their flavor and texture is noticeably better, and they are much less salty.

CHRISTMAS LIMA BEAN TACOS

Gigantic buttery beans are paired with bitter greens and tangy salsa in a newfangled taco

This wonderful take on vegetarian tacos is thanks to Amy Scattergood, a food writer from Los Angeles. Christmas lima beans are large, meaty beans that have a slight chestnut flavor. Since they are not easily found in supermarkets, you can make these tacos with plump butter beans or large white lima beans, both readily available, dried or canned.

Pairing the rich sweet beans with sautéed bitter greens makes a perfectly balanced taco, perked up with some green salsa. Use arugula or turnip greens if you can't find fresh dandelion greens. *Yield: 18 tacos*

Ingredients

3 1/2 tablespoons olive oil, divided

1 large onion, finely chopped

2 cloves garlic, minced

2 cups dried Christmas lima beans (or regular white limas or butter beans)

Black pepper to taste

1 1/2 teaspoons salt, plus 2 pinches

4 tomatillos, finely chopped

1/2 large red onion, finely chopped

2 jalapeños, minced

1 large bunch cilantro, finely chopped

2 limes, juiced, plus additional limes for wedges

2 bunches dandelion greens, cleaned and roughly chopped

18 small corn tortillas

Christmas Lima Bean Tacos

- Cook the beans and make the salsa verde.

- Put 1 tablespoon olive oil in a large skillet over medium-high heat. Cook the dandelion greens with a pinch of salt, stirring frequently, until wilted, about 3 minutes. Remove from heat and set aside.

- Heat tortillas on a hot griddle or sauté pan. Turn them so both sides are slightly toasted.

- Assemble tacos: Place about 1/3 cup beans on each tortilla, top with 1/4 cup wilted greens and salsa verde to taste. Serve with lime wedges.

Smoky Black Bean and Spinach Tacos: In a medium saucepan heat 2 tablespoons olive oil. Add 2 scallions, minced, and cook 1 minute. Add 2 plum tomatoes, chopped; 1 mashed chipotle pepper in adobo; and 1 15-ounce can black beans, drained. Cover and simmer for 15 minutes. Cool slightly. Meanwhile, heat 1 tablespoon olive oil in a large skillet over medium-high heat. Cook ½ pound spinach leaves with a pinch of salt, stirring frequently, until wilted, about 3 minutes. Drain and toss with 1 tablespoon fresh lime juice. Warm corn or flour tortillas and fill with the smoky beans, a portion of spinach, sliced avocado, and some crumbled *queso fresco* cheese.

Cook the Beans

Make the Salsa Verde

BEANS

- Heat 1½ tablespoons olive oil in a medium pot over medium-low heat. Cook onion and garlic until soft, about 10 minutes.

- Add dried beans and water to cover. Bring to a simmer over high heat, then reduce heat to low and cover the pot, stirring occasionally.

- After 45 minutes, add black pepper, 1½ teaspoons salt, and additional water to cover the beans if necessary. Cover and cook, stirring occasionally, another 45 minutes to 1 hour.

- When beans are tender, remove from heat and cool slightly.

- In a medium bowl, combine the tomatillos, red onion, jalapeños, cilantro, 1 tablespoon olive oil, pinch of salt, and lime juice.

- Stir to combine and set aside. You should have about 2 cups salsa.

147

RED LENTILS WITH GINGER

Orange-tinged lentils cook down into a creamy mash when simmered with garlic and ginger

This is a classic recipe for *dal,* the popular Indian dish that pairs split lentils with onions, ginger, and garlic. Once the red lentils are softened, they quickly turn into a creamy puree. You can add any number of warm spices when you add the garlic. Consider 2 teaspoons total of any of the following: turmeric, garam masala, cumin, coriander, curry powder, and a

pinch of cayenne. Red lentils are actually orange in color and turn yellow when cooked. The butter here is clarified so that it doesn't burn. You can skip this step and use whole butter, watching closely and using low heat. Or use *ghee* (cultured clarified butter), found in Middle Eastern grocery stores and authentic to Indian cooking. *Yield: 6 servings*

Ingredients

2 cups red lentils

2 tablespoons butter, ghee, or vegetable oil

2 large onions, finely diced

1 teaspoon salt

1 teaspoon ground black pepper

2 tablespoons finely minced garlic

2 tablespoons finely minced ginger

5 cups chicken broth or water

Red Lentils with Ginger

- Inspect lentils and pick out any small stones. Rinse in a fine strainer or bowl until water runs clear. Drain.

- Heat butter, ghee, or oil in a medium saucepan over medium heat; sauté onions with salt and pepper until golden brown.

- Add garlic and ginger; cook 3 minutes, stirring occasionally. Add lentils and broth or water. Bring to a boil, reduce heat, and simmer, covered, 20 minutes. Serve immediately.

Red Lentil Soup with Coconut Milk and Fresh Spinach: In a large saucepan over medium heat, melt 2 tablespoons butter. Add ½ onion, minced; 1 tablespoon minced ginger; and 2 garlic cloves, minced, and cook until soft, 5 minutes. Add 1 tablespoon curry powder and a pinch of cayenne and cook 1 minute. Add 3 carrots, cut in ½-inch rounds; 2 cups lentils; 6 cups chicken or vegetable broth; and 1 cup coconut milk. Bring to a boil, reduce heat to low, cover, and simmer until lentils are tender, about 20 minutes. Stir vigorously with a whisk to break up the lentils, then season to taste with salt. Add 2 cups shredded spinach leaves just before serving and stir until wilted. Serve hot or warm.

Make the Clarified Butter

- Clarified butter has a higher burning point than regular butter because the milk solids are removed.

- To separate the solids, melt butter in a saucepan over medium heat. Simmer until butter foams, then skim and discard the white froth.

- Carefully pour the remaining butter through a cheesecloth, leaving any remaining white sediment in the pan.

- You'll lose about a quarter of the volume by clarifying.

Red Lentils

- Red lentils are beautiful to look at and have a lighter, sweeter taste than brown or dark green lentils, and they cook in about half the time.

- You can use them when you're in a hurry for soups and so forth, but be careful when you substitute—they very quickly turn into a mash once they are cooked.

- Keep an eye on them and add them later in the recipe.

BEANS

BRAISED BLACK LENTILS
Nutty lentils are stewed with aromatic vegetables and thyme

This recipe is from Chef Judy Rodgers of the beloved Zuni Café in San Francisco. Her technique for cooking whole lentils (not split ones that turn soft and mushy when cooked) creates a nutty, rice-like dish, using a much smaller amount of liquid than is normally used to cook lentils.

The broth is also added in small increments (much like in risotto) to cook the lentils to perfection. Make sure your vegetables are very finely chopped so they blend into the lentils instead of overwhelming them with their size and flavor.

You can also use French lentils (also called green lentils) in place of the black beluga. Avoid the flat brown lentils and red lentils, which will not hold their shape during cooking. *Yield: 6 servings*

Ingredients

¹/₄ cup olive oil, plus 2–3 tablespoons more to finish the dish

¹/₂ cup finely diced carrots

¹/₂ cup finely diced celery

³/₄ cup finely diced onion

Salt

1 ¹/₄ cups black beluga lentils or tiny French green lentils

1 bay leaf

2 sprigs fresh thyme (optional)

1 cup red wine

2 ¹/₂ cups chicken broth or water, divided

Braised Black Lentils

- Warm ¼ cup olive oil in a medium pot over medium-low heat. Add carrots, celery, onion, and a few pinches salt.

- Stir about 5 minutes, then add lentils, bay leaf, thyme, wine, and 1 cup broth or water.

- Raise heat to a gentle simmer and cook, uncovered, stirring occasionally and adding ½ cup water or broth at a time until lentils are nutty and tender and not mushy, about 20 minutes.

- Season with salt. Add 2 or 3 tablespoons olive oil and simmer a minute longer.

Spiced Lentils with Sweet Potatoes: In a medium stockpot, heat 2 tablespoons olive oil over medium heat. Add 1 small onion, minced, and 2 garlic cloves, minced, and cook until golden brown, about 8 minutes. Stir in 1 teaspoon ground cumin and ½ teaspoon ground coriander and cook until fragrant, about 1 minute. Add 1 sprig fresh thyme; 1 sweet potato, cut into ½-inch cubes; 1 cup French or beluga lentils; and ¼ cup red wine (optional). Add 2 cups chicken broth and enough water to cover the mixture by ½ inch. Bring to a boil, reduce heat, and simmer, covered, until lentils and vegetables are tender and the liquid has almost evaporated, 30 minutes. Stir in the vinegar. Season to taste with salt and serve warm.

Dice the Vegetables

- This is a dish with surprising nuance if you take the time to dice the vegetables uniformly and very fine.

- You want pieces almost as small as the lentils themselves so the flavors meld seamlessly in every bite.

- The dish is still good with a rougher chop, but not nearly as elegant.

Braise the Lentils

- Unlike most bean dishes, these lentils are cooked with a scant amount of liquid, in a method that's almost like making risotto.

- Start with just 1 cup broth and 1 cup wine, and when that is absorbed, stir in a bit more broth. Once that is absorbed, add more, and so on, just until the lentils are nutty and tender (about 30 minutes).

- It's possible that you may not use all the broth.

BEANS

BLACK-EYED PEA SALAD

Smoky stewed peas are tossed with wilted greens and crispy bacon

Dried beans are excellent economy food. Food writer Amy Scattergood offers up this delicious salad idea using creamy black-eyed peas, smoky bacon, and wilted bitter greens to make a salad that is fit for a meal. With a hunk of crusty bread on the side, it is a hearty dinner. For extra flavor, rub the toasted bread with a raw garlic clove and "shave" it into the bread. Drizzle with olive oil and a sprinkling of salt, and you have "real" garlic bread to serve alongside the salad.

You need to serve this with sturdy salad greens, or the warm greens and heavy beans will overwhelm the lettuce. Stay away from mesclun and soft red leaf lettuce and opt instead for romaine. *Yield: 4 servings*

Ingredients

3 tablespoons olive oil, divided

1 medium onion, finely chopped

1 garlic clove, minced

1 cup (6 ounces) dried black-eyed peas

1 small bay leaf

2 small sprigs fresh thyme

³/₄ teaspoon salt

6 ounces thick bacon, cut into 1-inch strips

1 large bunch mustard greens, stems removed and roughly cut

4 slices crusty white bread

2 tablespoons sherry vinegar

2 cups sturdy salad greens

Black-Eyed Pea Salad

- Cook the black-eyed peas. Meanwhile, cook the bacon and the greens.

- Toast or grill the bread. In a large bowl, whisk together 2 tablespoons olive oil and the sherry vinegar.

- Add 3 cups cooked and cooled beans, the warm mustard greens, the bacon, and the salad greens.

- Toss until combined, divide among 4 plates and top with a slice of toasted bread.

You will see many recipes that call for bitter greens in this cookbook, and that is no mistake: They are our favorite type of leafy green. Their uniquely bitter flavor is a great complement to rich dishes (ones with sausages and bacon or even creamy sweet beans), because it offers a flavor counterpoint. Rich dishes are more easily enjoyed with a bit of bitterness in place.

• • • • RECIPE VARIATION • • • •

Black Eyed Peas, Southern Style: In a large pot, heat 2 tablespoons olive oil. Add 1 onion, minced, and 2 garlic cloves, minced; cook 5 minutes. Add 1 bay leaf, 1 ham hock, and 1 pound black-eyed peas. Add enough chicken broth to cover beans by 1 inch. Simmer until tender, 45 minutes. Remove the hock, cool, and return shredded meat to pot. Season with salt. Serve with rice.

Cook the Black-Eyed Peas

Cook the Bacon and Greens

- Heat 1 tablespoon olive oil in a medium pot and cook onion and garlic over medium-low heat until soft, about 10 minutes.

- Add dried black-eyed peas, bay leaf, thyme, and enough water to cover by 1 inch. Bring to a simmer over high heat, then reduce heat to low and cover.

- After 40 minutes, check to be sure there's still enough water to cover. Add more if needed, and add ¾ teaspoon salt.

- Cook until tender, about 20 minutes more. Remove from heat and set aside.

- Cook the bacon strips in a soup pot over low heat until crispy. Remove and set aside.

- Turn heat to medium and add the mustard greens, a little at a time, stirring constantly.

- When all the mustard greens are added, stir and cook over medium-low until they are wilted, dark green, and very tender, about 10 minutes.

- Remove from heat and set aside.

PASTA AL FAGIOLI
A hearty bean and pasta dish straight from Italy

Author Michalene's mother, Rose Busico, has made this dish for years. The fact that it includes mostly inexpensive pantry staples made it a shoe-in for inclusion in this cookbook.

This is the meal you make when you don't know what else to cook for dinner. With a well-stocked kitchen, you will always have these ingredients on hand. Bacon adds smokiness to basic aromatic vegetables (onions, garlic, and celery)

and the rest of the ingredients are courtesy of your pantry: canned tomatoes, canned beans, and dried pasta. It couldn't be simpler (or cheaper).

The pasta and beans release their creamy starch during cooking, creating a rich, luscious soup. Top the dish with grated cheese, pepper flakes for spice, or a dollop of pesto. *Yield: 4 servings*

Ingredients

2 slices bacon

1 small onion, finely chopped

1 rib celery, finely chopped

1 clove garlic, minced

Pinch of rosemary

1 15-ounce can chopped tomatoes, undrained

1 15-ounce can chicken broth

1 15-ounce can chickpeas (ceci) or cannellini beans, drained and rinsed well

1 cup small dried pasta, such as shells

Chopped fresh parsley

Red pepper flakes

Grated Parmesan cheese

Pasta al Fagioli

- Fry bacon in a medium pot over medium heat. When crisp, remove to a paper towel and set aside.

- Add onion and celery to the pot and cook 2 to 3 minutes. Stir in garlic and rosemary; cook 1 minute (do not let garlic brown).

- Add tomatoes and mix thoroughly. Add broth and beans, bring to a boil, and add pasta. Cook at a low boil until pasta is al dente. Crumble in bacon and stir.

- Serve in bowls; top with parsley, red pepper flakes, and Parmesan to taste.

Tuscan White Bean Soup: In a large pot, heat 2 tablespoons olive oil. Add 1 onion, chopped; cook 5 minutes. Add 2 garlic cloves, minced; 2 anchovies, mashed; and 1 bulb fennel, sliced and cook until tender, 6 minutes. Stir in 1 15-ounce can tomatoes; 1 quart chicken or vegetable broth; 3 15-ounce can beans; pinch of thyme; ½ head green cabbage, shredded; and 2 turnips, cut in ½-inch pieces. Bring to a boil, reduce heat, and simmer until all the vegetables and beans are tender, about 30 minutes. Season to taste with salt and pepper and a little lemon juice, if needed. Serve the soup hot or at room temperature with a drizzle of extra-virgin olive oil and a generous grating of Parmesan cheese.

Bruise the Rosemary

Ceci Beans

- "Bruising" herbs is a common technique designed to release as much flavor as possible, without cutting things into tiny bits.

- In this dish, rub the rosemary as you add it to the pot.

- In other recipes you can release a little more flavor by rubbing, bending, or crushing the leaves in your hand, or thwacking them with the side of a knife.

- Ceci beans (pronounced *chee-chee*) are what Italian cooks call garbanzo beans. They are especially good in this recipe.

- You can easily make them from scratch—same with the broth, for that matter. But part of the beauty of this recipe is its ease.

- Spend a few cents more on a can of good organic beans. It's worth it for this dish.

PASTA WITH GARLIC & PROSCIUTTO

A classic Italian pasta dish gets new life from ribbons of salty prosciutto

This simple dish is much more than the sum of its parts. The key here is quality, and it is worth getting some aged grated Parmesan (or look for Grana Padano, for a less expensive alternative) to crown your pasta instead of the packaged stuff from the supermarket shelves. FYI: The real stuff is in the refrigerated cheese case, not the dry-foods aisle. In a pinch, you can skip the prosciutto and save your pennies for the Parmesan.

To give cheese the longest life, store it (in a block or grated) in the freezer. It will never mold, and you will not have to worry about losing out on your worthwhile investment in the "real stuff." *Yield: 4–6 servings*

Ingredients

1 pound spaghetti, linguini, or other long thin pasta

2–3 tablespoons olive oil

3 cloves garlic, thinly sliced

¹/₄ pound prosciutto, thinly sliced, and cut into rough ¹/₂-inch strips

¹/₂ cup chopped parsley or basil, or a mixture

Grated Parmesan cheese

Spaghetti with Garlic and Prosciutto

- Bring a large pot of salted water to a boil. Add pasta and stir; cook until al dente.

- Reserve 1 cup pasta water; set aside. Drain pasta and return empty pot to stove. Lower heat to medium.

- Add oil to pot, then sliced garlic. Cook for 1 minute. Add pasta and prosciutto and enough pasta water so you can stir the ingredients and coat pasta with "sauce." Mix herbs through.

- Serve with a grating of Parmesan.

Aglio Olio Peperoncino: This classic Italian dish is a staple meal. Proceed with the recipe as directed, adding ¼ teaspoon hot pepper flakes along with the garlic and upping the olive oil to ¼ cup. Omit the prosciutto and serve with a shower of chopped parsley and grated Parmesan cheese. Season well with salt to bring out the flavors of the olive oil and garlic.

Penne with Garlicky Greens and White Beans: Boil 1 pound penne pasta; drain (reserving ½ cup water). Heat ¼ cup olive oil and 4 garlic cloves, sliced, in a large skillet. After 1 minute, add 1 cup chopped cooked greens (spinach, kale, broccoli rabe) and 1 can cannellini or roman beans, drained. Stir until heated through. Add penne and pasta water as needed to moisten.

Cook the Pasta

- All pasta dishes—but especially one this simple—rely on firm, perfectly cooked pasta.

- Start with plenty of water--5 or 6 quarts for a pound of pasta—so it can quickly return to a boil after you add the pasta. Salt the water until you can taste it.

- Forget about setting a timer. The only way to test for doneness is to taste. Start tasting after about 5 minutes. It's ready when it's soft but still chewy, with a tiny white dot at the center.

Reserve Pasta Water

- Italian cooks know that pasta water is a fabulous free dividend. Instead of thoughtlessly dumping it down the drain, reserve a small portion.

- Tossed with the cooked pasta, reserved pasta water helps distribute and meld flavors so you get the most out of your ingredients.

- And you can use a little to arm the serving dish before you add the cooked pasta. It will help keep the pasta moist, too.

LINGUINI WITH SHRIMP MARINARA

A simple pasta dish is upgraded to a celebratory meal with the addition of shrimp

Forget what you might have thought about all shellfish being prohibitively expensive. Shrimp is actually quite affordable, especially when you buy the frozen kind in the supermarket, which also has the added bonus of storing for a long time for whenever you need it. Make sure to buy the frozen, uncooked variety in their shells (don't by frozen cooked, they are quite dry when thawed). Also, watch for fresh shrimp on sale—they're a popular "loss leader" at supermarkets (the money-losing deal they offer customers to get them into the store). The Italian cliché about no cheese with seafood is true in this case—grated parmesan would ruin the dish. *Yield: 4–6 servings*

Ingredients

1 pound shrimp in shells (25-30 to the pound)

¹/₂ cup olive oil

2 cloves garlic, thinly sliced

3¹/₂ cups canned tomatoes, pressed through a strainer or put through a food mill to get rid of the seeds

1 teaspoon salt

1 teaspoon oregano

Black pepper to taste

1 tablespoon chopped parsley, plus more for topping

1 pound dried linguini

Linguini with Shrimp Marinara

- Prepare the shrimp. Make Marinara Sauce; while the sauce cooks, heat a large pot of salted water to a vigorous boil and cook the linguini.

- When linguini is nearly done, drop shrimp into sauce. When sauce returns to a low boil, cook 1 minute, more or less, until shrimp are cooked through but not tough.

- Remove sauce from heat. Drain pasta and put on warm plates. Top with ladles of sauce and distribute shrimp among them. Sprinkle with a little chopped parsley.

Prepare the Shrimp

- Peel shells and tails from shrimp. Discard or reserve to make broth.

- Using a sharp paring knife, cut a shallow slit down the back and remove the dark vein.

- Then cut all the way through the shrimp, making two crescent-shaped halves.

- Be vigilant when cooking—they will be done within seconds of hitting the hot tomato sauce.

Marinara Sauce

- Heat the oil in a medium saucepan over medium heat. Add garlic and cook until very lightly golden.

- Stir in the tomatoes, salt, oregano, black pepper, and 1 tablespoon parsley.

- Raise heat to a very low boil and cook 15 to 20 minutes, until thickened, stirring occasionally.

- If sauce becomes too thick, add up to ¼ cup pasta cooking water to thin it. You want it thick enough to cling to the spoon, but not nearly as thick as a long-cooked ragu.

PASTA & RICE

TRENETTE WITH PESTO

This hearty pasta pairs fresh basil-walnut pesto with red potatoes and string beans

This recipe is based on a creation of chef and cookbook author Nancy Harmon Jenkins, who makes a particularly delicious version of this classic Northern Italian dish. While it may seem uncommon to pair pasta with potatoes, the potatoes add an unexpected soft, creaminess to this bowl of pasta. You can make a fresh pesto out of any herb in the market in place of or in addition to the basil: flat-leaf parsley, cilantro, or mint. Make this dish when basil is abundant and inexpensive, particularly in the summertime. While basil pesto is traditionally thickened with pine nuts, we use walnuts here, which are much more economical and have a less assertive presence that we like. *Yield: 6 servings*

Ingredients

2 cups packed fresh basil leaves

3 tablespoons chopped walnuts

2 cloves garlic, roughly sliced

¹/₂ teaspoon salt

6 tablespoons olive oil, or more to taste

2 tablespoons grated Parmesan, or more to taste

¹/₂ pound new potatoes, peeled and sliced ¹/₄-inch thick

¹/₄ pound young green beans, cut into 1-inch segments

1 pound trenette, or other long thin pasta

Trenette with Pesto

- Set a large pot of salted water over high heat and bring to a vigorous boil. Meanwhile, make the pesto.

- Add potatoes to the boiling water and cook until they soften but are not cooked through. Add green beans and cook 2 minutes.

- Add pasta and cook until al dente. Drain pasta and vegetables and put into a warm serving bowl.

- Add pesto and mix until coated. Serve immediately.

Make several batches of pesto and then store it away in the freezer until you crave a breath of summer. Since fresh basil oxidizes (turns black) when it is cut and exposed to air, you need to store extra pesto in a container with a thin layer of olive oil poured over the surface to seal it. It will store in the freezer for months and in the refrigerator for weeks, as long as the olive-oil barrier is in place.

• • • • RECIPE VARIATION • • • •

Pesto-Roasted Portobello Mushrooms: Preheat oven to 400°F. Brush both sides of 3 large portobello caps with olive oil. Lay the caps, bottom side up, on a baking sheet. Spread 2 tablespoons pesto on the underside (which is now facing up) and roast until bubbly and soft, 10 minutes. Cool and serve over a bed of rice. Drizzle with balsamic if you wish.

Make the Pesto

Saucing the Pasta

- Put the basil leaves, walnuts, garlic, and salt into a food processor (you can use a blender if you don't have one).

- Pulse until ingredients are a uniformly coarse texture and well combined. Add

oil a little at a time, pulsing continually. Add cheese and pulse to mix through.

- If pesto is too thick, add more oil. Taste and adjust salt and Parmesan if needed.

- This dish, like the others in this chapter, is sauced in the traditional Italian way—that is, more lightly than what many Americans are used to.

- The idea is to let the toothsome, wheaty flavor of the pasta shine through as an element in itself.

- The flavor of the pasta itself is an important component to each dish—it is never just a flavorless shape carrying the sauce.

- Once again: Finesse equals economy.

PENNE WITH SAUSAGE

Sweet sausage and sharp broccoli rabe combine to make a satisfying pasta dinner

Sausages provide a good foundation for gourmet cooking on a budget. Their wonderful meaty flavor comes in small, affordable packages. It pairs particularly well with mildly bitter greens like broccoli rabe and escarole, whose sharpness is a good foil for sausages' rich but mellow flavor. Broccoli rabe resembles traditional broccoli only somewhat; both have florets (the rabe has small ones), but the rabe also has long thin stalks and big bushy leaves, both of which are edible. Remove and discard the bottom 3 inches of the bunch before using; it's too fibrous to enjoy. If you prefer a less bitter green, substitute red chard leaves, which are flavorful and add a lovely pink tint to your final dish. *Yield: 4 servings*

Ingredients

6 tablespoons olive oil, divided

1 small onion, diced

1 pound (about 4) sweet Italian sausages, sliced into $1/2$-inch rounds

3 cloves garlic, chopped

1 bunch broccoli rabe (also called rapini), trimmed

1 pound penne or other small pasta shape

Red pepper flakes (optional)

1 cup grated Parmesan cheese, or to taste

Penne with Sausage

- Heat 5 tablespoons oil in a large skillet over medium heat. Add the onion, sausages, and garlic. Cook slowly, stirring occasionally, for 10 minutes.

- Add the broccoli rabe and cook until it is tender.

- Bring a large pot of salted water to a boil and cook penne until al dente. Reserve a little cooking liquid, then drain penne.

- Add penne and 1 tablespoon olive oil to the sausage mixture, toss and sprinkle with a pinch of red pepper flakes. Serve with Parmesan.

Sausage with Braised Escarole: Heat 2 tablespoons oil in a large skillet over medium heat. Add 1 small onion, chopped; 3 garlic cloves, minced; pinch of hot pepper flakes; and ½ pound sweet or hot Italian sausage (removed from casings). Cook until the sausage is browned and heated through, about 10 minutes. Add thickly sliced escarole leaves (from 1 small head), in batches if necessary, until wilted. Add ½ cup chicken broth, cover, and braise until the escarole is tender, about 5 minutes. Serve over pasta, rice, or creamy polenta.

Cook the Sausages and Vegetables

- The sausages, onion, and broccoli rabe cook slowly together to meld their flavors and create a kind of sauce.

- Keep the heat to medium or medium-low so the ingredients don't brown.

- The sweetness of the onion will deliciously offset the bitterness of the broccoli rabe.

Toss Everything Together

- After the penne is cooked, and the broccoli rabe is tender, add the penne to the pan with the remaining 1 tablespoon olive oil.

- Toss everything together. If it needs more moisture, add more oil or a little reserved pasta water. Taste for seasoning.

- Divide pasta mixture among four bowls, and if you like, sprinkle a pinch of red pepper flakes on top. Serve with Parmesan cheese on the side.

PASTA & RICE

RISOTTO WITH BUTTERNUT SQUASH

Learn the secret to making this creamy rice dish delicious every time

Despite its finicky reputation, risotto is surprisingly easy to make. And since practically all its ingredients are pantry staples (rice, chicken broth, and Parmesan cheese), you will find yourself making it again and again once you make your first batch. Risotto is a dish worth learning to make well, as it is suited to both a weeknight dinner (30 minutes to make) and a special occasion meal, when you might splurge on pricier ingredients like shrimp and wild mushrooms, which both make terrific risottos.

Make sure you add hot broth to the cooking risotto; using cold broth prolongs the cooking time dramatically. *Yield: 6 servings*

Ingredients

1 butternut squash (about 1 pound), peeled, seeded, and cut into small cubes

7 cups chicken broth, divided

Sage leaves or dried sage

5 tablespoons butter, divided

1 medium onion, chopped fine

2 cups arborio rice

$1/2$ cup dry white wine

$1/2$ cup grated Parmesan cheese, plus more for garnish

Risotto with Butternut Squash

- Cook squash with 1 cup broth and a few sage leaves or a pinch of dried sage, until tender and just cooked. Heat remaining broth in another saucepan.

- In a large pot, melt 3 tablespoons butter. Sauté onion and a pinch of dried sage or a few chopped sage leaves until translucent; do not brown. Add rice; cook 2 minutes, stirring. Add the wine and stir until absorbed.

- When risotto is finished cooking, add squash, remaining broth, 2 tablespoons butter, and Parmesan. Stir 1 minute. Serve.

• • • • RECIPE VARIATION • • • •

Asparagus-Lemon Risotto: Cook risotto as directed, using the asparagus broth and adding ½ teaspoon grated lemon zest and 1-inch pieces steamed asparagus at the end in place of the squash. Serve the risotto topped with grated Parmesan and a few thinly sliced leaves of basil.

Cook the Rice

- After the rice has absorbed the wine, add hot broth to just cover the rice and cook at a low simmer, stirring regularly, until broth is mostly absorbed.

- Add another ladle of hot broth and continue cooking, stirring and adding more broth, until rice has absorbed most of the liquid, about 15 minutes.

- Add squash and remaining broth, 2 tablespoons butter, and Parmesan.

Know When It's Perfectly Done

- Adding the liquid a little at a time lets you control the final consistency of the risotto.

- It should be slightly liquid and not a solid mass.

- A good test is putting a little in a dish and running a spoon through the center. The risotto should slowly flow black into place.

- The rice itself should be tender but still chewy.

VEGETABLE FRIED RICE

Leftover rice gets a second life when stir-fried with crisp vegetables and sweet sausage

This dish was designed for leftover rice, since good fried rice can only be made with the day-old kind. Only an overnight rest in the refrigerator will yield grains that are dry enough to crisp up in the pan. Fresh rice is just too moist. And any kind of leftover white or brown rice will do, but avoid using day-old converted rice, which will not hold its shape.

You can vary the vegetables and meat you use, opting for whatever you have in your refrigerator: leftover chicken, carrots, zucchini, fresh or frozen corn, bell peppers, eggplant, a handful of cashews. If you don't use the Chinese sausages, you may need to up the oil by a tablespoon or two; they render some of their own fat during cooking. *Yield: 8 servings*

Ingredients

1 tablespoon vegetable oil

2 Chinese sweet pork sausages, diced (or 1 cup chopped ham or leftover roast pork)

2 scallions, trimmed and thinly sliced, including greens, plus more for garnish

1 cup peas, fresh or frozen, thawed

1/2 Napa cabbage head, or other Asian green, leaves cut into thin slices

4 cups day-old cooked rice

2 eggs, lightly beaten

2 tablespoons soy sauce, or more to taste

Black pepper to taste

Salt to taste

Vegetable Fried Rice

- Heat the oil in a large nonstick skillet or wok over high heat. Add the sausages, scallions, peas and cabbage and stir-fry 5 minutes.

- Add rice and continue to stir-fry, tossing ingredients to thoroughly combine.

- Add eggs to rice, stir-frying until cooked.

- Add soy sauce and some black pepper. Stir-fry a few minutes more, add salt if needed, and serve sprinkled with chopped scallions.

Cashew Chicken Fried Rice: Heat 2 tablespoons each vegetable oil and toasted sesame oil in a large nonstick skillet over medium-high heat. Add 4 scallions, chopped; 1 tablespoon chopped ginger; 1 green pepper, diced; and ½ cup cashews. Stir-fry until brown. Add 4 cups cooked rice and stir-fry until crispy. Stir in 1 cup shredded chicken and 2 tablespoons soy sauce.

ZOOM

The distinctly sweet-salty flavor of a Chinese sausage sets it apart from Western varieties. They are available both fresh and dried; the dried sausage has a much stronger flavor than the fresh. Look for both kinds in Asian markets, at the butcher counter (for fresh), or in the freezer section (for dried). The dried variety will keep for many months in the freezer.

Stir-Fry the Rice

- To avoid clumps of rice or gummy rice, be sure to use cooked rice that has been refrigerated at least overnight.

- When you add it to the pan, rub it between your fingers to break up the grains.

- Once it's in the pan, keep it in motion.

Add the Egg

- Give the eggs a light beating to break up the yolks before you add them.

- Pour them into the rice and stir continuously as they cook; you don't want big chunks of egg.

- You want to incorporate the egg with the rice, so think in terms of mixing it in.

- With fried rice, almost anything can be added or omitted, including the egg. So if you don't like egg, skip it.

PASTA & RICE

CHICKEN & ORZO CASSEROLE

Meaty drumsticks are stewed with lemon, olives, and tender orzo pasta

The beauty of a casserole is that all the food cooks together in one pot. Not only does this help tremendously with cleanup, it also allows the foods to season each other as they cook.

Here, inexpensive chicken legs are browned and then braised with chicken broth, salty olives, and whole lemon wedges to render their tough meat soft and tender. You can also substitute chicken thighs. For braising, dark meat is better than white, which dries out more easily (and is more expensive).

The orzo is cooked directly with the chicken legs, allowing it to absorb the flavors from the meat as it cooks. *Yield: 6–8 servings*

Ingredients

8 chicken drumsticks

1 1/2 teaspoons salt

1 teaspoon pepper

2 tablespoons olive oil

1 1/2 cups orzo

3 cups chicken broth

1 large garlic clove, minced

1 small lemon, cut into 8 wedges

1/2 cup pitted Kalamata olives

1 bay leaf

1 teaspoon oregano

Chicken and Orzo Casserole

- Preheat oven to 350°F. Season the chicken legs with salt and pepper.

- In a large pot or Dutch oven, heat oil over medium-high heat. Brown legs on all sides and remove from pan.

- Add orzo, broth, garlic, lemon wedges, olives, bay leaf, and oregano. Combine well, then return chicken to pan. Cover and place in the oven.

- Bake 25 to 30 minutes, until chicken is done—the juices will run clear. Taste to adjust seasoning, and serve.

Arroz con Pollo: Heat oven to 350°F. Season 8 chicken legs with salt and pepper. In a large pot or Dutch oven, heat 2 tablespoons olive oil over medium-high heat. Brown legs on all sides and remove from pan. Add 1 onion, minced, and 2 garlic cloves, minced; cook until soft, 3 minutes. Add 1 each green and red pepper, chopped; cook 3 minutes. Add 2 cups chicken broth, 1 15-ounce can crushed tomatoes, 1 tablespoon tomato paste, 1¼ cups long-grain rice, and ½ teaspoon salt. Add browned legs on top, cover, and bake until chicken is cooked and rice is tender, about 25 minutes. Sprinkle with ½ cup frozen peas, cover, and steam 2 minutes. Serve with fresh cilantro or parsley.

Season and Brown the Chicken Legs

- Season the chicken legs on all sides with salt and pepper.

- Heat the olive oil in a large stockpot or Dutch oven over medium-high heat.

- Working in batches, brown the chicken legs well on all sides.

- Remove from pan as they finish browning.

Pit the Olives

- There are a number of ways to remove the stubborn pits from olives, but we think this is the easiest.

- Simply place the olives on a cutting board and give each a good whack with a meat pounder or the flat side of a chef's knife.

- Then separate the pit from the olive flesh.

CASSEROLES

POTATO-ONION GRATIN
Layers of thinly sliced potatoes are baked with sweet caramelized onions and goat cheese

This is a variation of potatoes au gratin, but without all the heavy cream and cheese. The potatoes (russets bake up the creamiest) are thinly sliced and layered with a tangle of sweet caramelized onions and tangy goat cheese before being covered and cooked to perfection. The dish is then uncovered and baked again to create a crisp, bread-crumb topping.

This is an excellent entertaining dish because the potatoes can be cooked ahead of time and the bread crumbs sprinkled on top and browned just before serving. You can substitute sweet potatoes or butternut squash for some or all of the potatoes for a tasty fall and winter gratin. *Yield: 6 servings*

Ingredients

1 tablespoon unsalted butter, plus more for the dish

3 tablespoons olive oil, divided

2 large onions, sliced thin

Coarse salt to taste

4 large russet potatoes (about 1 1/2 pounds), peeled and sliced 1/8-inch thick

1/2 cup chicken broth

1 teaspoon thyme

Black pepper to taste

2 ounces fresh goat cheese, crumbled (optional)

3/4 cup fresh bread crumbs

Grated zest of 1/2 lemon or orange

1 garlic clove, finely minced

Potato-Onion Gratin

- Preheat oven to 375°F. Caramelize the onions; set aside.

- In a large bowl combine potatoes, broth, and thyme. Butter a 9-inch baking dish. Layer half the potatoes, sprinkling every other layer with salt and pepper. Cover with onions and dot with goat cheese.

- Top with remaining potato slices; salt and pepper. Pour over remaining broth from potatoes, cover with foil and bake 45 minutes.

- Make Bread-Crumb Topping, and sprinkle it over tender potatoes. Bake uncovered until crisp, about 15 minutes.

Sweet Potato Gratin with Caramelized Fennel:
Heat oven to 375°F. Heat 3 tablespoons olive oil over medium heat. Add 1 fennel bulb, thinly sliced (core removed), and cook until soft and golden, 20 minutes. In a bowl toss together 1½ pounds sweet potatoes, peeled and thinly sliced, and ½ cup chicken broth. Butter a 9-inch baking dish. Layer half the potatoes, sprinkling every other layer with salt and pepper. Cover with fennel and dot with 1 tablespoon butter. Top with remaining potato slices. Pour over remaining broth from potatoes, cover with foil, and bake 45 minutes. Sprinkle with bread-crumb topping (from recipe), and bake uncovered for 15 more minutes. Let stand 15 minutes before cutting and serving.

Caramelize the Onions

- In a large skillet over medium heat, melt the butter with 1 tablespoon olive oil.

- Add the onions and a sprinkling of coarse salt. Cover and cook for 5 minutes to release their juices.

- Uncover and cook until onions are lightly golden and tender, about 20 minutes more.

- Set the onions aside until ready to layer with potatoes.

Bread-Crumb Topping

- While gratin is baking, prepare Bread-Crumb Topping.

- In a small bowl, combine the bread crumbs, citrus zest, garlic, a generous pinch of salt and pepper, and enough olive oil to give the mixture the texture of wet sand—you'll need about 2 to 3 tablespoons.

- Set aside until potatoes are tender. Then sprinkle potatoes with bread crumbs and bake, uncovered, until topping is crisp and golden, about 15 minutes more. Let stand 15 minutes before serving.

171

MAC & CHEESE

Using uncooked pasta makes this creamy macaroni and cheese a real one-pot dish

This magical rendition of creamy baked macaroni and cheese is inspired by a particularly delicious one from food writer Julia Moskin at *The New York Times*.

The beauty of this recipe is that it truly embodies the casserole ideal: one-pot cooking. The elbows are added raw and cook as the dish is baked. An extra-large quantity of milk is added to help "cook" the pasta, and the dish is further enriched with creamy ricotta cheese and a whole ¾ pound grated cheddar.

It is a rich dish and needs only a crisp salad or a side of steamed broccoli to make it a full meal. Double the recipe to ensure leftovers, which freeze beautifully (wrapped well) for future meals. *Yield: 6–8 servings*

Ingredients

2 tablespoons butter, divided

1 cup ricotta cheese or cottage cheese

2 cups whole milk

1 teaspoon dry mustard

Pinch cayenne

¹/₂ teaspoon salt

¹/₄ teaspoon pepper

³/₄ pound sharp or extra-sharp cheddar, grated

¹/₂ pound uncooked elbow macaroni

Mac and Cheese

- Place an oven rack in the upper third of the oven. Preheat to 375°F. Butter a 9-inch baking pan with 1 tablespoon butter.

- Puree ricotta or cottage cheese, milk, and seasonings. Set aside ¼ cup grated cheddar for topping. In a large bowl, combine remaining cheddar, the puree, and uncooked macaroni.

- Pour into prepared pan, cover with foil, and bake 30 minutes. Uncover, stir, and sprinkle with remaining cheddar and butter. Bake uncovered 30 minutes, until browned.

Classic Macaroni and Cheese: In a saucepan, melt 4 tablespoons butter over medium heat. Add 4 tablespoons flour, whisking 1 minute. Add 1 teaspoon dry mustard and a pinch of cayenne; cook 1 minute more. Slowly add 2¾ cups hot milk, whisking constantly until the mixture is thickened, 1 to 2 minutes. Remove from heat and stir in 1 teaspoon salt, ½ teaspoon ground pepper, 1½ cups grated cheddar and 1 cup grated Gruyère or Swiss. Boil 1 pound elbow pasta until al dente; drain and rinse lightly. Toss pasta with cheese mixture and transfer to a buttered 2-quart baking dish. Top with ½ cup grated cheddar and bake at 350°F until bubbly.

Puree the Cottage Cheese

- Instead of a white sauce, this recipe uses a ricotta or cottage cheese puree to bind the cheese and macaroni.

- Put the ricotta or cottage cheese in a blender with the milk, dry mustard, cayenne, salt, and pepper.

- Puree mixture until smooth.

Bake the Mac and Cheese

- The uncooked macaroni will absorb the rich flavors as it cooks.

- Simply pour the mac and cheese mixture into the prepared pan, cover it tightly with foil, and bake 30 minutes.

- Uncover and give the mac and cheese a gentle stir. Sprinkle on the reserved cheddar for a topping and dot with 1 tablespoon butter.

- Bake uncovered 30 minutes longer, until browned. Let rest 15 minutes before serving.

CASSEROLES

MOM'S LASAGNA
The last word in classic Italian lasagnas, straight from mother's kitchen

It's big. It's gutsy. It is, as Mom would say, a real crowd-pleaser. And since Mom knows best (in this case Michalene's mom, Rose Busico, who generously donated this recipe), we suggest you make this right away.

The key here is the rich, meaty tomato sauce that is layered between the traditional lasagna noodles and mozzarella and ricotta cheeses. She uses hot or sweet Italian sausages and ground beef, along with a healthy dose of tomato paste, to intensify the flavor of the sauce. Basil, fennel, and a full $^1/_2$ cup chopped fresh parsley add another bright layer of flavor.

Leftovers, wrapped very well, make terrific freezer meals.
Yield: 8–10 servings

Ingredients

1 pound sweet or hot Italian sausage

$^1/_2$ pound ground beef

$^1/_2$ cup finely chopped onion

2 garlic cloves, crushed

1 tablespoon sugar

1 $^1/_2$ teaspoons salt, divided

$^1/_4$ teaspoon black pepper

1 $^1/_2$ teaspoons dried basil

$^1/_2$ teaspoon fennel seed

$^1/_2$ cup chopped parsley, divided

4 cups canned tomatoes, undrained

6 ounces tomato paste

$^1/_2$ cup water

12 curly edge lasagna noodles, cooked until just tender

1 pound ricotta cheese

1 egg

1 pound mozzarella, sliced thin, divided

$^3/_4$ cup grated Parmesan, divided

Mom's Lasagna

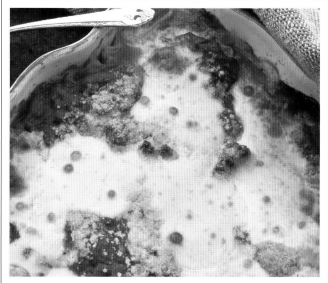

- Make the sauce. Cook the noodles, rinse under cold water, and drain on paper towels.

- Preheat oven to 350°F. In a small bowl, combine ricotta with ¼ cup parsley, egg, and ½ teaspoon salt.

- In a 9 x 13-inch baking pan, layer the sauce, noodles, ricotta, mozzarella, and Parmesan.

- Cover tightly with foil and bake 25 to 30 minutes. Remove foil and bake another 30 minutes. Let rest 15 minutes, cut into squares, and serve.

Baked Ziti: Boil 1 pound ziti until al dente; drain. Toss pasta with 3 cups sausage marinara sauce (follow recipe). In a bowl, combine 1 pound ricotta cheese, ½ pound grated mozzarella, ½ cup grated Parmesan, and ½ cup chopped parsley. Lay half the sauced pasta in the bottom of a greased 9 x 13-inch baking dish. Top with the ricotta mixture, then the rest of the sauced pasta.

Stir a few times to blend the ingredients (shouldn't be completely mixed). Top with 2 more cups sauce and ½ pound grated mozzarella and a few tablespoons grated Parmesan. Bake, covered, at 350°F until bubbly, 30 minutes.

Make the Sauce

- Remove sausage from casing. In a skillet over medium heat, brown it with the ground beef, onion, and garlic, breaking up the meat with a wooden spoon, for about 15 minutes.

- Mix in sugar, 1 teaspoon salt, pepper, basil, fennel, and ¼ cup parsley. Add tomatoes, tomato paste, and water. Mash tomatoes with the spoon as you stir.

- Bring to a light boil, reduce heat, cover, and simmer, stirring occasionally, until thick, about 90 minutes. Season for salt.

Layer the Lasagna

- In a deep 9 x 13-inch baking pan, put 1 to 1½ cups sauce in the bottom of the pan. Layer on 6 lasagna noodles lengthwise, overlapping slightly and centered in the pan.

- Spread half the ricotta mixture on top of the noodles, then a third of the mozzarella, then about 1 cup sauce. Sprinkle with ¼ cup Parmesan.

- Repeat, starting with noodles and ending with sauce and Parmesan.

- Spread on any remaining sauce, then another layer of mozzarella and Parmesan.

CASSEROLES

PUMPKIN TIAN

A savory baked dish that uses sweet winter squash and leftover rice

Tian refers to the browned topping that covers a finished dish, in this case crispy bread crumbs. For this dish, adapted from cookbook author John Thorne, it is best to use fresh bread crumbs (see page 89) instead of store-bought dry bread crumbs. There is not a lot of moisture in this tian, so you don't want a dry topping to add to that.

Make sure you use an eating pumpkin (often called pie pumpkins or cheese pumpkins) and not one destined for carving. Large pumpkins are stringy and watery and would make a terrible gratin, although likely an excellent jack-o'-lantern.

Butternut or kabocha is an excellent substitute when pumpkins aren't readily available. *Yield: 4 servings*

Ingredients

1 small (about 2 pound) pumpkin or kabocha squash

¹/₂ cup olive oil, divided

¹/₄ cup fresh bread crumbs

1 onion, minced

1 cup cooked white or brown rice

¹/₂ cup grated Gruyère or Swiss cheese

2 tablespoons chopped parsley

1 egg, beaten

Salt and pepper to taste

Pumpkin Tian

- Preheat oven to 375°F. Prepare the pumpkin.

- Sauté the bread crumbs, then the pumpkin and onion in olive oil. Set aside.

- In a large bowl combine the rice, cheese, parsley, egg, salt, and pepper. Mix in onion and pumpkin.

- Rub the inside of a 9- or 10-inch casserole dish with 1 tablespoon oil. Pour in the pumpkin mixture, sprinkle evenly with toasted bread crumbs, and drizzle the rest of the olive oil on top.

- Bake 20 minutes; serve.

Baked Pumpkin Risotto: In an ovenproof saucepan heat 2 tablespoons butter over medium-high heat. Add ½ onion, minced, and cook 2 minutes. Add ¾ cup arborio rice and toast 1 minute. Add 2 cups ½-inch cubes pumpkin and cook 2 minutes. Add ¼ cup white wine; cook until completely evaporated, about 1 minute. Stir in 2¼ cups chicken broth, ½ teaspoon salt, and some pepper. Bring to a boil. Cover, transfer to a 425°F oven, and bake until most of the liquid has been absorbed by the rice, 20 to 25 minutes. Thin with extra chicken broth (the risotto should be creamy), if needed, and stir in 2 tablespoons butter and ⅓ cup grated Parmesan. Serve immediately.

Prepare the Pumpkin

- Cut the pumpkin in half and scoop out the seeds and strings.

- Rest the flat, cut surface on a cutting board; with a sharp knife, pare off the skin.

- Or, cut the pumpkin into smaller pieces and then remove the skin—this is a little more time-consuming, but easier.

- Cut the flesh into ¾-inch cubes.

Sauté Bread Crumbs, Pumpkin, and Onion

- Heat 1 tablespoon olive oil in a large skillet over medium-high heat.

- Add the bread crumbs and toast, stirring, until golden. Remove to a small bowl.

- Add another 2 tablespoons olive oil and sauté the onion until tender.

- Add the pumpkin cubes, lower the heat, and gently sauté, turning, until just tender, about 15 minutes. Let cool.

CASSEROLES

COWBOY CASSOULET

Tender lamb stars in this version of France's beloved meat and bean dish

Traditional cassoulet takes the better part of a day to make and requires a plethora of expensive ingredients. In this version of the dish, lamb shoulder meat is used to create a dish that is just as rich and delicious as the original.

This particular recipe comes courtesy of Russ Parsons, food editor and columnist at the *Los Angeles Times*.

The whole, unpeeled garlic cloves are cooked in boiling water for a few minutes before being used in the dish. This softens their sharp flavor and allows you to use a whole head of cloves without having their garlicky flavor overwhelm the dish. *Yield: 8 servings*

Ingredients

3 tablespoons olive oil, plus more for drizzling

3 pounds lamb shoulder blade chops, bones and excess fat removed, meat cut in large pieces

1 carrot, peeled and diced

1 medium onion, diced

1 cup white wine

1 cup crushed tomatoes

1 pound Great Northern white beans or navy beans

2 medium fennel bulbs, trimmed and quartered

1 head garlic, cloves separated but not peeled, blanched in simmering water 5 minutes, then peeled

1¹/₂ teaspoons salt

1¹/₂ teaspoons black pepper

¹/₂ baguette, to get 1³/₄ cup fresh bread crumbs

8 fresh sage leaves

Cowboy Cassoulet

- Preheat oven to 325°F. Heat olive oil in a large heavy pot over medium-high heat. Brown lamb; remove to a plate.

- Make the vegetable-bean base. Cover pot with lid and bake 1 hour. Season with salt and black pepper. Stir gently; return to oven.

- Cook until beans are soft and lamb is tender, 2 to 2½ hours more. After 1½ hours, if cassoulet is dry, add up to 1 cup water.

- Remove pot from oven. Finish the cassoulet.

Lamb Ragout: In a large Dutch oven with 2 tablespoons olive oil, brown 2 pounds ½-inch-cubed lamb shoulder until browned; set aside. Drain off all but 2 tablespoons fat. To the pot add 1 onion, minced; 2 carrots, minced; 2 garlic cloves, minced, and cook 3 minutes. Add 1 tablespoon tomato paste and cook until caramelized, 3 minutes. Return lamb to pot and add 1 14-ounce can crushed tomatoes, 1 strip orange zest, 2 sprigs fresh thyme or rosemary, 1 cup red wine, and 2 cups chicken broth. Bring the liquid to a boil; simmer on medium low, covered, until the lamb is very tender, about 1½ hours. Remove the thyme sprigs before serving over barley or polenta.

Make the Vegetable-Bean Base

Finish the Cassoulet

- Turn heat under pot to medium low, add carrot and cook without stirring until it caramelizes lightly. Stir and cook 3 minutes more.

- Add onion; cook until soft. Add wine; bring to a boil and cook until it reduces to a syrup. Add tomatoes, cook until thickened, 5 minutes.

- Add 5 cups water and beans. Gently stir in fennel and whole garlic. Layer browned lamb on top. Bring to a simmer, press aluminum foil close to the surface to form a loose cover, cover with lid.

- Raise heat on oven to 400°F.

- Cut away crust from baguette and cut bread into cubes. Put in a blender with sage leaves and pulse to form crumbs.

- When oven has reached 400°F, spoon sage crumbs evenly over cassoulet.

- Drizzle with a thin thread of olive oil and return to oven for about 20 minutes, until crumbs are brown.

- Serve immediately.

CASSEROLES

SMOKY BLACK BEAN SOUP

Bacon rind is the secret ingredient for making a rich and smoky bean soup

This is a terrific dish for entertaining a crowd on a dime. A bag of dried black beans will set you back about $1.20, and slab bacon (with the smoky rind) provides a cheap way to get a maximum amount of flavor into your soup. The unsoaked beans are simmered, uncovered, for a long time, which helps to concentrate the flavor of the soup base, as much of the bland water content will evaporate during cooking.

The toppings served with this bean soup are an important part of its appeal, so don't omit them. Bright cilantro, lime juice, sour cream, and salsa all perk up the flavor of the soup and take the edge off the rich smokiness of the bacon. *Yield: 6–8 servings*

Ingredients

1/2 pound smoked slab bacon, rind removed (reserved)

1 large onion, finely chopped

3 stalks celery, finely chopped

3 carrots, diced

1 bay leaf

2 garlic cloves, minced

1 1/4 teaspoons thyme

2 tablespoons cumin powder

1 teaspoon black pepper

1 tablespoon oregano

2 tablespoons tomato paste

2 quarts chicken broth

1 pound black turtle beans or other black beans, rinsed

6 tablespoons freshly squeezed lime juice

1/4 teaspoon cayenne pepper

Salt to taste

1/2 cup chopped cilantro

Sour cream, for topping

Salsa, for topping

Smoky Black Bean Soup

- Cut bacon into ¼-inch cubes and cook in a large, wide pot over medium heat until crisp.

- Add onion, celery, carrots, bay leaf, garlic, thyme, 1 tablespoon cumin, pepper, and oregano. Stir, cover, and cook 5 minutes over medium-low heat.

- Stir in tomato paste, add broth, and bring to a boil. Add beans to pot along with bacon rind. Cook until beans are tender and discard the rind and bay leaf; add remaining ingredients.

- Serve garnished with sour cream and salsa.

Cook Beans Tender

- Add the beans and cook uncovered over medium-high heat for 1½ to 2 hours, skimming occasionally.

- The soup is ready when the beans are very soft—some will have melted into the broth.

- Stir in the lime juice, remaining 1 tablespoon cumin, cayenne, salt, and cilantro.

- Discard rind and bay leaf.

Garnish with Salsa

- Any salsa will work with this recipe. Use your favorite recipe or a refrigerated store-bought salsa, or make this simple salsa:

- Mix together ½ cup finely chopped onions, 2 cups cubed tomatoes, 1½ teaspoons minced seeded jalapeños, ¼ cup chopped fresh cilantro, 2 tablespoons lime juice, and salt to taste.

- Taste and adjust seasonings.

181

CHICKEN SOUP WITH DIVIDENDS

Two extra meals are the rewards you reap from cooking this soup just one time

This version of tortilla soup is by Thomas Schnetz and Dona Savitsky of Doña Tomás in Oakland, California. They are to be credited for coming up with this dish's brilliant twist: You cook the chicken for an hour, remove the meat, and then return the bones to the pot to cook for another hour. Unlike other chicken broths, where the chicken is cooked until the flavor is entirely leeched out, this one will give you incredibly tender and moist shredded chicken that's full of flavor. With this, you get both a great broth and great leftover chicken—your dividend. One bird, three meals. Now that's budget cooking. *Yield: 6 servings soup, plus enough extra meat for two other dishes*

Ingredients

1 whole chicken, about 4 pounds

1 white onion, diced, divided

1 carrot, chopped

1 celery stalk, chopped

2 bay leaves

7 peppercorns

3 sprigs thyme

1 tablespoon vegetable oil

3 quarts cold water

1 teaspoon chopped garlic

1/2 jalapeño pepper, seeded and chopped

2 tomatoes, diced

Juice of 2 limes

1 bunch cilantro, stemmed and chopped, divided

Salt to taste

2–3 cups crushed tortilla chips

Chicken Soup with Dividends

- Cut legs and wings off the chicken, cut the carcass in half, and put all in a large soup pot. Add half the onion, plus the carrot, celery, bay leaves, peppercorns, and thyme. Cover with water and bring to a boil.

- Lower heat and simmer 1 hour, skimming, until chicken is cooked through.

- Remove chicken and shred the meat from the bones. Discard skin. Return bones to pot and simmer 1 hour more.

- Pass broth through a fine strainer and make Chicken Soup with Dividends.

•••• RECIPE VARIATION ••••

Chicken & Zucchini Quesadillas: Heat 3 tablespoons olive oil in a skillet. Cook 1 large zucchini, cut into ½-inch slices, and 1 minced jalapeño pepper until softened, 7 minutes and salt. Divide zucchini between 4 flour tortillas and top with grated Jack cheese and shredded chicken. Top with another tortilla and brown in same skillet (adding extra oil if needed).

MAKE IT EASY

When you have more leftover broth than you can use in a few days, store it in the freezer. The key is to store it in small portions so you defrost only the amount you need. Store 1-cup portions in small freezer bags and pour the rest into an empty ice-cube tray (each well is 2 tablespoons). When frozen, transfer cubes to a large freezer bag and use for recipes that call for less than 1 cup.

Make Soup

- Heat the oil in a soup pot over high heat. Add the remaining onion and sauté until translucent. Don't brown. Add garlic, sauté 30 seconds, stirring constantly.

- Add jalapeño and tomatoes, sauté 5 minutes. Stir in lime juice and half the cilantro, remove from heat.

- Pour in broth and bring to a boil. Add salt to taste and simmer gently for 30 minutes. Add a fourth of the shredded chicken, simmer 5 minutes, adjust salt.

- Serve topped with crushed tortilla chips and remaining cilantro.

Shred the Chicken

- Halfway through making the broth, remove the chicken and let it cool until you can safely handle it.

- Shred the meat from the bone and discard the skin.

- Return the bones to the pot and continue cooking them to extract maximum flavor.

- By taking the chicken out early, you end up with much more flavorful meat.

GINGERED BUTTERNUT SQUASH SOUP

Sweet and creamy squash soup is infused with the heat of fresh ginger and jalapeño

This is another winner from Regina Schrambling, food writer and blogger on Epicurious.com. She calls for leeks instead of onions, which add a noticeably mellow flavor to the soup. Since leeks are a bit more expensive, you can use scallions or shallots in their place.

Butternut squash is available year-round in the supermarket since it stores very well (in fact all hard winter squashes do when properly stored).

Topping it with toasted pecans makes this soup fit for a holiday first course, perhaps with a few dried cranberries for color. This soup can be made at least 2 days ahead and stored in the refrigerator until needed. *Yield: 6–8 servings*

Ingredients

4 tablespoons butter

2 medium leeks, wash well and coarsely chopped

3 stalks celery, coarsely chopped

2 large carrots, peeled and coarsely chopped

1 1-inch piece fresh ginger, peeled and chopped

1 jalapeño, seeded and chopped

1 teaspoon thyme, or to taste

Salt to taste

1 butternut squash (about 2 pounds), peeled, seeded, and cut into rough cubes

4 cups chicken broth or water

1/2 cup heavy cream

Pepper to taste

A few toasted chopped pecans (optional)

Gingered Butternut Squash Soup

- Melt butter in a soup pot over medium heat. Add the leeks, celery, carrots, ginger, jalapeño, and thyme. Season with salt and cook, stirring, until vegetables wilt.

- Stir in squash and broth or water and bring to a boil. Reduce heat, cover, and simmer 20 to 30 minutes, until vegetables are soft.

- Puree in a blender until smooth. Pour puree into a clean pot, stir in cream and gently heat (do not boil). Salt and pepper to taste, and serve sprinkled with pecans if you like.

• • • • RECIPE VARIATION • • • •

Curried Butternut Soup with Apples: Follow the recipe below using 1 chopped onion in place of the leeks and omitting the carrots. Add 1 tablespoon curry powder after the vegetables have wilted. Add 2 peeled and cubed apples (any kind) when you add the broth; cook and puree as directed. Garnish with chopped pecans and dried cranberries if you wish.

MAKE IT EASY

Instead of using cubes of raw butternut squash, you can substitute the same amount of roasted butternut squash. Roasting the squash beforehand intensifies its sweetness and flavor. To roast the squash, preheat oven to 425°F. Place the squash halves, cut side down, on an aluminum foil–lined baking sheet. Roast until very tender, about 45 minutes. Allow to cool and then scrape out the soft flesh.

Washing the Leeks

- Leeks require a little extra attention to remove the last bits of grit hiding among their leaves.

- Trim off most of the green top and then cut verti-cally, but not through the root, dividing the leek into quarters.

- Rinse this floppy mop of a leek under running water until all the grit is gone.

Peel and Cut the Squash

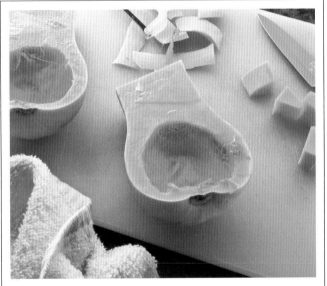

- Butternut squash are noto-riously difficult to peel. To make it easier, cut it in half first and then use a sturdy vegetable peeler to remove the leathery skin.

- Cut the flesh into thick slices and then cut into rough cubes. The cubes don't need to be the same shape, but they should be approximately the same size so they are all tender at the same time.

- Some supermarkets sell pre-peeled butternut squash. Although it costs a bit more, it is a terrific con-venience item if you want to save time.

MINESTRONE

This hearty white bean and vegetable soup satisfies all year long

It feels like there's a whole vegetable patch in this meal-in-a-bowl soup. Serve it as is or with homemade garlic croutons: Toast a slice of crusty Italian bread, rub it with garlic, put it on the bottom of the bowl, and ladle soup on top.

This is even a great soup for warm-weather dining. Author Jennifer's mother always serves this soup for summer lunch guests: She ladles the hot soup into bowls, sprinkles it with grated Parmesan or pecorino cheese, covers the bowls with

a clean dish towel, and then serves it at room temperature with a dollop of pesto on top (dabbed on just before serving) and some crusty bread on the side. *Yield: 12 servings*

Ingredients

¹/₂ cup olive oil

2 carrots, finely chopped

2 celery stalks, finely chopped, including leaves

1 large onion, finely chopped

2 garlic cloves, minced

2 large potatoes, peeled and finely chopped

1¹/₂ cups fresh or canned Italian plum tomatoes, peeled, seeded, and chopped

1 teaspoon thyme

2 cups dried cannellini beans, rinsed and drained

1 small bunch kale, coarsely chopped

¹/₂ small head cabbage, coarsely chopped

3 small zucchini, coarsely chopped

6 cups chicken broth, plus more to thin soup, as needed

Salt and pepper to taste

Slices of stale, crusty Italian bread (optional)

1 garlic clove, cut in half (optional)

Minestrone

- Heat oil in a large pot over medium-high heat. Sauté carrots, celery, onion, and garlic until onion is soft but not brown. Add potatoes; cook 8 minutes. Stir in tomatoes and thyme. Bring to a boil.

- Add beans and then the remaining vegetables and broth. Cook, partly covered, 2½ hours, until soup is very thick.

186

Oven-Roasted Cabbage: Leftover cabbage? Rejoice! You can make sweet and addictive roasted cabbage. Preheat oven to 400°F. Cut the cabbage in 2-inch chunks (don't separate the leaves, although it's okay if they fall apart, too). Toss cabbage with 3 tablespoons olive oil and spread in an even layer on a baking sheet. Sprinkle lightly with salt and roast until caramelized, 20 to 30 minutes. Drizzle with 1 tablespoon apple cider or wine vinegar before serving. Roasted cabbage is terrific served alongside grilled or roasted pork or served at room temperature as a summer party side dish with anything coming off the barbecue grill.

Add Beans and Vegetables

- After adding the tomatoes and thyme and bringing the soup to a boil, add the beans.

- Then stir in the kale, cabbage, and zucchini—you may need to do this in batches, letting vegetables cook down.

- Add broth. Season with salt and pepper. Bring to a boil and simmer, covered, until vegetables are very well cooked, about 2½ hours.

- Add more broth only if needed, the soup should be quite thick.

Serve the Soup

- The soup is deeply satisfying served just as it is. You can also garnish with a sprinkling of Parmesan or any chopped fresh herbs you like.

- And you can make a different kind of a dish by serving it ladled over crisp garlic crouton.

- For each serving, toast a slice of slightly dry, crusty Italian bread. Rub it with a halved garlic clove, put it on the bottom of the bowl, and ladle soup over the top.

PROVENÇAL BEEF STEW
Braised brisket is infused with the Southern French flavors of olives, fennel, and thyme

This delicious beef stew is based on the classic Southern French daube, a similar braised beef dish with wine, herbs, and vegetables. Here we chose to use brisket (which is a richly flavored and inexpensive cut) instead of cubed stew meat. The ingredients list of a traditional daube can often be a bit overwhelming in length, so we have streamlined it here,

making it a one-pot dish with an abundance of flavors, from fresh thyme and salty olives to sweet fennel and fragrant allspice. Like all good beef stews, this one is meant to be made ahead of time to allow the flavors to deepen as the dish sits.

This stew is a perfect entertaining dish for the cold winter months. *Yield: 8 servings*

Ingredients

4 pounds brisket, cut into 1½-inch cubes

Salt and pepper to taste

2 tablespoons olive oil

3 onions (about 1 pound), cut in eighths

6 garlic cloves

3 carrots, peeled and cut diagonally into ½-inch slices

½ cup small green olives or more, prepared (see recipe)

2 bulbs fennel, tops trimmed, cut into eighths (optional)

3 tablespoons flour

1 bottle robust red wine (or half wine, half broth)

1 cup water

1 teaspoon thyme

1 bay leaf

2 whole cloves

2 allspice berries

1 tablespoon tomato paste

Noodles or polenta, for serving

Provençal Beef Stew

- Brown the beef in oil.

- In heavy casserole combine the browned beef, onions, garlic, carrots, prepared olives, and fennel. Cook over medium heat 5 minutes; stir in flour and cook 1 minute more.

- Stir in the wine and/or broth, water, spices, and tomato paste. Bring to a simmer, then cover and cook over low heat 3 hours, or until meat is tender. Remove the bay leaf and skim fat. Serve stew over noodles or polenta.

• • • • RECIPE VARIATION • • • •

Beef Bourguignon: In a heavy casserole, crisp 4 slices bacon until brown; remove and crumble. Add 3 pounds cubed brisket (seasoned with salt) and brown all over (in batches). Remove meat and add 1 onion, chopped; 3 garlic cloves, sliced; and 3 carrots, cut into 1-inch rounds. Cook until browned, 5 minutes. Add 3 tablespoons flour and cook 1 minute. Add 1 tablespoon tomato paste and cook 1 minute. Add 1 bottle red wine, 2 cups beef or chicken broth, 2 sprigs thyme, bacon, and 1 bay leaf. Cover and simmer until beef is very tender, 2 hours. Meanwhile, heat 3 tablespoons butter in a large skillet. Cook ½ pound sliced mushrooms until lightly browned, 7 minutes. Season with salt. Stir cooked mushrooms into finished stew.

Brown the Beef

- Sprinkle the beef with salt and pepper.

- In a skillet large enough to hold the meat in a single layer, heat the oil over high heat.

- Add the beef and cook, stirring until it is well browned, and add to the heavy casserole.

- The browning adds flavor—so don't be timid about getting a nice sear on the surface.

Prepare the Olives

- Before you add the olives to the stew, they must be pitted and blanched to remove some of their salt.

- Bring a small pot of water to a boil.

- Lay the olives on a cutting board and crush them with the side of a chef's knife. Pull out the pit.

- Drop pitted olives briefly into boiling water, then drain.

SILKY CAULIFLOWER SOUP

Follow this classic technique for making smooth pureed soups from any vegetable

It doesn't get more economical, or versatile, than vegetable soup! It is the best solution for any vegetable wilting in your refrigerator.

You can make a smooth soup from practically any vegetable: carrots, zucchini, cauliflower, mushrooms, fennel, asparagus, tomatoes, butternut squash. Pureed soups also make a

good canvas for a variety of toppings: minced fresh herbs, a dab of sour cream, toasted nuts, or croutons. Perk up bland soups with a squeeze of fresh lemon or lime juice. *Yield: 4 servings*

Ingredients

1 quart chicken broth

1 bay leaf or sprig of any herb you like (optional)

3 cups roughly chopped cauliflower or other raw vegetable, alone or in combination, such as carrots, broccoli, or asparagus

Salt and pepper to taste

Crème fraiche or cream, to taste (optional)

Grating of nutmeg (optional)

Silky Cauliflower Soup

- Pour the broth into a medium soup pot over medium-high heat. Add the bay leaf, if using, and the cauliflower and/or other vegetables.

- Bring to a simmer and cook until cauliflower is tender.

- Remove bay leaf and puree soup in a blender (or use an immersion blender or food processor).

- Return puree to a clean pot and adjust salt and pepper. If you like, swirl in a little cream or crème fraiche. Serve topped with a grating of nutmeg.

········· YELLOW ● LIGHT ·········

Since many vegetable soup recipes call for an approximate amount of vegetables (1 head broccoli, 1 bunch asparagus), it is always good to err on the side of caution when adding your liquid (water, broth, wine). A good rule of thumb is to *just* cover the raw vegetables with liquid, then cover and cook until tender. Any leftover broth can then be used to thin the pureed soup if it is too thick. Thin soups are much harder to rescue.

• • • • RECIPE VARIATION • • • •

Carrot Ginger Soup: In a medium pot melt 2 tablespoons butter. Add ½ onion, chopped; cook until soft. Add 1 tablespoon chopped ginger; cook 1 minute. Add 2 pounds carrots (in rounds) and 3 cups chicken broth. Simmer, covered, until carrots are tender; 15 minutes. Puree in blender. Season with 2 tablespoons fresh lime juice and salt. Serve hot or chilled.

Trim and Chop the Cauliflower

- Tear the green leaves off the cauliflower's base and use a paring knife to cut around the underside to remove stems. Discard stems and leaves.

- Cut a kind of cone shape into the underside to remove most of the core. Detach the florets.

- Cut florets into quarters or halves, depending on their size, so you have a uniform rough chop and the pieces cook evenly.

Puree the Soup

- The smoother the puree, the more elegant the soup.

- A blender is the best tool for the job because its shape forces solid pieces onto the blade. But an immersion blender or food processor will also work well.

- If you'd like to go an extra step, pass the puree through a strainer.

CREAM SCONES

Whipped cream instead of butter makes for the lightest of scones

No, they won't keep you on a diet. But making scones with whipped cream in place of butter transforms them from the heavy pucks you buy at coffeehouses into meltingly tender ones you can make at home for the same price.

These scones are based on a recipe by Judith Jones, the lauded cookbook editor who was responsible for launching Julia Child's first cookbook. They freeze extremely well; just place them frozen on a baking sheet and warm in a 375°F oven until crisp and heated through.

Since they are ridiculously easy to assemble, consider them for a special-occasion work morning or certainly for your next brunch gathering, where everyone will be begging you for the recipe. *Yield: about 18 scones*

Ingredients

3 cups flour

¹/₂ cup sugar

4 teaspoons baking powder

¹/₄ teaspoon salt

6 tablespoons currants or raisins, chopped candied ginger, or dried cranberries

2 cups heavy cream

2 tablespoons melted butter (optional)

2 tablespoons brown sugar (optional)

Cream Scones

- Preheat oven to 375°F. Sift the flour, sugar, baking powder, and salt together. Mix in the currants or other dried fruit.

- In a separate bowl, beat the cream until it holds soft peaks, then fold it into the dry ingredients and knead just until it holds together.

- Pull off rough rounds of dough, about the size of a billiards ball, and place on a lightly greased baking sheet. Brush tops with butter and sprinkle with brown sugar, if you like.

- Bake 35 minutes, until golden.

• • • • RECIPE VARIATIONS • • • •

Assorted Flavors: Try adding a whole array of ingredients to vary the flavor: grated orange zest and small pieces of dark chocolate (or chocolate chips), toasted pecans and dried cherries, raspberries (not frozen), or grated lemon zest and fresh blueberries. You can also make a small indentation in the top of each scone and fill it with a dollop of jam (apricot or raspberry) before baking. The jam becomes sticky and sweet.

Assorted Shapes: Instead of rolling each scone you can vary the shape to suit the occasion like stars, hearts, or even gingerbread men. Lightly dust the work surface with flour and roll out the scones to be 1-inch thick. Increase the baking time to about 45 minutes.

Fold in the Whipped Cream

- Whip the cream until it holds soft peaks. Add about a quarter of it to the dry mixture, cutting it in.

- Add the remaining whipped cream, gently folding it into the flour mixture. Not every bit of flour may be incorporated, but don't worry, it will come together when you knead the dough.

- You don't want to add too much moisture—that will make the scones heavy.

Knead the Dough

- Take the ragged dough out of the bowl and put it on a work surface, gathering up all the stray bits and any unincorporated flour.

- Using the heel of your hand, push the dough away from you as you attempt to bring it together into a unified mass.

- Using a rubber scraper, if needed, flip the dough and repeat one or more times, just until it holds together.

- Overkneading will make scones tough!

ORANGE-BANANA BREAD

Classic banana-walnut bread updated with a hint of orange zest

From an economical standpoint, banana bread cannot be beat. Often enough, you have a few bananas that have past their prime sitting on your counter. It is time to make banana bread! Or if you don't have a hankering for it, just toss the bananas in the freezer and defrost them when you do. Then make as many batches as you have bananas, and freeze the extra baked loaves.

You can toast the walnuts beforehand for a more intense flavor, or substitute pecans if you like.

This cake-like bread can easily be made into muffins, just reduce the baking time to about 35 minutes or until a tester comes out clean.

Serve for breakfast with a smear of cream cheese. *Yield: 1 loaf*

Ingredients

1 cup sugar

$^1/_2$ cup butter, softened

2 eggs

1 cup mashed ripe banana

$^1/_2$ teaspoon baking soda

2 teaspoons baking powder

2 cups flour

$^1/_3$ cup orange juice

Zest of 1 orange (optional)

$^1/_2$ cup chopped walnuts

Orange-Banana Bread

- Preheat oven to 325°F. In a large bowl, cream the sugar and butter. Add eggs one at a time, beating well after each addition. Add banana; mix well.

- In another bowl sift dry ingredients and add to butter mixture, alternating with orange juice. Stir in zest, if using, and the nuts.

- Bake in a greased loaf pan 60 to 75 minutes, until a toothpick or cake tester comes out clean.

- Cool in the pan 10 minutes; run a knife along the edge, pop out, and cool completely on a rack

• • • • RECIPE VARIATIONS • • • •

Chocolate Banana Bread: It is hard to beat the flavor combination of chocolate and bananas. Try adding ⅓ cup grated dark, bittersweet, or semisweet chocolate (or use chips) into the batter when you add the walnuts. Allow the bread to cool completely before slicing it, or molten chocolate will coat your knife. Then again, maybe you want to cut it while it's still warm!

Leftover Banana Bread: The best way to serve leftover banana bread is toasted in the morning with a thick smear of cream cheese. It's almost like eating a banana cupcake with cream cheese frosting, but a little on the healthier side, so you won't feel guilty at breakfast time. Leftovers also make amazing bread pudding, mixed with cubes of eggy challah bread.

Cream the Sugar and Butter

- Let the butter come to room temperature. Don't try to heat it, or it will break into liquid and solids.

- To speed things up, cut it into bits or rub it lightly between your fingers.

- Then add the sugar and, using either a mixer or a wooden spoon, beat the butter and sugar together until they are fully incorporated and light.

Ripe Bananas

- Bananas need to be very soft and fully ripe—or even overripe—for this recipe.

- If you find any browned parts, you can cut them away. But they are fine to eat, too.

- Overripe bananas can be stored in the freezer until you have enough to make this bread.

- Never throw a banana away again!

195

MAPLE BUTTERMILK BISCUITS

A touch of salt brings out the sweetness in these maple biscuits

When baking these light maple biscuits, try to find Grade B maple syrup. It has a stronger maple flavor and is often a bit cheaper than the lighter Grade A variety.

The secret to making fluffy biscuits is not to overknead them, which will make them heavy and dense. Just combine the ingredients until they hold together (it is fine if they are not completely incorporated).

These biscuits also benefit from a short rest in the freezer before baking, which chills the butter and produces a tender and flaky crumb. The finished biscuits are treated to a drizzle of fresh maple syrup before being transferred back to the oven for a few minutes, producing a caramel-like glaze on top. *Yield: 2 dozen*

Ingredients

3¹/₂ cups flour

2 tablespoons sugar

1 tablespoon baking powder

¹/₂ teaspoon baking soda

³/₄ teaspoon salt

2 sticks butter, cut into ¹/₂-inch cubes

³/₄ cup plus 2 tablespoons maple syrup, divided

³/₄ cup plus 2 tablespoons buttermilk

1 egg yolk (optional)

1 egg (optional)

1 tablespoon cream or milk (optional)

Coarse salt or sea salt

Maple Buttermilk Biscuits

- Whisk together flour, sugar, baking powder, baking soda, and salt in a large bowl. Cut in butter until mixture looks like small peas. Add ¼ cup plus 2 tablespoons maple syrup and the buttermilk.

- Roll, cut, and chill biscuits. Prepare the egg wash, if you like. See optional ingredients.

- Preheat oven to 350°F. Bake biscuits until barely brown, about 25 minutes. Remove from oven, quickly drizzle 1 teaspoon maple syrup over each biscuit, then return to oven 3 minutes more. Serve warm.

• • • • RECIPE VARIATION • • • •

Orange-Honey Buttermilk Biscuits: In a bowl, combine 2 cups cake flour, 1 tablespoon baking powder, grated zest of half an orange, and ½ teaspoon salt. Cut 5 tablespoons butter into the flour mixture until crumbly. Add ¾ cup chilled buttermilk; finish biscuits as below, substituting honey for the maple syrup as the final drizzle.

YELLOW ● LIGHT

Biscuit Scraps: The more you handle the dough the tougher the biscuits become, so keep that in mind when reusing the scraps. Gently press the scraps together (don't pack into a tight ball) and pat down your hands (don't roll) until the dough is 1-inch thick. Cut out more biscuits, but don't reuse those scraps again. Or avoid scraps altogether by making (gasp!) square or triangular biscuits.

Roll, Cut, and Chill

- Dough is ready to roll when it comes together but is still clumpy. Don't overwork it.

- On a lightly floured surface, gently press or roll out dough to a 1-inch thickness.

- Cut biscuits into 2-inch rounds. Place on a lightly greased or parchment-lined baking sheet 2 inches apart.

- Freeze 10 minutes; then coat with egg wash, if using, and bake.

Prepare the Egg Wash

- While the biscuits are in the freezer, whisk together the egg yolk, egg, and cream until everything is incorporated.

- Brush the tops of the chilled biscuits with the egg wash and top each with a tiny pinch of salt.

- The biscuits are ready for the oven.

197

CLASSIC CORN BREAD

A pan of corn bread amounts to a whole lot of options for breakfast, lunch, and dinner

There is practically no end to the things you can do with fresh or day-old corn bread. Created from staples you always have on hand (flour, cornmeal, eggs, milk, and butter), every occasion or meal calls for corn bread on the side. For breakfast enjoy it with butter and honey alongside fried eggs, for lunch it makes any bowl of soup a full meal, and at dinnertime it is the obvious side dish for a serving of seasoned beans with sautéed greens. Crumbled day-old corn bread gets new life as a dressing (stuffing that isn't actually stuffed into anything), when seasoned with fresh herbs, sausage, and cooked vegetables. *Yield: 1 8-inch-square corn bread*

Ingredients

1 cup flour

1 cup fine cornmeal

2 tablespoons sugar

3 teaspoons baking powder

$^1/_2$ teaspoon salt

2 eggs

1 cup milk

2 tablespoons melted butter or bacon drippings

Classic Corn Bread

- Preheat oven to 400°F and grease an 8-inch-square cake pan.

- In a large bowl, mix together the flour, cornmeal, sugar, baking powder, and salt.

- In a separate bowl, beat eggs, then add milk and butter or bacon drippings. Pour into the flour mixture and stir just until combined. Don't overmix.

- Pour batter into the pan and bake until golden and crisp and a toothpick comes out clean, about 30 minutes.

Herbed Corn Bread Stuffing: Give your staling corn bread new life with a savory batch of herbed corn bread stuffing. If you aren't up for stuffing right away, pack away leftover corn bread in the freezer for Thanksgiving. Toast ½ cup pecans in a 350°F oven for 8 minutes. Transfer to a mixing bowl and add 5 cups crumbled corn bread. Heat 4 tablespoons butter in a skillet. Add 1 onion and 2 stalks celery, both minced; cook until soft, 3 minutes. Add 1 teaspoon each thyme and rosemary; cook 1 minute. Add ¼ cup sherry or white wine and cook until evaporated. Add vegetables to corn bread, along with ⅓ cup each heavy cream, chicken broth, and dried cranberries and the pecans. Use to stuff or bake, covered, at 350° for 35 minutes.

Don't Overmix the Batter

- When you add the liquid ingredients to the dry, be careful to stir them together just until they are combined.

- Overmixing will make the corn bread tough.

- You want a light, fluffy texture to contrast with the grittiness of the cornmeal.

Grease the Pan

- You can grease the pan with any shortening, although butter adds a nice note of flavor.

- If you used bacon drippings in the recipe, they will work on the pan as well.

- And of course you can also use this recipe to make corn muffins. Just pour the batter into greased or paper-lined muffin tins.

LEMON-GINGER MUFFINS

Fresh ginger and lemon zest create a flavorful morning treat

These delectable muffins are from Marion Cunningham's Bridge Creek restaurant, which was a marvelous breakfast spot in Berkeley, California. These are Michalene's favorite muffins ever—delicate and buttery with a bright kick of citrus and ginger. By melting the sugar instead of using it raw, you create a flavorful ginger-lemon–infused syrup, which packs much more flavor than when the ingredients are used separately (sugar syrup is a terrific conductor of flavor). The

sour buttermilk and spicy ginger temper the muffins sweetness. Be careful when melting the sugar in a dry pan, as it does brown in spots. To avoid that, add a tablespoon or two of water to the sugar to help it melt more smoothly. *Yield: 16 muffins*

Ingredients

³/₄ cup plus 3 tablespoons sugar

4 ounces fresh gingerroot, finely minced

Zest of 2 lemons, finely grated or chopped

1 stick butter, softened

2 eggs

1 cup buttermilk

2 cups flour

¹/₂ teaspoon salt

³/₄ teaspoon baking soda

Lemon-Ginger Muffins

- Preheat oven to 375°F. Grease 12 muffin tins.

- Melt ¼ cup sugar with the ginger. Let cool. Rub lemon zest with 3 tablespoons sugar and add to ginger mixture.

- Beat butter in a medium bowl. Add ½ cup sugar;

beat until smooth. Add eggs and beat well. Mix in buttermilk, then add flour, salt, and baking soda. Add ginger-lemon mixture; mix well.

- Fill muffin tins ¾ full and bake 15 to 20 minutes. Serve warm.

Believe it or not, you don't need to peel fresh ginger. It's thin, papery skin is not bitter or coarse and will blend right into the finely minced ginger you use in most recipes. Better yet, store fresh ginger in the freezer, where you can easily grate it (still frozen) on a sharp grater, and you won't notice the peel at all. When grated frozen, the tough fibers are left behind—another plus!

When a recipe calls for buttermilk and you don't want to buy a whole quart for just one dish, consider making it yourself. Gently warm the equivalent amount of milk (whole is preferable but not necessary) until warm to the touch. Stir in 1 tablespoon neutral-tasting vinegar (white is best) and let sit 10 minutes. Voila! There is also dried buttermilk powder on the market; just store in the refrigerator and reconstitute when needed.

Melt the Sugar

- Cut the unpeeled ginger into large chunks, then chop it fine—or pulse it in a food processor until fine.

- You should have ¼ cup ginger; a little more is good, but not less.

- Put the ginger and ¼ cup sugar in a small pan and cook over medium heat until sugar melts and begins to brown. Remove from heat and transfer to a sheet of wax paper or parchment to cool a bit.

Beat Ingredients Together

- In a medium bowl, beat the softened butter for a minute.

- Add ½ cup sugar and beat until smooth. Add the eggs and beat well.

- Add the buttermilk and mix it through.

- Add flour, salt, and baking soda. Add ginger-lemon mixture, mix well, and fill muffin tins.

GOUGÈRES
Classy cheese puffs are elegant and a snap to make.

These light, bite-size gems are also known as cheese puffs. They are a classic from the Burgundy region of France, and they're having a bit of a revival right now, showing up in some of the trendiest restaurants and bars coast to coast.

They're wonderful to nibble with a glass of wine or a cocktail—and awfully classy for something that's actually very inexpensive to make.

They are made from the same dough used to make éclairs, called *pâte à choux,* a wonderfully simple pastry dough made with just eggs, butter, and flour.

You can drop the dough on cookie sheets or, for more uniform puffs, use a pastry bag or large plastic storage bag with one corner snipped to make a pastry "tip." *Yield: about 32 cheese puffs*

Ingredients

1 cup water

³/₄ teaspoon salt

¹/₂ cup butter, cut into bits

1 cup flour, sifted

4 eggs

4 ounces Gruyère cheese, grated, divided

Gougères

- Preheat oven to 400°F. In a medium saucepan over medium-high heat, combine water, salt, and butter. Bring to a boil, stirring constantly.

- Remove from heat and add flour all at once. Beat vigorously to create a smooth dough.

- Put pan over low heat and beat constantly with a wooden spoon for 1 minute to dry the dough a little.

- Beat eggs into the dough, one at a time. Beat in cheese, reserving 3 tablespoons for topping. Bake 25 minutes.

· · · · RECIPE VARIATION · · · ·

Cocktail Sandwiches: Gougères make great cocktail sandwiches. Just use the split gougères like a "bun," stuffing them with things that will complement their flavor, like smoky ham or turkey breast, roast beef, cured meats, or roasted red peppers. If you substitute Parmesan for the Gruyère, stuff with fresh mozzarella, tomato, and basil.

Beat the Dough

Bake the Gougères

- After the water-butter mixture boils, remove the pan from heat and add flour all at once. Beat vigorously to create a smooth dough that pulls away from the sides of the pan.

- Put pan over low heat and beat constantly with a wooden spoon for 1 minute to dry the dough a little.

- Beat eggs into the dough, one at a time.

- Set aside 3 tablespoons of the cheese for topping; beat in the remaining cheese.

- When the cheese has been incorporated into the dough, it is ready to bake.

- Gently drop tablespoons of dough onto a lightly buttered or parchment paper–lined baking sheet.

- Sprinkle the gougères with the remaining cheese and bake until golden and crisp, about 25 minutes.

- Immediately after removing them from the oven, pierce the side of each gougère with a sharp paring knife. This releases steam and keeps them crisp.

CHICKEN FAUX GRAS

Luxurious pâté at a fraction of the price

Chef Michel Richard developed this brilliant recipe for a chicken liver pâté. It is called *faux gras* because the flavor is just as rich and complex as pricey (and controversial) *foie gras*, a smooth pâté made from duck livers. Here inexpensive chicken livers are used to create an equally luxurious treat for very little money. You can purchase chicken livers very inexpensively or just save the livers that come inside a whole chicken until you have a pound (without spending a dime!).

Topped with an emerald parsley gelée, it's a really beautiful dish, too. Serve with thin slices of crispy white bread for a great first course or appetizer. *Yield: 12 servings*

Ingredients

2 sticks unsalted butter, room temperature, divided

1 cup finely chopped onions

1 garlic clove

1/2 cup heavy cream

1 pound chicken livers

1 teaspoon salt, plus a pinch for gelée

1/2 teaspoon pepper

1/2 English cucumber, cut into 2-inch pieces

1 teaspoon powdered gelatin

1 teaspoon lemon juice

1 teaspoon sugar

1–2 drops Tabasco sauce

2 tablespoons finely minced Italian parsley

Chicken Faux Gras

- Prepare onion mixture, then add to blender with livers, salt, and pepper. Blend until combined. Heat oven to 300°F. Bring a pot of water to a boil.

- Put 4 1-cup ovenproof crocks into a deep baking dish. Strain liver mixture into crocks.

- Cover each crock with foil and pour boiling water in the baking dish to reach halfway up the crocks. Bake 30 minutes, until mousse is set.

- Cool to room temperature, then refrigerate. When cool, make gelée.

A savory wine gelée (jelled liquid) is commonly served with foie gras. But instead of springing for a pricey sweet white wine to make the jelly, this recipe calls for the juice of a pureed cucumber instead. Its bright vegetal flavor, combined with a bit of lemon juice and fresh parsley, makes a terrific complement to the chicken liver richness. The jelly is spooned on top of the cooked livers and then chilled so a beautiful speckled layer of gelatin comes with every bite. Make sure you don't heat the gelatin mixture to a boil, which will destroy it. You can also dissolve the gelatin using a microwave, at 10-second intervals on high.

Prepare the Onion Mixture

- Melt 2 tablespoons butter over medium heat. Stir in onions. Cover and cook about 5 minutes, stirring occasionally, until onions are translucent.

- Grate garlic into the onions. Add the cream; bring to a simmer. Reduce heat and cook gently for 6 minutes, until onions are very soft.

- Remove pan from heat and add remaining butter. Return to heat and stir until butter melts and onion mixture is completely combined. Set aside.

Make the Gelée

- Put cucumber in a blender and liquefy. Strain into a measuring cup (should be about ½ cup).

- In a small saucepan, heat gelatin and ¼ cup cucumber liquid until gelatin just melts, stirring constantly. Do not boil!

- In a separate bowl, combine lemon juice, sugar, pinch of salt, Tabasco, and remaining cucumber liquid. Add gelatin mixture; slowly stir in parsley.

- Spoon 2 tablespoons gelée on each crock. Refrigerate until set, 1 hour. Let stand 30 minutes before serving.

WINE-BRAISED SHORT RIBS

Meaty short ribs are cooked to tender perfection in an herbed wine sauce

These classic French braised short ribs come courtesy of Chef Daniel Boulud. He serves them with a celery root puree topped with braised celery (fancily termed *celery duo*). They can also be served with your favorite mashed potatoes. These ribs are best made a day ahead so the fat can be scraped off and the rich flavors in the sauce can develop.

While two bottles of wine doesn't feel terribly economical, you can always find an inexpensive bottle to cook with for around $6 to $8. Plus, this is the showstoppers chapter, and these luxurious braised ribs will surely stop the show. Julia Child always reminded us to cook with the same wine we would drink. *Yield: 8 servings*

Ingredients

2 bottles dry red wine

2 tablespoons vegetable oil

8 short ribs, fat trimmed

Salt and pepper to taste

Flour for dusting

10 garlic cloves, peeled

3 medium onions, peeled and quartered

2 medium carrots, peeled and cut into 1-inch rounds

2 stalks celery, cut into 1-inch segments

1 medium leek, coarsely chopped

6 sprigs Italian parsley

1 teaspoon thyme

2 bay leaves

2 tablespoons tomato paste

3 quarts chicken broth

Wine-Braised Short Ribs

- Heat wine in a large saucepan over medium-high heat. Boil lightly until reduced by half. Set aside.

- Preheat oven to 350°F. Brown the short ribs and the vegetables. Add the reduced wine and broth.

- Bring to a boil, cover tightly, and braise in the oven 2½ hours, until meat is fork-tender, skimming fat every 30 minutes.

- Remove ribs. Make the sauce; serve.

Celery Root Mashed Potatoes: Celery root is a terrific complement to potatoes and mashes up just as smooth. Peel and cube 2 pounds celery root and 1 pound baking potatoes. Cover with water and boil until tender. Drain, reserving ½ cup cooking water. Mash vegetables, adding 4 tablespoons butter and a little cooking water to moisten. Season with salt and pepper.

Braised Celery: Trim 2 inches off the bottom and top of 1 bunch celery, then cut in quarters. In a saucepan, cover celery with 2 cups chicken broth, 1 tablespoon olive oil, 1 carrot (for flavor), and pinch of salt. Simmer until celery is tender and broth reduced to a glaze, about 25 minutes.

Brown the Short Ribs and Vegetables

Make the Sauce

- Heat the oil in a large Dutch oven or casserole over medium heat. Season the ribs with salt and pepper. In batches, dust the ribs with a little flour and sear on all sides—be sure to brown them well, about 5 minutes per side.

- Remove all but 2 tablespoons fat from the pot. Lower heat to medium and add vegetables and herbs. Brown lightly, then stir in tomato paste and cook 1 minute.

- Return ribs to pot and continue.

- You can cook the ribs a day in advance. Cool and refrigerate, then when you are ready to continue, scrape off the fat and rewarm.

- Carefully transfer the ribs to a heated serving platter with a lip; keep warm.

- Boil the pan liquid until it thickens and reduces to about 1 quart. Season with salt and pepper and strain through a fine-mesh strainer. Discard solids.

- Pour the sauce over the short ribs; serve.

SHOWSTOPPERS

MOZZA CAPRESE

Fresh tomato, basil, and mozzarella salad gets a winter makeover

Chef Nancy Silverton isn't one to pass off an inferior tomato—so she came up with a brilliant variation on the fresh tomato caprese salad to serve during the long months when tomatoes aren't at their peak.

This is her version of a "winter" caprese salad, where the tomatoes are roasted on the vine to boost their flavor, and fresh pesto is used in place of fresh basil leaves to further amp up the flavor. It is gorgeous to behold. And it is so good that it is now being served year-round at her Osteria Mozza restaurant in Los Angeles.

To cut down on the tomato roasting time, look for cherry tomatoes on the vine, which roast into tenderness more quickly. *Yield: 4 servings*

Ingredients

For the pesto:

3 tablespoons pine nuts

2–3 cloves garlic, finely chopped

1/3 cup fresh basil leaves

1/3 cup chopped Italian parsley leaves

1 teaspoon salt

1/2 cup olive oil

1/4 cup grated Parmigiana Reggiano

1 tablespoon lemon juice, or to taste

For the salad:

1 pound small tomatoes or cherry tomatoes, on the vine

1 tablespoon olive oil, plus more for drizzling

1 pound fresh mozzarella

Salt and pepper to taste

4 large basil leaves

Mozza Caprese

- Make the pesto. Roast the tomatoes.

- Slice the mozzarella and distribute evenly among four plates. If you like, season lightly with salt.

- Spoon about 1 tablespoon pesto over each portion. Use scissors to cut a basil leaf over each plate. Top with the tomatoes, leaving a bit of the vine intact.

- Drizzle with olive oil; serve.

Using Leftover Pesto: It is always a good idea to make a few extra batches of pesto since it doesn't take any extra time to double the ingredients. That way, you will always have a batch on hand for when you need it. Since basil leaves oxidize when the cut leaves come in contact with air, you will need to cover your extra pesto with a thin layer olive oil to make an airtight seal. Then the pesto can be stored in the refrigerator for up to 1 week, or frozen for up to 3 months. Use extra pesto when serving salmon (mixed with a bit of sour cream or yogurt to make a thick sauce) or toss with shredded chicken and mayonnaise for a pesto chicken salad.

Make the Pesto

- Heat oven to 325°F and toast pine nuts until lightly browned, about 8 minutes. Let cool.

- Put pine nuts in a mortar and pestle or food processor along with the garlic, basil, parsley, and salt, and grind to a smooth paste.

- Drizzle in the olive oil and add the Parmigiana Reggiano. Just before serving, season with lemon juice and more salt, if needed.

Roast the Tomatoes

- Heat oven to 200°F.

- Set the tomatoes—still attached to the vine—on a wire rack set on a baking sheet. Brush with 1 table-spoon olive oil and season with salt and pepper.

- Roast tomatoes 4 to 4½ hours, until the skins begin to shrivel but the tomatoes are still plump. (If you use cherry tomatoes, it will take much less time, about 2 hours.)

- Cool to room temperature.

ZUNI ROAST CHICKEN

Herb-roasted chicken is served with a warm savory bread salad

This is a roast chicken dinner taken to the limit. It is the signature recipe of Judy Rodger's Zuni Café in San Francisco. The chicken itself is cooked to perfection thanks to a few extra flips while it is roasting. As the chicken roasts, you assemble a bread salad (very similar to a dressing) seasoned with currants, pine nuts, and garlic. It is the best use for leftover bread we can think of. The warm bread salad is seasoned with the

pan drippings from the roast chicken, so not a drop of flavor is lost.

Toasting the bread beforehand allows the bread to absorb the maximum amount of delicious chicken juices. The salad is completed with a handful of bitter baby greens to complement the lusciousness of the bread salad. *Yield: 4 servings*

Ingredients

1 3½-pound chicken

4 ½-inch sprigs fresh thyme, rosemary, marjoram, or sage

2½ teaspoons salt, plus more to taste

¼ teaspoon pepper, plus more to taste

8 ounces slightly stale rustic bread (not sourdough), bottom crust and most of top and side crusts removed

6-8 tablespoons olive oil, divided

1½ tablespoons white wine vinegar

1 tablespoon dried currants

1 teaspoon red wine vinegar, or as needed

1 tablespoon warm water

2-3 garlic cloves, slivered

¼ cup slivered scallions, including some green

2 tablespoons pine nuts, toasted

2 tablespoons chicken broth or lightly salted water

2 cups arugula, curly endive, or red mustard greens, washed and dried

Zuni Roast Chicken

- Season chicken. Start bread salad. Preheat oven to 475°F.

- Heat a large skillet over medium heat. Wipe chicken dry and set breast up in hot pan, then put in oven 30 minutes. Flip chicken breast down and roast 20 minutes. Flip again breast up and roast 10 minutes.

- Remove chicken to cutting board. Pour off fat from drippings and toss juices with greens, warm bread mixture, and more vinaigrette. Spread on a warm platter.

- Carve chicken, arrange pieces on top, and serve.

Dressing is what a stuffing is called when it is baked outside the bird. Since it doesn't have the benefit of absorbing the juices from the chicken or turkey while it cooks, it is often seasoned with the pan juices after the bird is cooked. To make an even richer bread dressing than the one here, you can omit tossing the toasted bread pieces with the ¼ cup olive oil and instead toss it with all the drippings from the chicken (instead of pouring off the fat beforehand). For more flavor, remove chicken from skillet and set over medium heat. Add ¼ cup chicken broth (or wine) and scrape up browned bits; reduce liquid by half. Pour over assembled dressing.

Season the Chicken

- Remove fat from cavity; rinse and dry inside and out.

- Approaching from the edge of the cavity, make 4 pockets by sliding a finger under the skin of each breast and at the thickest portion of each thigh. Shove an herb sprig into each.

- Season chicken liberally with salt and pepper. Put a little salt inside the cavity on the backbone.

- Tuck wing tips behind shoulders, cover loosely, and refrigerate 2 to 3 days.

Start the Bread Salad

- Cut bread into 2 chunks, brush with olive oil, and crisp in broiler. Tear into bite-size pieces and crumbs.

- Combine ¼ cup olive oil with white wine vinegar, salt, and pepper. Toss a quarter of this mixture with the bread. Adjust seasonings.

- Moisten currants in red wine vinegar and warm water. While chicken roasts, soften garlic and scallions in 2 tablespoons olive oil over medium-low heat. Toss with bread mixture, drained currants, pine nuts, and broth. Tent with foil in baking dish, and warm in oven for last 10 minutes.

ANIMAL'S CUBAN ROAST PORK

Slow-cooked Boston butt is heady with the flavors of citrus and garlic

Jon Shook and Vinny Dotolo, the chefs behind Animal restaurant in Los Angeles, have a thing for pork. They're known to put it in just about every dish—even dessert (chocolate bacon bar, anyone?).

This is a rather restrained dish for them, but delicious—and made with the supremely economical Boston butt, which is roasted at a very low temperature until it is falling-off-the-bone tender. The meat is served shredded with a crown of thinly sliced white onion. Serve it with a side of white rice, black beans, and an avocado salad for a superb meal.

To make it extra delicious, top the shredded meat with a mojo sauce just before serving. *Yield: 12 servings*

Ingredients

1 6–8-pound boneless Boston pork butt, fat trimmed and tied into a roast

1 cup olive oil, divided

2 cups orange juice

1/2 cup lemon juice

1/2 cup lime juice

20 garlic cloves, smashed, divided

5 white onions: 4 very thinly sliced, 1 sliced into 1/2-inch-thick rings

1 1/2 teaspoons thyme

2 bay leaves

1 tablespoon cumin

1 1/2 teaspoons red pepper flakes

4 tablespoons salt, divided

5 limes, cut into wedges

Animal's Cuban Roast Pork

- Marinate pork at least 24 hours ahead. Preheat oven to 450°F.

- Separate the ½-inch-thick onion rings and put them on the bottom of a roasting pan with 5 smashed garlic cloves. Drizzle with 2 tablespoons olive oil.

- Remove roast from marinade and discard marinade. Pat roast dry, set it on the onions and garlic, and rub with salt.

- Roast pork until tender.

Mojo Sauce: To make a piquant sauce, heat ¼ cup canola oil with 2 tablespoons finely chopped garlic in a small saucepan over low heat. When garlic is soft, about 10 minutes, turn off heat and cool. Stir in 2 tablespoons lime juice, 1 tablespoon orange juice, 2 teaspoons lemon juice, ½ teaspoon cumin, and ¾ teaspoon salt. Serve at room temperature.

Avocado Salad: Lay a bed of shredded romaine lettuce on a plate. Top with thin slices of avocado (at least a quarter of an avocado per person). Top with thinly sliced red onion and whole cilantro leaves. For a dressing, combine 4 tablespoons olive oil, 2 tablespoons lime juice, salt, and pepper. Pour over salad.

Marinate the Pork

- Reserve 2 tablespoons oil.

- In a large bowl, whisk the remaining oil with the orange juice, lemon juice, lime juice, 15 smashed garlic cloves, half the thinly sliced onions, thyme, bay leaves, cumin, red pepper flakes, and 2 tablespoons salt.

- Pour marinade into a large plastic bag and add the pork. Seal the bag and set it in a large bowl to catch any leaks.

- Marinate at least 24 hours and up to 3 days.

Roast Pork Until Tender

- Reduce oven to 425°F and put the pork roast in the oven.

- Roast 45 minutes. Reduce the temperature to 250°, cover the roasting pan with foil, and roast another 4 to 4½ hours, until the meat is falling-apart tender.

- Shred the pork and serve it with remaining thinly sliced onions and lime wedges.

SHOWSTOPPERS

AUNTIE EM'S COCONUT CUPCAKES
Almond-scented cupcakes are topped with fluffy sweet coconut

These divine cupcakes are from Auntie Em's Kitchen in Eagle Rock, California, outside of Los Angeles. We thought we'd had it up to here with cute cupcakes—cute, overpriced cupcakes. Then we tasted these. There's some kind of alchemy that happens with the simple ingredients—they're moist, with a tender crumb, and not too sweet. They have a subtle hint of almond, too. They bake up into a high dome, crowned with

cream cheese frosting and a jaunty cap of shredded coconut. It's the cupcake, grown-up at last.

To intensify the coconut flavor, you can lightly toast the coconut before sprinkling it on top. In a large dry skillet over medium heat, toast 1 cup shredded coconut until lightly golden, shaking frequently, about 3 minutes. *Yield: 18 cupcakes*

Ingredients

2¹/₃ cups flour

1 teaspoon baking soda

1 teaspoon salt

1 cup vegetable oil

1 cup buttermilk

3 eggs

2¹/₂ teaspoons vanilla extract, divided

2 teaspoons almond extract

1¹/₃ cups sugar

1³/₄ cups shredded sweetened coconut, plus more for decoration

¹/₂ pound cream cheese, room temperature

10 tablespoons butter, room temperature

3¹/₃ cups powdered sugar, sifted

Auntie Em's Coconut Cupcakes

- Preheat oven to 325°F. Sift together the flour, baking soda, and salt.

- In another bowl combine the oil, buttermilk, eggs, 1½ teaspoons vanilla, almond extract, and sugar. Using a mixer on low speed, slowly add dry ingredients, mixing just until smooth. Fold in the coconut.

- Line a muffin tin with paper cups and fill each three-quarters full. Bake 20 to 25 minutes, until a cake tester comes out dry. Cool on a rack.

- Make the frosting and finish the cupcakes.

Coconut Birthday Cake: You can easily adapt the recipe below to make a showstopping triple-layer cake for any occasion. You will need to double the recipe for the cupcakes and frosting. Pour the cupcake batter into 3 8- or 9-inch cake pans and bake just until a tester inserted in the center of each cake comes out clean (start checking after 30 minutes). Allow the layers to cool completely before stacking and layering with frosting. Save enough frosting for the sides. Crown the top and sides of the cake with sweetened shredded coconut, either plain or toasted. You can also decorate the top with sliced almonds, to highlight the hint of almond flavor in the cake.

Make the Frosting

- In a medium bowl, beat the cream cheese until smooth.

- Scrape down the sides, add the butter, and continue beating on medium speed until smooth.

- Scrape down, and add a third of the powdered sugar. Beat on low until combined. Add another third of the powdered sugar, beat until combined; beat in the last third.

- Add 1 teaspoon vanilla and beat until fluffy.

Finish the Cupcakes

- When the cupcakes are completely cool and the frosting is ready, frost each cupcake with about 3 tablespoons frosting.

- Sprinkle the tops with extra shredded coconut for decoration.

- The cupcakes will stay fresh at room temperature for 2 days.

APPLE BREAD PUDDING

Stewed apples and raisins stud this creamy and comforting dessert

Bread pudding, rich with apples and cream—what better use for day-old bread? Save the ends of your baguettes and crusty loaves in the freezer until you have enough for this rustic dessert from the Normandy region of France, adapted from Chef Pierre Franey, the late and beloved French chef and food writer.

Baking the bread pudding in a water bath just keeps the bread pudding from browning along the side and bottom edges. However, you can omit this step entirely and bake the pudding directly in the oven; you will be rewarded with a caramelized crust all around.

You can also substitute pears and dried cranberries for the apples and raisins.

Using a combination of whole eggs and yolks creates a more luscious pudding. *Yield: 10 servings*

Ingredients

2 tablespoons butter

1 pound apples, peeled, cored, and sliced very thinly

1 1/4 cups sugar, divided

1/4 cups currants or raisins

1/4 cup Calvados or apple juice

12–14 1/4-inch-thick slices day-old baguette

3 egg yolks

2 whole eggs

1 teaspoon vanilla

1 cup heavy cream

3 cups milk

1/4 teaspoon salt

Powdered sugar, for dusting (optional)

Apple Bread Pudding

- Preheat oven to 400°F. Cook the apples and currants or raisins.

- Arrange bread slices in a single layer and top with cooked apple mixture.

- Lightly beat yolks and eggs with 1 cup sugar, vanilla, cream, milk, and salt. Pour over apples and bread.

- Set baking dish in a larger baking dish and pour boiling water in the larger dish. Bake 40 minutes. When pudding is still warm, sprinkle with sifted powdered sugar, if you like, and serve.

Chocolate-Cherry Bread Pudding: Chocolate and cherries are a classic combination—and for good reason. They are delicious together! This is a great recipe when cherries are in season, but you can even substitute frozen dark cherries for fresh with very good results. Just thaw the cherries in a colander before using so they aren't quite so juicy. Following the recipe here, just omit the step of sautéing the apple, and sprinkle 1½ cups halved cherries over the first layer of bread. Then grate a few ounces of dark chocolate over the cherries (or sprinkle with ½ cup chocolate chips) before covering cherries with the top layer of bread. Pour over cream mixture and bake as directed.

Cook the Apples and Raisins

- Heat the butter in a large nonstick skillet over medium-high heat.

- Add the apple slices and ¼ cup sugar. Sauté 2 minutes, stirring.

- Add the currants or raisins and Calvados or apple juice; cook a minute or two more.

- Layer over the bread slices.

Layer the Bread and Apples

- Arrange bread slices in a single layer over the bottom of a 9 x 13-inch baking dish.

- The pieces should slightly overlap, but don't crowd them; make just one layer.

- Spoon the cooked apples and currants evenly over the top.

DESSERTS

CHOCOLATE CAKE

This light cake is flavored with cocoa powder instead of pricey block chocolate

This light and spongy chocolate cake derives its airiness from the beaten egg whites folded into the batter. The small bubble of air trapped inside the beaten whites expands in the heat of the oven to create a cake with a lot of volume.

We use cocoa powder as a more affordable option to dark chocolate. But like good chocolate, buy the best cocoa powder you can afford. It makes all the difference.

This is a simple cake and can be embellished with any number of frostings, icings, and toppings. When berries are in season, serve the cake with plenty of softly whipped cream and a handful of sliced strawberries and raspberries. *Yield: 8 servings*

Ingredients

1 cup flour, sifted

1 cup sugar

1 tablespoon baking powder

4 tablespoons cocoa powder

$1/2$ cup vegetable oil

$1/2$ cup boiling water

4 eggs, separated

1 teaspoon vanilla

Pinch of salt

Powdered sugar, for dusting

Chocolate Cake

- Preheat oven to 400°F. Combine the dry ingredients. Add vegetable oil and boiling water. Beat with a handheld mixer for 3 minutes.

- Mix in the egg yolks and vanilla. In a separate bowl, add salt to the egg whites and beat to snowy peaks.

- Fold egg whites into the chocolate mixture and pour batter into a greased and floured 9-inch cake pan. Bake 30 minutes.

- Cool 10 minutes in pan, then remove and cool on a rack. Dust with powdered sugar and serve.

Raspberry Coulis: When fresh raspberries aren't in your budget, you can opt for a berry coulis instead. *Coulis* refers to a thick puree or sauce, which is generally made out of fruit or vegetables. To make a raspberry coulis, combine 1 16-ounce package frozen raspberries (or black berries or blueberries, which are really terrific with chocolate) with 1 tablespoon lemon juice and ¼ cup sugar. Bring to a boil, reduce heat to low, and simmer 5 minutes. Strain the mixture through a fine sieve to remove the seeds, pressing down on the seeds with the back of a spoon to release all the juice. Taste and add more sugar or lemon juice as needed.

Combine the Dry Ingredients

- In a large bowl, add the flour, sugar, baking powder, and cocoa.

- Mix with a wooden spoon until thoroughly incorporated.

- Be sure to use a bowl large enough to allow you to combine these ingredients with everything else—including the room to fold in the egg whites without compressing them.

Fold in the Egg Whites

- Place the egg whites in a perfectly clean, medium bowl.

- Add a pinch of salt—to help them develop structure—and beat with a handheld mixer or a whisk until they form snowy peaks.

- Gently fold the beaten whites into the chocolate mixture by adding about a quarter of it to first loosen the batter, then gently folding in the rest.

DESSERTS

PUMPKIN SPICE CAKE

A warmly spiced holiday dessert served with boozy whipped cream

This cake recipe from Chef Jeremiah Tower, one of California cuisine's pioneering chefs, is very easy to make, and its homey and inexpensive ingredients combine to make a very sophisticated fall dessert.

The pumpkin adds moisture and earthy sweetness to the cake, which is seasoned with a gingerbread spice mix.

You can substitute 1 tablespoon finely minced fresh ginger in place of the dried for a huge flavor boost. Fresh ginger also adds a bit of welcome spiciness to the cake.

Crowning the cake with a softly whipped cream spiked with a little brandy or rum makes this dessert fit for all your fall and winter holidays. Top with a few bits of crumbled candied ginger for a finishing touch. *Yield: 8 servings*

Ingredients

2 cups flour, sifted

1 teaspoon baking soda

1/4 teaspoon salt

1 egg

1/2 cup sugar

1/2 cup canned pumpkin

1/2 cup vegetable oil

1/2 cup molasses

2 teaspoons ground ginger

1/2 teaspoon cinnamon

1/2 teaspoon cloves

1/2 teaspoon allspice

1/2 cup boiling water

1 cup heavy cream (optional)

2 tablespoons rum or brandy, or 1 teaspoon vanilla (optional)

Pumpkin Spice Cake

- Preheat oven to 350°F. Butter and flour an 8- or 9-inch cake pan.

- In a medium bowl, sift together the flour, baking soda, and salt.

- In a large bowl, beat the egg and sugar, then mix in the pumpkin, oil, molasses, and spices. Mix in the boiling water. Mix in the dry ingredients.

- Pour batter in the pan; bake 35 to 40 minutes, until a cake tester or toothpick comes out clean.

- Serve warm, with the whipped cream, if you like.

It is simple enough to make a batch of whipped cream, but there are a few tricks to making the best whipped cream you can. First, chill your ingredients. Cold whipped cream beats up more quickly and to greater volume. Also, try to buy heavy cream (also called heavy whipping cream) that is not ultrapasteurized. This may be a bit of a challenge to find, but just read all the cartons at the supermarket. The high temperature the cream is subjected to increases its shelf life (which is why it is the preference in supermarkets), but it also makes it more difficult to beat into fluffy peaks and it doesn't hold its shape for very long.

Prepare the Cake Pan

- Smear the bottom and sides of the pan lightly but evenly with soft butter. Be sure to get butter along the grove where the sides meet the bottom.

- Put about ¼ cup flour into the pan and shake and turn the pan so the surface is completely dusted with flour.

- Bang the pan on the side of the sink or counter to remove extra flour.

Whip the Cream

- A rum- or brandy-spiked whipped cream is a delicious complement to this cake—one that makes it festive enough for a holiday table.

- Just whip the cream with the spirits or vanilla (you may also want to add a little sugar, but it isn't necessary).

- Stop whipping when the cream is barely whipped and pillowy. It looks wonderful "draped" over a slice of the cake.

WARM FRUIT COMPOTE
Never throw out fruit that is past its prime again!

Nothing could be simpler or more appreciated than a warm bowl of fruit compote. It is infinitely versatile and can reflect the seasons or whatever you have in your produce drawer.

Even better: You can take advantage of the sale bags of browning fruit at the supermarket or farmers' market and use them to make compote. It is actually preferable to make it with older fruit. Save your blemish-free produce for eating in hand.

You can serve this compote for breakfast, too, as a topping for pancakes and waffles or stirred into plain yogurt and served as is or topped with a handful of granola.

This particular compote was adapted from Chef Jeremiah Tower, one of California's pioneering chefs. *Yield: 4 servings*

Ingredients

¹/₂ cup sugar

¹/₄ cup water

2 teaspoons lemon juice

3 cups ripe fruit (in the summer, use a variety of berries; in the fall, a mix of pears, quinces, red or green seedless grapes, apples, and figs; or try ripe tropical fruits such as mangoes and papayas)

4 tablespoons butter, cut into pieces

1 pint vanilla ice cream

Warm Fruit Compote

- Heat the sugar and water in an 8-inch sauté pan, stirring until the sugar is dissolved.

- Add the lemon juice and fruit and cook over medium heat. As the fruit cooks, shake the pan gently to coat it with syrup.

- When the fruit is almost done, add the butter and swirl it through, until melted.

- Spoon the compote and juices into 4 shallow bowls or deep-rimmed plates and drop a scoop of ice cream in the center.

Dried Fruit Compote: To intensify the flavor of the compote, add some dried fruit in place of fresh (visit the bulk aisle of a health food store for the most economical compote). Dried plums (prunes), raisins, unsulphured apricots, dried pears, dried cherries, and dried cranberries all make marvelous compote.

Fruit Compote for Dinner: You can use the same method to make a less sweet compote to accompany roast pork or chicken. Just reduce the sugar to ¼ cup and add 2 tablespoons apple cider or wine vinegar to the fruit as it stews. Use any fruit (pears, plums, peaches, and apples are great), but not berries. You will have a terrific sweet-and-sour condiment.

Cook the Fruit

Choosing the Fruit

- After the sugar has dissolved, add the lemon juice and fruit and cook over medium heat. If you are using berries, they will be done in about 3 minutes (if your mix includes raspberries, add them at the last second just to heat through).

- Other fruits will take longer.

- As the fruit cooks, shake the pan gently to coat it with syrup. When the fruit is nearly cooked, add the butter and swirl it through, until it melts.

- This is an infinitely flexible recipe—it works for most any fruit that is ripe and on hand.

- It is best if you stick with what's in season. Fall fruits harmonize with fall fruits, summer fruits with other summer fruits, and so on.

- Cut harder fruit, such as pears and quinces, into thin, uniform slices.

- If you're using berries, hull and split any strawberries so they are about the same size as the others.

DESSERTS

223

ORANGE-SCENTED COOKIES

Tender orange-scented cookies get their tang from sour milk

Here is a great reason to rejoice when your milk sours in the refrigerator. No matter that the expiration date has passed, "turned" milk is terrific in baking, where its sour flavor is greatly appreciated (think about buttermilk's appeal as a baking ingredient). It makes for a tender crumb in cakes and cookies and adds a delightful tang.

These cookies are exceptionally good and very cake-like in their texture. They aren't too sweet either, which makes them an excellent treat for serving with a hot cup of tea or cold glass of milk. *Yield: 5 dozen*

Ingredients

³/₄ cup butter

¹/₄ cup vegetable shortening

1¹/₂ cups sugar

2 eggs

1 cup sour milk

1 teaspoon baking soda

4 cups flour

3 teaspoons baking powder

3 small oranges, juice and zest

Juice of ¹/₂ lemon

2 cups powdered sugar

Orange-Scented Cookies

- Preheat oven to 375°F. Cream the butter, shortening, and sugar. Beat in the eggs one at a time, beating well after each addition.

- Mix the sour milk with the baking soda in a small bowl.

- Add the dry ingredients in alternating batches. Mix in the juice and zest of 2 oranges. Refrigerate 15 minutes.

- Drop rounded teaspoons of dough onto lightly greased cookie sheet and bake 13 to 15 minutes.

- Cool on rack. While still warm, frost with icing.

Chocolate and Orange Cookie Sandwiches: Make a thick chocolate ganache (a mixture of cream and chocolate) and spread it on the underside of one orange cookie, then sandwich with the underside of another cookie. To make ganache, heat ½ cup heavy cream until almost boiling. Place 6 ounces semisweet chocolate chips in a small, heatproof bowl. Pour the hot cream over the chips, cover with a plate, and let sit (without stirring) for 10 minutes. Remove plate and stir until smooth (put in microwave for 20 seconds if it doesn't melt completely; stir until smooth). Let cool to room temperature before spreading on cookies.

Add Milk and Dry Ingredients

- Combine sour milk and baking soda.

- In a separate bowl, mix the baking powder with the flour.

- Alternate adding the sour milk mixture and the dry ingredient mixture to the creamed butter and sugar mixture.

- Then add the juice and zest of 2 oranges and refrigerate dough 15 minutes.

Make the Icing

- Put juice and rind zest of 1 orange and the juice of ½ lemon into a medium bowl.

- Whisk in the powdered sugar until completely smooth. Add a little more powdered sugar, if needed, to get a consistency thick enough to spread.

- When cookies have cooled a little, but are still warm, spread icing on the tops.

- Then cool completely on a rack. Wait until icing is dry to store.

DESSERTS

BERRY PAVLOVA

A crisp meringue shell is piled high with fruit and whipped cream

This is a spectacular summer dessert, especially when berries are in season and cheap. When they're not, buy perfectly soft ripe peaches or nectarines, or any combination of summer fruit that you like.

Tossing the berries with balsamic vinegar adds a wonderful sweet acidity to the fruit, making for a nice counterpoint to the creamy sweet meringue. Fresh strawberries and balsamic vinegar are classically paired together. Make sure the egg whites are at room temperature so they can beat up to their maximum volume (cold whites don't beat up as high).

This recipe can easily be cut in half to serve a smaller crowd; leftovers aren't as spectacular the next day. *Yield: 10–12 servings*

Ingredients

8 large egg whites, room temperature

2 cups superfine sugar

4 tablespoons cornstarch

2 teaspoons white wine vinegar

2 teaspoons vanilla extract

¹/₄ cup shelled pistachios (optional)

2 pints strawberries, hulled and halved

1 pint blueberries, blackberries, or raspberries, or a mix

¹/₂ cup sugar

1 tablespoon balsamic vinegar

1 pint whipping cream, chilled

1 teaspoon vanilla

Berry Pavlova

- Make the shell. If using pistachios, toast in a 350°F oven until lightly golden.

- Combine all the berries in a bowl with sugar and vinegar and let macerate 30 minutes. Whip cream with 1 teaspoon vanilla until soft peaks form; chill until ready to assemble Pavlova.

- Put the cooled shell on a platter.

- Mound whipped cream in center, then spoon macerated berries over the cream. If using pistachios, crush lightly and sprinkle on top. Serve immediately.

Crème Anglaise: Leftover yolks are wonderful for making custards. The simplest is crème anglaise, a rich custard sauce used as the base for homemade ice cream (just flavor and pop in your ice-cream maker!) or for a sweet topping for fresh berries. In a small saucepan over medium heat, combine 2 cups milk, 1 teaspoon vanilla, and ⅓ cup sugar and bring just to a boil. While milk is heating, whisk 6 egg yolks in a large bowl with 2 tablespoons sugar until the yolks fall from the whisk in thick ribbons, 4 minutes. Slowly pour hot milk into yolks, whisking constantly (so they don't curdle). Return mixture to saucepan and cook, stirring, until custard coats a spoon, 3 minutes. Serve warm or chilled and serve with fruit.

Make the Shell

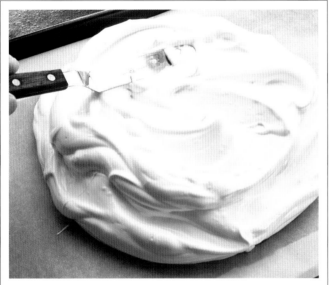

Assemble the Pavlova

- Preheat oven to 350°F. Draw an 8-inch circle on a sheet of parchment paper and line a baking sheet with it.

- Beat egg whites to soft peaks, then beat in super-fine sugar a little at a time, then cornstarch and vinegar, then vanilla. Spread it onto the parchment circle, slightly higher at the edges.

- Put in oven and reduce temperature to 300°F. Bake 90 minutes, turn off oven, prop open door, and cool completely in the oven. The shell can rest uncovered several hours.

- This is a terrific dinner-party dish, because you can make the time-consuming components ahead and assemble it at the last minute.

- Be sure the meringue shell is slightly higher at the edges to help hold in all the cream and berries.

- Don't be afraid to use a different mixture of berries or even other summer fruit such as ripe peeled and sliced peaches or nectarines. You just need the same total volume of fruit.

DESSERTS

227

EQUIPMENT RESOURCES

Here are the best places to track down essential kitchen equipment

Stores

Bed, Bath & Beyond
www.bedbathandbeyond.com
Beyond must refer to the kitchen, as this place is stocked to the ceiling with every conceivable gadget and pot.

Discount Department Stores
Stores like Kohl's, Marshalls, and T.J. Maxx often have excellent buys on top-name kitchen equipment.

Local Kitchenware Stores
Remember to patronize any small local kitchenware stores or bookstores in your area. You will get much more personal attention and a resource to return to again and again.

Macy's The Cellar
www.macys.com
Its famous Cellar on the bottom floor is stocked with everything yo need to get started.

Restaurant Supply Stores
Almost every city has one. It is the best place to look for professiona grade pots and pans and all sorts of fun kitchen gadgets, like larg skimmers and mandolines. The prices will always be better than far cier cookware stores.

Web Sites

www.bedbathandbeyond.com
Just as good as going to the store, but perhaps much easier.

www.bowerykitchens.com
Online home of the Bowery Kitchen Supply in New York City, which equips its famous neighbor—TV's Food Network—with everything it needs. A great place to find inexpensive restaurant cookware and cooking and baking equipment.

www.broadwaypanhandler.com
Online home of New York City's famed Broadway Panhandler store, where author Jennifer got her start doing cooking demonstrations. They have an excellent selection of knives and always have terrific sales going on. Check out their Kid's Corner for little chefs.

www.chefscatalog.com
A wide assortment of kitchen tools, cookware, and bakeware.

www.ebay.com
A great place to start when looking to buy expensive cookware, like Le Creuset enamel-coated cast-iron pots and All-Clad stainless steel pans. They are so well made that the fact they are secondhand is negligible.

www.kingarthurflour.com
A great resource for all things baking, including baking tips and recipes.

www.localharvest.com or www.ranchogordo.com
Two excellent sources for finding Christmas limas

www.surlatable.com
Kitchen equipment along with dishes, serving utensils, and flatware.

COOKBOOKS & MAGAZINES

Having a collection of essential go-to cookbooks lining your shelves will ensure you have the answers to all your cooking questions at your fingertips. Treat yourself to one or two food magazine subscriptions, which will refresh your recipe ideas every month, ensuring you are always learning and trying new things in the kitchen.

Cookbooks

Here are a few of our favorite cookbooks, the ones filled with stained fingerprints and broken spines from so much use in our own homes.

Aidells, Bruce and Denis Kelly. *The Complete Meat Cookbook*. Houghton Mifflin Harcourt, 2001.
Everything you'll ever need to know about cooking pork, beef, veal, and lamb. Includes in-depth, illustrated information on the different cuts and how to cook them. This one's very accessible.

Bittman, Mark. *The Best Recipes in the World*. Broadway, 2005
Like *How to Cook Everything* from a global perspective.

Bittman, Mark. *How to Cook Everything*. Wiley, 2008
Includes the basic recipe, along with plenty of variations, for practically every dish you can think of.

Corriher, Shirley. *CookWise*. William Morrow, 1997 and *BakeWise*. Scribner, 2008
Answers all your questions about the science behind cooking and baking.

Jenkins, Sara and Mindy Fox. *Olives & Oranges*. Houghton Mifflin Harcourt, 2008.
This book offers flat-out some of the most deliciously rustic Mediterranean recipes. The recipes call for simple ingredients with powerful flavor and texture.

Food Lit

In this day and age, there is plenty of food literature beyond the realm of cookbooks. To help you best understand the science and global/local issues behind today's food, take a peek at the following:

McCullough, Fran. *The Good Fat Cookbook.* Scribner, 2007.
Details the difference between the good fats and bad fats. Plenty of recipes, too. You'll be surprised—and delighted—at the research. Hello butter, good-bye margarine!

Parsons, Russ. *How to Read a French Fry.* Houghton Mifflin Harcourt, 2003.
A fascinating collection of food science stories and supporting recipes, with answers to questions ranging from "How does a roux work?" to "How do you perfectly brown a steak?"

Pollan, Michael. *The Omnivore's Dilemma.* Penguin, 2007.
The journey from farm to plate, on a local and industrial level, is explored in this book. It's a must read for anyone who wants to be current on food issues facing us all today.

Monthly Magazines

Cook's Illustrated
www.cooksillustrated.com
A terrific teaching magazine, with no ads (!), which breaks down the simplest recipes (fried chicken, for example) into meticulously researched articles about how to make the best version of it (they will fry 100 pounds of chicken just to give you the answer).

Eating Well
www.eatingwell.com
Keeps you up-to-date on all the latest nutritional advice and is filled with ideas for incorporating the healthiest foods into your meals. Excellent recipes, too.

Food & Wine
www.foodandwine.com
Filled with recipes for simple dinners to showstopping entertaining dishes. Also keeps you up-to- date on the latest in food news and wine.

Martha Stewart's Everyday Food
www.everydayfoodmag.com
Like a toned-down version of *Martha Stewart Living,* but solely dedicated to the simple art of cooking good food and understanding ingredients. Incredibly readable format and well-tested recipes make this a gem. It's also filled with many good kitchen tips.

Saveur
www.saveur.com
One of the best magazines to explore the culture and history behind all things food. It also highlights farmers and vintners. Gorgeous photography and excellent recipes. Like curling up with a good novel.

GROCERY CHECKLIST
Weekly Shopping List

When you head to the grocery store each week, keep these items in mind to ensure your pantry and refrigerator are stocked with all the items you need for a week's worth of meals.

Dairy
- ❑ **Milk, cheese, yogurt, eggs**

Leafy Greens
- ❑ **collard greens**
- ❑ **kale**
- ❑ **salad** (green leaf, red leaf, romaine, arugula, radicchio, baby spinach, Boston)
- ❑ **spinach**
- ❑ **Swiss chard**

Green Vegetables
- ❑ **asparagus**
- ❑ **broccoli**
- ❑ **broccoli rabe**
- ❑ **brussels sprouts**
- ❑ **snap peas**
- ❑ **snow peas**
- ❑ **string beans**

Other Vegetables
- ❑ **avocados**
- ❑ **onions** (garlic, scallions, leeks, shallots)
- ❑ **potatoes** (russet or baking for mashing and baking; smaller potatoes, such as fingerling, red potatoes, and Yukon Gold, for roasting and boiling)
- ❑ **root vegetables** (carrots, sweet potatoes, parsnips, beets, turnips, celery root, rutabaga)
- ❑ **summer squashes** (zucchini, yellow, patty pan)
- ❑ **tomatoes**
- ❑ **winter squashes** (butternut, acorn, delicate)

Citrus Fruits
- ❑ **grapefruit**
- ❑ **lemons**
- ❑ **limes**
- ❑ **oranges**

Other Fruits
- ❑ **apples**
- ❑ **bananas**
- ❑ **berries**
- ❑ **grapes**
- ❑ **mangoes**
- ❑ **peaches**
- ❑ **pears**
- ❑ **plums**

Meats And Seafood
- ❑ **beef:** ground, steaks (look for rib eye and New York strip for best flavor), chuck roast (for beef stews and braising)
- ❑ **fish:** wild salmon, sea bass, trout, flounder, Arctic char, cod, halibut, tuna steaks
- ❑ **poultry:** boneless chicken breasts, chicken pieces on the bone, whole chickens, turkey breasts, ground turkey
- ❑ **pork:** tenderloin, bone-in roasts, chops, ground
- ❑ **shellfish:** scallops, shrimp, mussels, clams, squid

Pantry Items
- ❑ **canned beans:** black beans, garbanzo (chickpeas), cannellini, pinto, kidney
- ❑ **canned tomatoes:** whole peeled, diced, crushed, paste
- ❑ **flavorings:** coconut milk, toasted sesame oil, capers, olives, roasted red peppers, pesto, hot sauce
- ❑ **grains:** barley, quinoa, couscous, polenta
- ❑ **pasta:** shapes, spaghetti, linguini
- ❑ **oils and vinegars:** extra-virgin olive oil, coconut oil, red wine and sherry vinegars, balsamic vinegar
- ❑ **rice:** long grain, short grain, brown, basmati, arborio

CULINARY WEB SITES

The Web is filled with culinary content in the form of recipes, cooking videos, ingredient information, and blogs. Here are a few that we visit on a regular basis.

Cooking on a Budget, the blog!
Also on www.epicurious.com
Regina Schrambling, a pithy food writer (and contributor of more than a few recipes in this book) writes a blog on Epicurious about how to eat well on a budget. Search for her name on the site's Epi-Log, which covers food and news from around the world.

Epicurious.com
This is a great resource for recipes that hail from the test kitchens of *Bon Appétit* and the now-defunct *Gourmet* magazines. Not every recipe Web site (except those connected to a magazine or some TV shows) has recipes that are actually tested before being posted. Here you can trust the recipes before you spend your money on groceries. It also has a useful culinary dictionary.

www.foodtv.com
Includes the tested recipes from every beloved show on the Fo Network. Our favorites are from Alton Brown, who exhaustiv researches the simplest things, from roasting beets to making pick

Wednesday Newspaper Food Sections
Wednesday is food day in most major (and minor) newspapers. Ma it a habit to read the paper on Wednesday if only to get some fre new recipe ideas for the week. We love www.nytimes.com and ww .latimes.com if you can't get to the newsstand.

RESOURCES

Seafood Watch

www.montereybayaquarium.org/cr/seafoodwatch.aspx

You can download a wallet-size file of the best and worst fish choices at the market. Best refers to those species that are sustainable, abundant, and low in PCBs or other toxins. Worst is reserved for species that are overfished or are high in toxins or whose farming or harvesting methods create hazards for the environment. There is also a "good alternatives" column for fish that fall in between.

www.youtube.com

Want to how to knead bread properly, cure bacon, or perfectly dice an onion? YouTube has videos on every cooking subject you can think of.

METRIC CONVERSION TABLES
Approximate U.S. Metric Equivalents

Liquid Ingredients

U.S. MEASURES	METRIC	U.S. MEASURES	METRIC
$1/4$ TSP.	1.23 ML	2 TBSP.	29.57 ML
$1/2$ TSP.	2.36 ML	3 TBSP.	44.36 ML
$3/4$ TSP.	3.70 ML	$1/4$ CUP	59.15 ML
1 TSP.	4.93 ML	$1/2$ CUP	118.30 ML
$1^1/4$ TSP.	6.16 ML	1 CUP	236.59 ML
$1^1/2$ TSP.	7.39 ML	2 CUPS OR 1 PT.	473.18 ML
$1^3/4$ TSP.	8.63 ML	3 CUPS	709.77 ML
2 TSP.	9.86 ML	4 CUPS OR 1 QT.	946.36 ML
1 TBSP.	14.79 ML	4 QTS. OR 1 GAL.	3.79 L

Dry Ingredients

U.S. MEASURES	METRIC	U.S. MEASURES		METRIC
$1/16$ OZ.	2 (1.8) G	$2^4/5$ OZ.		80 G
$1/8$ OZ.	$3^1/2$ (3.5) G	3 OZ.		85 (84.9) G
$1/4$ OZ.	7 (7.1) G	$3^1/2$ OZ.		100 G
$1/2$ OZ.	15 (14.2) G	4 OZ.		115 (113.2) G
$3/4$ OZ.	21 (21.3) G	$4^1/2$ OZ.		125 G
$7/8$ OZ.	25 G	$5^1/4$ OZ.		150 G
1 OZ.	30 (28.3) G	$8^7/8$ OZ.		250 G
$1^3/4$ OZ.	50 G	16 OZ.	1 LB.	454 G
2 OZ.	60 (56.6) G	$17^3/5$ OZ.	1 LIVRE	500 G

GLOSSARY
The language of cooking

Blanch: To briefly cook food, primarily green vegetables, to soften, remove skin, or fix color.

Braise: To cook food (as in a stew) by simmering it in a flavorful sauce or broth.

Brown: Cooking step that caramelizes food and adds color and flavor before cooking.

Deglaze: Adding a liquid to a pan used to sauté meats; this removes drippings and brown bits to create a flavorful sauce.

Dice: To cut food into small, even portions, usually about ¼-inch square.

Extra-Virgin Olive Oil: The oil that is release from olives during the first pressing. It is the strongest in flavor, aroma, and color of all the olive oils.

Fold: Combining two soft or liquid mixtures together using an over-and-under method of mixing.

Instant read thermometer: Slim tool with a digital read or clock face that will tell you more-or-less instantly when your meat is cooked to the desired temperature. Better than "meat thermometers" or your ones that go into the oven inserted in the roast, causing a large escape hold for precious juices.

Kosher salt: The coarse, flaky salt preferred by chefs and cooking professionals. Called "kosher salt" because its flat surface is ideal for koshering (drawing blood from) meat. Its crystals don't melt right away when sprinkled on food (unlike table salt), making it less likely that you will oversalt your food.

Marinade: A mixture that includes an acid such as citrus, oil, and seasonings used to flavor meat, fruits, and vegetables before cooking.

Non-reactive cookware: Includes pots and pans whose surfaces do not react with the strong acids in certain foods, like tomatoes and wine. Stainless steel and enamel-coated cast-iron are both non-reactive. Aluminum and cast-iron are highly reactive and shouldn't be used when simmering tomato sauces or wine-based sauces, or the acid will draw out a bit of the metallic tang from the cookware.

Panfry: To cook quickly in a shallow pan in a small amount of fat over relatively high heat.

Silicon baking mat: A great way to avoid greasing and cleaning baking sheets when baking cooking, biscuits, or breads. This non-stick and reusable mat is made of oven-safe silicon and last virtually forever. Also great for rolling out pie doughs and cookie dough; it grips the countertop and the dough won't stick to it, saving you from over-flouring the dough as you roll it out.

Simmer: A gentle state of cooking liquid in which it is kept just below a boil to prevent the food from being tossed around.

INDEX

INDEX